CW00482534

Also from Camphor Press

KYOTO: A LITERARY GUIDE

THE SAME MOON

INAKA: PORTRAITS OF LIFE IN RURAL JAPAN

Inaka

Portraits of Life in Rural Japan

Edited by John Grant Ross

A Camphor Press book

Published by Camphor Press Ltd
83 Ducie Street, Manchester, M1 2JQ
United Kingdom

www.camphorpress.com

ISBN   978-1-78869-219-9 (paperback)
          978-1-78869-220-5 (hardcover)

The moral right of the authors have been asserted.

Set in 11 pt Linux Libertine

inaka 田舎 (*ee-nah-KAH*)

n. rural area; the countryside; the sticks

Contents

Notes on Romanization and Spelling

In general, Japanese words that are not widely used in English are italicized only upon first incidence in each chapter.

This collection employs the most common method of Japanese romanization, the Hepburn system, which employs a macron (a flat line above a vowel) to indicate a long vowel sound. For familiar place names, however, this book does not use macrons: you'll see Kyushu, Honshu, and Hokkaido rather than Kyūshū, Honshū, and Hokkaidō, and Kyoto and Tokyo instead of Kyōto and Tōkyō. For other things, we've been flexible on usage, weighing various factors and personal preferences chapter by chapter while also striving for consistency throughout the anthology.

One intentional inconsistency is the book's mix of American English and British English. By coincidence, for the most part this follows a geographic pattern, with the Americans writing about southern Japan and writers in British English covering the north, and some intermingling in the center. So from the far south it's American English all the "kilometers" up to Kyoto, and British English "flavours" from Mount Fuji to Hokkaido.

JAPAN

18. Hokkaido

17. Tohoku

● 16. Ibaraki

3. Tsushima ●

● 1. Tanegashima

● 2. Okinawa

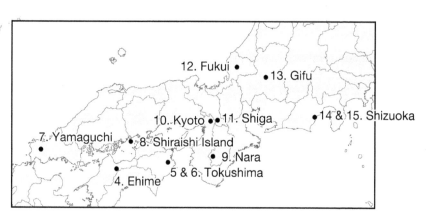

12. Fukui ●

● 13. Gifu

10. Kyoto ●● 11. Shiga

● 14 & 15. Shizuoka

7. Yamaguchi ● 8. Shiraishi Island

● 9. Nara

4. Ehime ● 5 & 6. Tokushima

Numbers refer to chapters

Introduction

IT's easy to fall under the spell of rural Japan. On top of the countryside's essential beauty, there seems to be some beguiling combination at work in the balance of aesthetic elements; it's colorful yet austere, simultaneously manicured and wild; and it contains human-scale warmth alongside grandeur.

And there are many ways to fall under the spell. Oftentimes the enchantment begins well before setting foot in Japan, long before those memorable moments of, for the first time, stepping out from a lonely train station, strolling around castle ruins, stumbling upon a rustic shrine in a grove of huge cedars, or catching sight of a billowing volcano. It starts from screen and page with landscapes seen in documentaries and dramas, in photographs and paintings, and in anime's Arcadian visions of nostalgia-tinged village life and animistic forests.

For others, the attraction to rural Japan may stem from cultural aspects such as pottery, poetry, tea, and religion, all of which and more are covered in this anthology. In my case, it started with a visit to Kyushu, made out of general curiosity, a more specific interest in history, and the practical fact that Japan is just a two-hour flight away from my home in Taiwan, a former Japanese colony. I was smitten by the people and bucolic scenes, and I started to wonder what it would be like to put down roots in the *inaka* ("countryside"). This isn't a matter of wanting to escape city life, as I already live in a small town, or wanting to exchange an office for a field, as I have two neglected farm plots to keep me busy. It's actually when I'm laboring on the family farm that I find myself thinking: *I chose the wrong country; I should have moved to Japan.* Many's the time catching my breath in the sweltering shade I've cursed my adopted home for being such a year-round jungle sauna. The mind wanders to an idealized Japan and I see myself working on a small farm in comfortable temperatures against an ever-changing backdrop of gorgeous seasonal flavors; the flowers of spring, lush summer greens, the rich reds and browns of autumn maples, and then a white winter respite from the weeds.

It's too late for a permanent move now, but one day I hope to rent for a year or two a quaint Japanese farmhouse with a good-sized garden of faded splendor. Financial and family obligations mean this won't be possible in the immediate future, but I can in the meantime at least periodically travel to Japan.

In a way, my frequent trips there over the past five years are making up for lost time after having lived nearby for many years without paying it a visit. I was for a long time put off by the high prices, the crowded urban environment, the small food portions, and by a fateful encounter with the writing of longtime Japan resident Alex Kerr. The American's books *Lost Japan* (1993) and *Dogs and Demons* (2002) describe a land ravaged by construction; Kerr's Japan is a fallen Eden where streams are lined with concrete, almost all the rivers are dammed, and the seashore is lined with cement slabs and tetrapods. Government pork in the form of construction boondoggles has, he asserts, turned Japan into "arguably the world's ugliest country."

For the first-time visitor who gets out of the cities and coastal plains, however, Japan strikes one as a land of trees, not concrete. It's a green archipelago of thousands of islands, with forest-covered mountains from one end to the other. This is not an exaggeration; compare, for example, the percentage of forest cover in Japan, 68.5 percent, with the 30 percent in my native New Zealand, 38 percent in Canada, and 13 percent in the United Kingdom. As well as the quantity of the trees, there is also a stunning variety of fauna. A telling indication of the inherent fecundity of Japan's natural setting is shown by a defining characteristic of the Jōmon era (14,000 to 1,000 BC). This prehistoric culture — named after a style of pottery — is remarkable for the degree of sedentarism and cultural sophistication it achieved while relying predominantly on hunting and gathering. The bounty of coast and forest was able to feed a settled density of people normally associated with agriculture.

Today the Japanese countryside makes the news for its inability to support viable populations. Headlines tell of "vanishing towns and villages," of shrinking settlements so desperate that they're offering abandoned houses for free to outsiders willing to relocate. One recent rural depopulation story to make the international rounds concerns the "doll village" of Nagoro. In a remote valley on Shikoku, an elderly returnee started compensating for departed residents by placing life-size dolls around the village. There are dolls of children in an empty classroom, farmers in fields, a road-repair crew, and so on, totaling about three hundred dolls, similar to the village's former population, and greatly outnumbering the current twenty-seven flesh-and-blood residents.

It's an extreme example — but one that no doubt misleads some foreigners into thinking the entire Japanese countryside is dotted with scarecrow human substitutes — yet the cold hard demographic facts are alarming. Approximately 91 percent of Japan's 126.5 million people live in urban areas. Twenty-eight percent of Japanese are sixty-five years old or over, by far the highest proportion in the world, and the population is at its grayest in the countryside, where the average farmer is sixty-seven. I suspect few nations have the need for a phrase such as *genkai shūraku* — "marginal village" — which describes a situation where more than half of the inhabitants are over the age of sixty-five.

But rural depopulation has at least been slow and gradual, allowing for a manageable decline, and there are also signs of rejuvenation, from both public and private initiatives. What are things really like on the ground in the countryside? Answering this question with an accessible, personal, and non-sensational look at life in rural Japan was a driving motivation for this book.

We've been misled by numbers and media reports before. Japan has for a long time been synonymous with economic stagnation, from its "lost decade" of the 1990s — which stretched into two decades, until the low growth of the present became the new normal. Any visitor to Japan then or now, however, encounters a society of enviable prosperity, social order, and civility, at odds with the talk of decline.

As well as the gloom of impending demographic disaster, coverage of Japan is also marred by a predilection for stories of the weird. In his memoir *Welcome Home, Master: Covering East Asia in the Twilight of Old Media*, former American freelance journalist J.D. Adams recalls how the reception to his Japan reporting prompted him to leave the profession. It was 2010 and the Taipei-based reporter was in Nagoya, home of Japan's auto-manufacturing industry, working on an in-depth series about the labor-market transition from lifetime employment to temporary contracts. Adams found himself with a free weekend, which coincided with a nearby town's annual fertility festival, one notable for the parading around town of a large wooden "male object." Adams flew back to Taipei and filed a four-part labor investigation story and also a piece on the festival. The phallus festival story went viral like none of his stories ever had, earning him a large bonus and lavish praise from editors and colleagues. His articles on labor trends died a silent, unread death.

Between the covers of *Inaka: Portraits of Life in Rural Japan* you will find some eccentric color but not the clichés of "wacky" Japan: there are no maid cafés, no love motels, no marginal trivia held up as mainstream trends, no fertility objects paraded about town. Instead, you'll enjoy an affectionate but unsentimental taste of authentic rural living: inconvenient superstitions, the tough realities of training to be a Buddhist monk, the mystery of an abandoned shrine, an ancient pilgrimage given new life, fishermen's tales, cycling adventures, examples of rural revitalization in tea farm tourism and the indigo dyeing industry, hypothermia-inducing housing, and friendly neighbors sharing old customs and local histories.

As Tom Gibb details in a chapter titled "Ibaraki, Inaka, and the In-laws," the Japanese word for the countryside, "inaka," carries a slightly pejorative meaning of "the sticks," of being far from culture and amenities; and "inaka" is applied not only to truly rural areas but also to small towns and cities away from metropolitan areas. Likewise, *Inaka: Portraits of Life in Rural Japan* includes a look at small-town life and areas in the urban–rural zone of interaction rather than only pure remote settings; a messy mix of city and country is much more representative than hermits hiding in the wilderness.

* * *

Once I had decided to compile an anthology on rural Japan, I embarked on the project with a wish list and a large dose of audacity. I contacted the authors of my two favorite Japan books: John Dougill (*In Search of Japan's Hidden Christians*) and Lesley Downer

(*On the Narrow Road to the Deep North*). I wrote to Rebecca Otowa, the author of *At Home in Japan*, the best title there is on country living. I contacted writers I knew from their frequent contributions to the *Japan Times* (and other publications): Amy Chavez, Stephen Mansfield, and Iain Maloney. I found a way to include Brian Burke-Gaffney, the premier history scholar of Nagasaki, by drawing on his earliest Japan experiences.

I wanted to balance these Japan Olympians with some mortal contributors, including new arrivals settling in and experiencing Japan through fresh eyes. I read numerous travelogues and memoirs, browsed blogs, and listened to podcasts. The people who made the cut had, on top of interesting content and storytelling skill, a commonality of good-natured humor, honesty, and a lack of ego.

For the book, I approached a total of eighteen people. Sixteen replied and were keen to come on board. I didn't get replies from two, but in perfect symmetry I was approached by two other writers who wanted to contribute. It was an astounding success rate — my most positive experience in publishing — and one I feel illustrates the overdue need for such an anthology.

When all the chapters were submitted, a framework was needed. One possibility, reflecting my initial daydreams of seasonal rural rhythms, was to go through a year: we could visit the tea farms of Shizouka for the prized first spring picking of leaves, experience the hottest summer while walking the ancient pilgrimage of eighty-eight Buddhist temples around Shikoku Island, and, at the other extreme, share a snow-lover's delight at the heaviest snowfall in a generation. Another possible framework was by subject area: farming, family, religion, island life, and so on. Or chronological: Lesley Downer traveling in the footsteps of a seventeenth-century haiku master, Brian Burke-Gaffney's study of Zen at a small temple in the 1970s, and all the way up to present-day adventures.

But I kept coming back to Japan's exceptional geography. Consider the ingredients: about three thousand islands, a coastline almost thirty thousand kilometers long, and mountains covering 73 percent of the land area. Throw in volcanoes for added spice and stretch everything along a three-thousand-kilometer arc from latitudes 24 degrees to 45 degrees north, the equivalent of going from Florida to Nova Scotia.

A trip through rural Japan it is then. Travel has never been easier: the transport infrastructure is excellent, with a rail network second to none, and driving a rental car is easier than you might think. And decades of English instruction by foreign teachers on the JET Programme, including by some of the contributors to this anthology, you can find — even in the most remote areas — numerous competent English speakers who are comfortable interacting with foreigners (Just kidding: When it comes to the English language, the Japanese remain a stubbornly tongue-tied tribe). The English you're most likely to hear is the repeated admonition of your rental car's navigational system to "Please drive safely," as you keep pushing past the fifty kilometers per hour speed limit on a straight expanse of highway.

So, we will undertake an epic journey the length of Japan, from the subtropical Ryukyu Island chain and head northwest all the way to the chilly wilds of Hokkaido. In this northern expedition we are retracing the general path of Japan's first human settlers, and also of the West's first interactions with Japan.

INAKA: PORTRAITS OF LIFE IN RURAL JAPAN

1

Tanegashima

By Silvia Lawrence

The Ryukyus, or the Nansei-shotō (Southwest Islands), arc from within sight of Taiwan eleven hundred kilometers to the island of Kyushu. The southernmost chapter of *Inaka* takes us to Okinawa on a visit to master potter Paul Lorimer, a Japan veteran of four decades living a rural idyll; but before that we will begin at the northern end of the Ryukyus with Tanegashima (Tanega Island). It is was here, in 1543, where the first Europeans to reach Japan set foot. In "Tanegashima" it's 2010 as we follow another kind of beginning familiar to many foreign residents in Japan, with young American graduate Silvia Lawrence heading to a remote posting to teach English.

* * *

How could I have ever thought majoring in philosophy was a good idea? Did I ever actually even think about it? Philosophy has to top the list of useless degrees.

That's how I found myself at the Japanese consulate in Boston, Massachusetts, waiting to be called in for an interview for an English-teaching position with the Japan Exchange and Teaching (JET) program. And while I wasn't sure how much use my degree in philosophy would be, I was hoping that the year I had spent as a kindergarten student in Japan might help get me the job. It's probably good that during all those years poring over textbooks as a high school and college student, no one told me that by my seventh birthday I had already completed the year of studies that would help most when entering the job market.

I flipped through a brochure in an attempt to calm my nerves and saw a picture of a smiling blonde girl standing on a beach surrounded by a group of Japanese students:

"Carly teaches on several small islands and takes a boat to her schools!"

The distraction worked; my mind drifted into a montage of me standing on a ferry deck with the wind in my hair, afternoon strolls along a sandy white beach, and evenings waiting for the fishing boats to come in so I could buy my dinner of fresh lobster. Fingers crossed these interviewers liked me!

After several nail-biting months of waiting, I received the news that I would be teaching at high schools on the islands of Tanegashima and Yakushima, with the port town of Nishinoomote (a population of sixteen thousand of the island's twenty-eight thousand) in northwest Tanegashima serving as my home base. The two islands are part of Kagoshima Prefecture, lying just south of Japan's southernmost main island of Kyushu.

In researching Tanegashima I came across an old blog written by an English teacher who had been part of the JET Programme several years before. His blog posts featured pristine beaches, surfers hanging out at cool seaside huts, and even some photos of rockets launching into space. If this guy's enthusiasm for Tanegashima was anything to go by, I was right in my excitement over being placed there. His posts did taper off after a few months, but I figured this must have been because he was too busy loving life on Tanegashima to be cooped up inside with his computer.

As for those rockets, it turned out Tanegashima was home to the largest launch site of the Japanese space agency, JAXA. How random! I imagined nights out at the local bar mingling with visitors from NASA — of course I would be invited along as one of the token English speakers on the island. Maybe I'd even meet my future husband, though I had once heard that one of the criteria for becoming an astronaut is having a family, to minimize risk-taking, so perhaps I'd be catching them too late.

The rocket launch site also happened to be on Tanegashima's most beautiful beach. Or at least from the photos it looked like it must be the most beautiful beach, but then each new photo I found of Tanegashima seemed to reveal another stunning stretch of coastline. How lucky was I?

Not very lucky, according to my Japanese colleagues. We were at my welcome party and I had just asked them how they enjoyed life on Tanegashima.

"I'm almost done with my third year of island duty!"

"I still have two years left."

Island duty?

Apparently high school teachers in Kagoshima Prefecture had to change schools every few years, and at least once in their careers they would have to spend three to five years on one of

Kagoshima's islands. Most teachers were not as enthusiastic about being placed on Tanegashima as I was. I do remember thinking how odd it was that I usually found myself alone on Tanegashima's gorgeous beaches.

However, two weeks later, on my first visit to my high school on the neighboring island of Yakushima, I learned that not all of Kagoshima's islands are viewed equally. The attitude at Yakushima High School was totally different. Teachers took pride in working there.

Yakushima is just an hour's boat ride from Tanegashima, but the islands look so different I might as well have sailed across the world. While Tanegashima is mostly flat, Yakushima rises out of the sea with Mount Miyanoura, Kyushu's highest peak, reaching 1,935 meters. As a result, the island gets a lot of rain; in fact, with rainfall of between five and ten meters, Yakushima is the wettest place in Japan.

Yakushima is over 90 percent forested and renowned for its cedar trees; one giant specimen — twenty-five meters tall and sixteen meters in circumference — is over two thousand years old. These trees are sacred to the Japanese people, and the cedar forests were the joint first natural area in Japan to be granted UNESCO World Heritage Site status. They've also provided inspiration for anime feature films such as Studio Ghibli's acclaimed *Princess Mononoke*.

The enchanted forests of Yakushima are home to a subspecies of deer and a monkey — the Yaku macaque. They are little terrors, but *kawaii* terrors, I have to admit.

Despite wanting to root for the underdog, Yakushima High School quickly became my favorite workplace. I enjoyed getting to know the teachers and students, and I felt lucky to visit this incredible island each month. I began to think that the generous monthly bonus I received for my trips out to Yakushima was less

Silvia (right) and friend wearing yukata

of a compensation for the inconvenience of spending two nights a month at a hotel and more a consolation for having to return to the much less esteemed Tanegashima.

It was a shame, because Tanegashima deserves to be loved. For a start, it's highly scenic, with a coastline both beautiful and varied: there are dramatic basalt rock formations, caverns, white sand beaches, and "black sand" — iron-rich sands that enabled the island to develop a metalworking industry nearly a millennium ago. This technology would be important. In the summer of 1543, a Chinese junk, blown off course and badly damaged by a storm, washed ashore at a bay at the southern end of the island, right next to where the rocket launch site stands today. Among the passengers were two Portuguese merchants, the first Europeans to land in Japan. The pair's firearms — matchlock arquebuses — drew attention and caused a sensation after a shooting demonstration was held. The ruler of Tanegashima ordered a copy to be made, something that was possible given the unlikely metalworking abilities the local smiths had developed after centuries of producing bladed weapons. The junk was repaired after two months and the Portuguese left on it. The copied guns were introduced to mainland Japan and kicked off an arms race there between warring clans. For the next few hundred years, guns in Japan would be colloquially referred to as "Tanegashima."

Nearly five centuries after that first Western–Japanese interaction, Tanegashima is still an adventurous off-the-beaten destination for foreigners. Being the only blonde woman on the island and a good head taller than most locals, I didn't exactly blend in. People seemed to be constantly watching me, and it became normal to meet someone for the first time and have them say that they had recently seen me in the supermarket. And then they would proceed to list everything that had been in my shopping basket, often commenting on my eating habits. "Do all Americans eat so much chicken?"

The Japan Exchange and Teaching (JET) Programme, which started in 1987, is intended not just to increase English-language proficiency, but to also promote internationalization and help the Japanese feel more comfortable dealing with foreigners (and less likely to spy and comment on their supermarket baskets). In 2019 there were 5,761 JET participants, over half of them from the United States. The vast majority of JETs are recent graduates from Western countries, 90 percent of whom work as Assistant Language Teachers (ALTs) in the school system, from kindergartens through high schools. Teachers sign a one-year contract, which can be renewed for a maximum of five years. The monthly salary starts at 280,000 yen (approximately US$2,600).

Working as an ALT, I was there to help the English teachers, and what that specifically entailed varied greatly from teacher to teacher, as well as from school to school. Some teachers would bring me to class solely to help students read drills, while others would hand over entire lessons for me to conduct on my own. At my main high school I could often go several days without visiting any classes, whereas at the schools I taught at less frequently my schedule might be booked solid from eight in the morning until four in the afternoon. I enjoyed the variety, though at times I found navigating Japanese approaches to education a challenge.

Tanegashima was also incredibly conservative compared to the rest of Japan. When gay comedians came on television, people would laugh and say that obviously it was all an act. A Japanese friend on Yakushima told me that she had once asked her doctor for birth control pills and, very begrudgingly, he had prescribed her one week's worth. Very few of the teachers I worked with gave their students much room for creative thinking, always stressing the importance of social harmony above all else. It was great for those who fit in, but the students who didn't really struggled.

At the same time, this remote island didn't feel completely foreign. During my JET interview the panel had asked how I thought my year in Japan as a child would help me as an adult teaching in Japan. I had explained how formative that year had been, and that I might now have an easier time adjusting to life in Japan and understanding the perspectives of my students and fellow teachers. Now, I don't know if that's exactly how it worked out — my Japanese-language skills didn't magically reappear in the way that I had hoped they would — but a lot about life in Japan was familiar and comfortable. And perhaps I did have a head start when it came to the language, as I seemed to pick up words and phrases more easily than I had with other languages.

I took pride in how attuned I was to social cues, which helped me a lot in a society that values social harmony so highly. I would note when someone looked uncomfortable or nervous and try to adjust my behavior accordingly, hoping I could learn to behave as "Japanese" as possible.

So when it came time to renew my contract in February, I decided to stay, partly because the job paid well and the cost of living on Tanegashima was quite low, but primarily because I knew I needed more time to find my feet in Japan. I was just beginning to get comfortable communicating in Japanese: I was finally able to sort my garbage without referencing the chart taped to the side of my refrigerator, and who knows, maybe soon I'd make a friend.

And then the tsunami hit. At 2:46 in the afternoon of Friday, March 11, 2011, a magnitude 9 earthquake, the largest ever recorded in Japan, struck off the coast of northeast Honshu, generating massive tsunami waves that devastated the coastal areas.

On the afternoon of the tsunami I went downstairs to the secretary's office to hand in paperwork and the whole office was watching television footage of what appeared to be a flood somewhere in Japan. I joined them in front of the television, and although my Japanese wasn't great at that point, I did understand the words *jishin* (earthquake) and *tsunami*.

I also understood when they told me the tsunami would arrive in a few hours. The secretary didn't say anything more, but she also knew that she had pretty much exhausted my Japanese-language capability with this short conversation. When I first started teaching at the school, she used to attempt to communicate with me through an online translator, though we never had much luck with it. Still, it was nice that she tried speaking with me, and I grew to enjoy our exchange of mystery phrases, which ranged from making very little to absolutely no sense. I would smile and nod, happy to have a person smiling and nodding back to me. But then one afternoon after the secretary energetically pointed at her computer screen, which was informing me that the green elephants would cascade after the sun (or something along those lines). My smile was cut off mid nod by the look of horror on her face. I tried to save the situation by shaking my head and frowning, but I was too late. The online translator would never be brought out again.

And so instead of attempting to explain the situation, the secretary silently offered me a banana cake *omiyage* — a colleague must have recently returned from a trip to Tokyo. Was it a goodbye banana cake? I couldn't tell. She certainly looked worried, but the television footage of the tsunami was worrisome regardless of what was going to happen to us. No one seemed to be organizing an evacuation, which suggested we weren't in any danger, but then again on a flat island reaching just ten kilometers across at its very widest point, where would we even go?

Thinking back to the afternoon of the tsunami it now seems crazy to me that I didn't ask for more answers. For the few hours before school ended I had no idea why people kept mentioning five p.m., and I was so caught up in my efforts to fit in that I didn't want to disturb any of the English teachers by asking them about it. (I learned later that five p.m. was the estimated time for the tsunami reaching Tanegashima.)

Instead I sat back down at my desk and unwrapped the banana sponge cake, assuring myself that once I got home I could investigate online and find out what was really happening. And maybe on my way home I'd stop by a FamilyMart convenience store to pick up some almond chocolates, as this gooey cake wasn't quite last meal material.

In the end, the wave lost force by the time it made its way down to Tanegashima. Even when I had feared it might be headed for my small island, the tsunami somehow never felt real. But the death toll reported in the news the next morning was very real. Over the coming weeks we'd learn that nearly nineteen thousand people lost their lives from the earthquake and resulting tsunami and nuclear disaster.

On Tanegashima I split my teaching time between the high school in Nishinoomote, the town where I lived, and the high school farther south in Nakatane. I had always loved the forty-five-minute drive to Nakatane, as the road took me along Tanegashima's sandy white coastline with its beautiful views out over the ocean. But after the tsunami that drive became hell. Staring at the water that had just taken so many lives, it took me a full month before I was able to get through the drive without pulling over in tears. I didn't understand how this beautiful ocean that I had grown to love could have betrayed us like that, and I didn't think I could ever admire those coastal views again. How were we supposed to go back to our everyday lives after this?

Two JET teachers were taken by the tsunami: twenty-six-year-old Monty Dickson and twenty-four-year-old Taylor Anderson, both from the United States. Monty and his students had sought shelter on the third floor of the town hall. The tidal wave swept him and most of his students away. Monty's body, one of the few found, was recovered a kilometer away almost three weeks later. Taylor had helped all of her elementary school students evacuate to safety and then bicycled home to get her phone to call her family in America.

I thought about my own confusion over what was happening as I drove home the day of the tsunami. Had the tsunami felt real to Taylor? I hoped that the waves came so quickly and she was so focused on cycling that she didn't have time to realize her impending fate before it was over. But there was no way to hope away the fear and dread her family must have felt in the two weeks they waited before receiving the official confirmation of her death.

I remembered my dad's panic the morning of the 1995 Kobe earthquake, trying to get in touch with family and friends back home in the States. My sister and I were playing in the large wooden wardrobe that had come crashing down next to the futon in my bedroom. Now we could pretend it was a boat! The phone lines were down, so my dad announced that he was going to his office to try to find out the extent of the earthquake damage.

The Kobe earthquake was my first introduction to death. I watched our neighbors come out of their homes, some covered in blood, all dazed from the shock of what had just happened. I felt sad when my parents told me that their friend had died, and I remember thinking how strange it was that I had just been at his house playing a game of stacking clementines, and now he was gone. And I felt happy when my parents told me that all of my classmates had survived, but then sad again when they said that we were leaving Japan. So, in a way, they were gone too.

Experiencing the aftermath of an earthquake as an adult, I saw the events of my childhood in a new light. Sure, I had realized it was upsetting for my father to drive the corpse of his friend to his family's home and to help dig out bodies from the rubble, but it wasn't until now that I really faced how heartbreaking the earthquake must have been for my parents.

And though this time around I was far away from the earthquake's damage, the devastation struck me harder.

But should it have? I admired how instead of discussing the tsunami and how it affected them personally, my Japanese colleagues were focusing more on their work and helping their students. In contrast, there I was, without any close friends or family in the affected areas, somehow making the disaster about me.

I could also understand that the teachers at my schools probably didn't want to discuss the earthquake with a foreigner. Japan was getting a lot of bad international press following the emergency at the Fukushima Daiichi nuclear power plant in the aftermath of the tsunami, and whenever I brought up the tsunami my colleagues would ask me to tell all of my friends back home that everything in Japan was fine.

I felt shut out by the other teachers, and in a way I was shutting myself out, or at least my feelings about the tsunami, trying to be as stoic as everyone around me. But it was also confusing being held at more of a distance, when the tsunami made me feel closer than ever to the people around me and in the country. A big reason I was so upset was due to the history I had with Japan; yet instead of bonding over our shared grief, no one wanted to talk to me about it.

After the Kobe earthquake my family briefly stayed at a shelter, as there was a chance our house might fall down. We were given futons to sleep on, and as time went by my family's allocated area grew with piles of gifts and blankets offered by our neighbors. Now, my mind might have embellished this with time, but as I remember it, by the end of our stay we were perched atop a stack of futons piled right up to the ceiling, covered in so many blankets, trinkets, and snacks that at one point we lost my sister Nina and my mother had to dive under packets of rice crackers to find her.

I still want to cry when I think about how sweet and generous everyone was to us after the earthquake, when so many around us had lost a lot more than we had, but I also remember thinking that this futon situation was really weird. Or perhaps I had heard my parents discussing it afterward. We had all just shared a traumatic experience, yet it was as if our Japanese neighbors were very kindly, and very gently, pushing us away.

And then we left.

Of course, this time I didn't leave. I had no need to leave, and I'd just signed the contract for another year. Just a few weeks later April arrived, and with it the start of a new school year. This brought a fresh start for me, mostly thanks to our new English teacher, Miyuki. Her mother was from the Philippines, so Miyuki understood what it was like to be an outsider in Japan. We quickly became friends, and she would often laugh over funny things that had happened during the day — usually involving my awkwardness or the awkwardness of the other teachers attempting to interact with me.

Seeing her laugh over my social stumbles made me realize that I had been taking myself too seriously, and that making mistakes here wasn't the end of the world, and even if I saw people around me look embarrassed, maybe they could laugh about it as well.

I also eventually learned to forgive the sea, once again appreciating the beautiful coastal drives to my schools. And while I was very excited when it was time for me to leave Japan, I left incredibly grateful for everything those two years had given me.

And one of those things was money.

I always credit my time in Japan for giving me the travel career and lifestyle I have now. JET paid the same salary to its English teachers regardless of where in Japan we lived. So while the salary might have just covered living costs for teachers in Tokyo and Osaka, life on Tanegashima was so cheap that I managed to save the bulk of my earnings. I left Japan with over forty thousand dollars in savings, which opened up a lot of opportunities for me. And because my time in Japan had been so difficult, I was very selective about how I wanted to spend that money. Was a dinner at a fancy restaurant or an expensive pair of boots worth all those lonely months on Tanegashima? Probably not. Was a weeklong horse trek through the Kyrgyz mountains worth it? Maybe.

At least that's what I usually tell people. My savings from Japan allowed me to travel for several years, which eventually led to my current job as a travel blogger, and the difficult time I experienced on Tanegashima motivated me to live life to the fullest, only pursuing experiences I was passionate about.

But there's actually more to it than that. In Japan I attempted to immerse myself in a culture so rich and complex that I couldn't possibly master it in only two years. This was the time in my life when I tried the hardest to fit in and to adopt a way of acting and even thinking foreign to my own. This inevitably led to frustration and disappointment, but it also opened my perspective to a new way of living and in some respects, a new version of myself.

This revelation set me on a journey to explore more lifestyles around the world, hoping that I might find a place that felt more like home than Japan, or even my home country of the United States, ever had. After leaving Japan I traveled full time for three years, visiting more than fifty countries.

My travel work also brought me back to Japan several times. And while those visits took me through emotional highs and again down into anxiety and self-doubt, they also reminded me that Japan will always be a part of who I am. No, I never considered Japan a true home, but over the years the country became a sort of adopted family member — one who continues to drive me crazy, but without whom my life would not be the life I have now.

About the Author

Silvia Lawrence was born and grew up in Worcester, Massachusetts, and studied philosophy at Williams College. After teaching in Japan, she traveled through over eighty countries on six continents, before finally settling in Tromsø, Norway, where she runs the popular travel blog *Heart My Backpack*.

2

Figure in a Landscape

By Stephen Mansfield

For no particular reason, except the insistent magnetism of the object itself, I am turning a *guinomi*, a sake cup, in the early morning light of my hotel room in Naha. Made from a mixture of feldspar and ash grass, the small object has a degree of weight and heft you would not expect, as if drawing its authority from deep geological strata.

Its pitted surfaces, umber and murky green, recall the *aburabei* walls of old Japanese gardens. Centuries of exposure to the elements, to rain and baking sunlight, cause the oil to seep out of the walls, creating surfaces akin to stained murals. The irregular surfaces of the walls are less defect than felicitous effect. A shallow crack on the lip of the cup has been sealed with untreated clay. Deformed or over-brittle objects removed from kilns are often reworked in Okinawa, transformed into pieces whose utility, and rustic beauty, is admired. If ceramicware is cracked or chipped, the debonair *artistes*, the Living National Treasures of mainland Japan, are more likely to dispose of the object or, in an act of aesthetic dilettantism, apply visible repairs by means of *kintsugi*, filling the flaw with a mixture of lacquer and 23-carat gold dust.

The guinomi I hold in my hands was made by Paul Lorimer, a potter from New Zealand. It's portable enough to fit in my rucksack and to remove when I have the occasion to sample *awamori*, Okinawa's strong, rice-based spirit. Made from clay dug on the southern island of Ishigaki-jima, the cup's fired, asymmetric surfaces draw the viewer into depths of raw, mineral earth, the heat of this torrid, sub-tropical zone. Much has been written about Okinawa's marine life, prosaic meditations and rhapsodic paeans on its translucent waters and coral gardens, but its most compelling stories speak of land and earth.

I have rented a small motorbike, and, with camera bag slung behind me, rucksack wedged between my legs, I will be riding up north to the sequestered village of Shinzato, on the Motobu Peninsula, where Lorimer makes his home. My hotel is located in one of the less salubrious districts of Naha, tucked into a crooked back alley near the port. It's early when I start out. It's high summer, the heat, engorged with vaporized steam and irradiated sunbeams.

Built by occupying Americans forces in the post-war years as a rapid corridor for the transportation of military convoys and hardware, Route 58 runs from Naha, the prefectural capital, to the northern extremity of the island. I have ridden it countless times. The early stage of this route, consisting of six lanes, is a veritable strip of Americana, a mash of fast food franchises, drive-in shopping centers, supermarkets, U.S. army surplus stores, tattoo studios, bars serving Miller draft and Kentucky bourbon, steakhouses hung with the Stars and Stripes, and dealerships with names like "Johnny's

Used Cars." A great deal of the signage along this section of the highway is in English.

Miles of razor wire surrounding Camp Kinser in the township of Urasoe represent the first of a series of U.S. bases that resemble briskly managed mini-cities. Resuming its northern progress, Route 58 transects the sealed peripheries of Marine Corps Air Station Futenma in the district of Ginowan, a massive installation whose existence depends more on the will of Washington and Tokyo, with their unassailable sense of entitlement, than the wishes of Okinawans. The next township, Chatan, hosts Camp Lester, a base that seems relatively small when compared, a little way up the highway, to Kadena Air Base, the largest such installation in the Asia-Pacific region. Old folks still remember the area when it was an expanse of sugarcane fields. Smidgens of village shrines and family tombs are said to lie within the borders of the base, reminders of communities that once lived there, a way of life that has been lost, drowned out by the noise from fighter jets and the rotary blades of low-flying helicopters. Some locals have complained of impaired hearing. I stop at the fence of an elementary school to watch children playing a lively game of catch ball, as a plane passes overhead in a corkscrew maneuver, and an attack helicopter banks and drops down onto the runway. It is clear from their excited gestures that the children are bellowing encouragement and taunts to each other in their loudest voices. Mouths agape, voices inaudible, they are like small actors in a medieval dumb play. The most sacrilegious acts of our time, the worst desecrations of all, I reflect, have been perpetrated not against churches, mosques, synagogues, or holy reliquaries, but against Mother Nature.

The dark matter of history lingers as Route 58 snakes northward, but, like a malodorous vapor, a mnemonic malediction, begins to wear off as I leave behind the vast bases that blight much of central

Okinawa. Gradually, the shabby ribbon of towns that forms a kind of urban bricolage, is replaced with farmland and salt breezes. Nature reasserts itself in belts of sub-tropical groves of sago palm and roadside napa, and glimpses into private gardens of flame tree, bougainvillea, and hibiscus. When the sea appears, I am reminded that this is an island, not an urban corridor. Here, the world seems a little fresher, a touch more natural and renewed for it. It is as if I have passed from a toxic zone to a bucolic one. In this more laconic world, you begin to sense the deceleration of time. And the light here, as I pass into Okinawa's rural fastness, is magnificent. One yearns for it long after leaving. Okinawans, unlike mainland Japanese, with their folk tales of forest ghouls, starving demons, and spirits wailing at the bottom of wells, are not much given to darkness and shade. The light is too relentlessly clear for that. One begins to understand why Lorimer, a craftsman whose working material is the earth itself, would choose to relocate to a region soaked in beauty and an appealing tropical lassitude. In the chain's outer islands, and in secluded parts of mainland Okinawa, it is still possible to travel back in time, to experience a slowing down of velocity, even gravity. It is still possible on islands like this to be woken by silence.

In our minds, islands should be counter worlds, autarchies unsullied by continental concerns. We should arrive spellbound, leave reinvigorated, anointed by their beauty. Mostly, this happens. It is almost impossible to set foot on an island without experiencing the sensation that you have been there before. These emotions of recognition come from their link to the idea of Creation, the opportunity to repeat the experiment on a small, more personal scale. Central and northern Okinawa offer a glimpse into this cauldron of creation.

Even on these green, rural roads I pass along, the humid, super-heated salt air is intense. It is good to be on the motorbike, runnels of breeze cooling me down. The roadside boundaries of forests here at the heart of the Motobu Peninsula are too lush to ignore, the prospect of rural serendipity under a canopy of giant fronds, sapanwood trees, and Ryukyu pine, too strong to resist. Stopping a little way beyond Izumi, a tiny village known for its orange groves, I follow the gurgle of a stream running beside a trail, a beaten track so faint it can have been used in recent days only by the likes of hunters and naturalists. Good levels of precipitation and sunlight, and soil rich in minerals and organic matter, make these verdant parts of Okinawa ideal for the growth of wildflowers. Within minutes I have spotted the red spathes of the anthurium, several kinds of cordylines, spiky wild costus, and the stunning inflorescences of the heliconia, whose pendant red and yellow bracts, growing from rhizomes, are erect. Brave the dark forest at night, I am told, and it is possible to detect the scent of flowering trees like *Amherstia nobilis*, whose golden petals are associated with plumeria and Indian laburnum.

The hardy sea hibiscus appears throughout the islands. Few gardens here are without a cluster or two of the flower. In the past, hibiscus might be planted beside a household's outside toilet, not for their fragrance, but because its large leaves, soft and round, could be crumpled in the hand and used as a substitute for toilet paper. The bright yellow flowers of the allamanda, a scrub-like woody vine, are often confused with the hibiscus. A staple in the tropics, it does well in salty air, making it an ideal flower for sea-facing gardens. It often creeps across the coral walls of Okinawan residencies. The flowers are sometimes seen growing over *hinpun*, a screen wall placed inside the main walls of a garden, between the entrance and the residence, its purpose to protect the home from malign spirits, which are thought to travel in straight lines. The walls, it is believed, deflect them. Many of these older gardens contain sealed wells. Fan palms can still be seen beside some wells, following an ancient belief that their roots could purify water as it passed through the earth. Okinawan flowers appear to have a photosynthetic energy that provides greater resistance to the withering effect of hard, direct sunlight. Not that dazzling sunshine is a prerequisite for appreciating flowers. Early morning, with its subdued light, is a fine time to be in the company of flowers. The highly active oils that provide their fragrance is most concentrated at this time, the warming sun gradually evaporating their perfume.

It is past noon, the air roasted but silk-like against the skin, as I wind through the peninsula en route to Paul Lorimer's home. The bedrock of this region, I am told, is composed of Permian and Triassic limestone, igneous rocks such as andesite and quartz porphyry, layers of phyllite, shale, and tuffaceous sandstone, something a potter would know.

Few people have reason to visit the village of Shinzato, its modest residencies and kitchen gardens attractive but unremarkable. Goat droppings on the roads outside the village are a reminder that this is rural Okinawa. When I eventually locate the property, tucked into the end of a lane, Lorimer steps out to meet me, extending a hand so massive that, for an instant, mine vanishes into its grip. It's fitting, I find myself thinking, that a craftsman's hands be coarse, roughly calloused, and marked with a lifetime of work, as Lorimer's are. Exposed to splintered wood, smoldering ash, astringent smoke, and heat trapped in the scorched brick walls of kilns, the working conditions of a potter can be pitiless. A tall, well-grounded figure, a colossus of healthy flesh, muscle, and bone, Lorimer's body, nevertheless, gives the impression of being slightly out of kilter, his movements like a man occasionally groping for

Lorimer in front of his kiln

a banister to steady himself. Decades of sitting at a potter's wheel, powering the contraption manually, damaged his hip, a condition requiring corrective surgery.

When Lorimer first viewed the house, there was little to see, the long-abandoned structure smothered in jungle vine and scree. One of his first tasks was to dig out a termite nest from the living room. It's a very different house today, with polished floors, antique cabinets, rooms lined with stoneware jars, vases, plates, incense burners, and flagons, and outside, a broad, garden-facing, hand-built deck. It's a craftsman's home, but a far cry from the exhibition elegance of a William Morris residence or the vernacular grandeur of potter Hamada Shoji's home in Mashiko.

Lorimer's roots are in the land, and his home reflects it. Raised on a farm on the outskirts of Auckland, he studied oceanography at university but soon dropped out in favor of traveling by yacht to Australia, Indonesia, and a number of other Pacific islands, before returning to New Zealand, where he was employed as a carpenter. Working on the construction of a home and workshop for the master potter Barry Brickell, Lorimer was exposed to wood firing and salt-glazing techniques, a European method in which vaporizing salt attaches itself to the surface of the clay, producing pleasing tones and textures. Lorimer moved to Bizen in Okayama prefecture in 1977, studying there for three years before moving to the warmer climes of Ishigaki-jima, part of Okinawa's Yaeyama chain, where he lived for sixteen years. The opportunity to exhibit more and reach a larger customer base brought him to mainland Okinawa some years ago.

A strong advocate of self-sufficiency, a reliance on the resources of nature, he refuses as a matter of principle to pay for raw materials like the wood he collects for his kilns. Making sure there are no traces of paint or creosote on the timber, he approaches sawmills, whose owners are happy to part with strips of wood made imperfect by the twisting and warping caused by typhoons. Lorimer builds his own kilns, a task that can take an entire month. The bricks for the type of kiln he prefers, the through-draft *anagama*, or "hole kiln," are obtained from waste dumps. A measure of Lorimer's commitment to his craft is evident in the fact that a kiln can take days to fire up, a process requiring a level of patience, stamina, and attention to detail many contemporary potters lack. Favoring a potter's wheel to the electrically operated type favored by many ceramicists, he is also fastidious about the clay types he uses, travelling all over the islands in search of raw materials. Examining bedrock and strata, he has developed a keen geologist's sense when it comes to identifying sites that might yield the dense red, iron-rich clay, often containing difficult-to-fire particles of coral, that is typical of Okinawa. Adamant that a potter should be able to access resources from the natural environment, he never purchases clay. In some instances, he simply locates a likely spot and sets about extracting the material himself. The method is not without its risks. Lorimer relates how, on one occasion, while digging a little too close to a U.S. military installation, a helicopter suddenly appeared, its irate pilot bellowing warnings. "I was out of there like greased lightning!" he recalls with a chuckle.

A small showroom on the grounds of Lorimer's home offers a representative sampling of his work. Its shelves contain sake cups and flasks, culinary dishes and plates, vases, tea bowls, incense burners, and his trademark awamori jars. He also creates *kara kara*, the traditional serving vessels for awamori. Many of these objects result from the *yaki-shime* stoneware technique learnt in his Bizen days. I notice a large jar on the floor of Lorimer's showroom with a sealed door motif. This turns out to be a burial urn that will house the skull of the deceased. Okinawan funeral rites and customs are closer to ancient Chinese practices than Japanese ones. Like many Okinawan potters, Lorimer makes his fair share of *shisa*, the lion-dog figures placed on rooftops or above gate pillars. Bodies of concentrated energy, these fierce, resolute sentinels protect the fortunes of the household. Unlike the shisa typical of souvenir shops, all of Lorimer's lion-dogs have different features. "I need to rest between bouts of making shisa," he says, "or the faces will show my fatigue."

Most of the items in Lorimer's showroom, though noted for their powerful forms, are paragons of virtuous frugality, aligned in their restrained astringency with the notion of rustic elegance. The forms may be contemporary, fresh in their inspirational sources, but the clay represents the sedimentation of time. The pieces are, therefore, at once new and ancient, straddling the immeasurable gulf between transience and immanence. I pick up a flagon, turn it in the light, marveling at the rough, uneven surfaces, by turns radiant and muted. With tonal strata of great complexity, it passes itself off ingeniously as an unschooled work of the utmost simplicity. Although I spy an upstart dish, glazed in Prussian blue, most of the pieces have burnt earth hues. Comparisons are difficult, but some of the pieces might be likened to darker, more brooding Shigaraki works or high-fired Bizen pottery. Each piece is unique, yet might be viewed as part of a homologous whole. Lorimer's work also reveals tastes, techniques, and influences that extend beyond Okinawan or Japanese design methods. These include modern tableware items, earthenware lampshades, wine coolers, and figurative vases that would not look out of place in a fashionable New York gallery or designer home in the south of France.

Like the difference between synthetic fiber and homespun cloth, there is a strong sense of authenticity to this work. Only by handling these objects can you feel their acute tactility. Pottery like this is called *keshiki* in Japanese, a term that refers to the resemblance the irregular surfaces, ash deposits, stains, cracks, and patterns caused by scorching, bear to landscaping. Lorimer's pottery is part of a long geological process, involving the decomposition of rocks into clay, and violent firing in brick kilns, the embers and ash saturations, producing surfaces resembling the deposits left by earth eruptions. One can only imagine the brutal temperatures inside his two kilns, the crackling and bursting, the storms of ash, the heat, all the callous randomness of nature, hardening and fixing clay into objects of understated beauty, deforming others. Under the intense heat and pressure of the kilns, the clay is volatile, altering form, asserting characteristics impossible to replicate. There is usually one spot, and Lorimer's pottery is no different in this regard, where the materiality of the clay is left unglazed, untouched by dribble glaze, running slips, or spur marks. On cups and bowls this area of untreated clay is commonly the *kodai*, the foot or base of the object. This reveals the intrinsic, artisanal qualities of the material, its *tsuchi-aji*, or "clay flavor." A most singular craftsman, Lorimer embodies in equal measure the elemental and urbane. A man who extracts his own clay, builds kilns by hand, firing them up in the summer, he is also a researcher, devoting part of his time to establishing the provenance of specific clay types. In this role, he may be instrumental one day in helping to reconfigure accepted theories of Okinawan ceramic history.

Much of his work involves producing unglazed storage jars for awamori. Based on distillation methods originating in the kingdom of Siam, awamori is unique for its use of black *koji* mold (*Aspergillus awamori*). Production is a year-round process, aided by the fact that black koji produces citric acid when the starch breaks down into sugars. The high acidic levels protect the fermenting rice mash from invasive bacteria. Only long-grain Thai indica rice is used, the preference a legacy of ancient trading links with Southeast Asia. A good deal of the floor space, shelves, and alcoves in Lorimer's main room are assigned to these jars. In this world of seasoned wood, polished surfaces, and subtle shadows, time itself seems to ripen. The darker tones of his powerful stoneware are well suited to the aging of the liquor. Lorimer, who stresses that flavors and aromas are influenced by clay types, stores identical awamori samples in different earth varietals to see how their internal composition is altered during maturation. Each jar is high fired to prevent leakage. Within the rows of awamori casks, a slow reaction, altering taste, depth and aroma, is taking place between chemical elements, such as manganese, calcium, and magnesium. I can attest, having been steered through a range of older liquors by Lorimer, that clay-matured awamori, in contrast to younger, bottled varieties, has the refining effect of soothing and teasing the palate rather than biting into it. Among the stoneware objects are one or two glass vessels like large bell jars, containing *habu-shu*, the dark liquor hosting the decomposing corpses of venomous serpents. They may have shrugged off their mortal coils in the service of maturation, but their faces, paralyzed in vicious death throes, are still alarming.

* * *

For this visit, I have brought salt from the island of Hamahiga as a gift. Lorimer is not a health zealot, but I know he follows, as a matter of course and habit, a well-established and conceived food regime based on the wisdom of Okinawan lifestyles and dietary concepts. Such is the health value of its traditional cuisine that Okinawa ranks among a select number of regions in the world — such as the Greek island of Ikaria, Pakistan's Humza Valley, and the Olestra region of Sardinia, designated as Blue Zones —where health and longevity have been directly connected to lifestyle and diet. In its healthiest form, Okinawan cuisine is found in *yakuzen*, or "medicinal food." An almost Ayurvedic approach to consumption and healing, it seeks to restore the body's energy levels and rebalance fluids.

While age-related diseases common to the West have not been eliminated among older islanders, they have been kept to a minimum, evinced in astonishingly clean arteries and low levels of cholesterol. Breast cancer, prostate cancer, and heart disease are rarities. As Okinawans have no particular predisposition to longevity, the reasons are assumed to be a combination of diet, regular exercise, and low-stress lifestyles. Longevity, naturally, loses its luster if it is synonymous with infirmity. And that's where the Okinawan model again surprises, with the elders not only living longer but enjoying persistently robust constitutions. Elderly Okinawans suffer far lower risks of arteriosclerosis than other Japanese, the lower level of heart and blood related diseases often linked to the quality of the water and soil, both of which are rich in alkaline, magnesium, potassium, and calcium. Unlike mainland Japan, whose acidic water is soft, Okinawa's underground and tap water is hard, a characteristic believed to have a softening effect on blood vessels. Calcium properties in the soil also differ, the Okinawan variety containing a higher lime content derived from its coral reefs.

Ingrained habits among the elders include taking a little time each day to commune with their ancestors, tending chemical-free kitchen gardens, maintaining strong family and community bonds, and belonging to *moai*, mutual support groups of five friends dedicated to each other for life. Many old folks begin the day with prayers for the well-being of their children and grandchildren. Those of advanced age tend to be physically active, many taking part in village events, volunteer activities, and senior citizens' clubs. Many continue tending their kitchen gardens until the end of their lives. A relatively high sun count throughout the year may explain the concentrated richness of its vegetables and tropical fruits, the stronger fragrance and taste of its herbs.

Lorimer, who pays exacting attention to the correlation between diet, lifestyle, and health, gained his early knowledge of plants and herbs some forty years ago, when he was employed cutting the undergrowth in the hills of Ishigaki-jima. "My coworkers," he explains, "were mostly older men who taught me which trees and seedlings to leave and which to cut out. I also observed several of them collecting different plants to take home." These were herbs, natural medicines, his co-workers pointing out what they were used for. This led to questioning elderly people about the use of medicinal plants. While medics and nutritionists debate the faintly narcotic effects of certain herbs, Okinawan elders have simply applied an inherited, applied wisdom, singling out the harmful from the efficacious.

At first glance, Lorimer's plot of land resembles nothing so much as a wilderness, an unkempt allotment, overrun with a riot of invasive plant life. Closer inspection reveals an emerging order in patches of greenery too delineated in their planting to be weeds. Medicinal herbs grow wild in Okinawa, so Lorimer only has to plant a small number of types, vary them through the year, and adjust his diet accordingly. He talks me through his garden, identifying *chomeiso* (long-life plant); Okinawan *sansho*; the spin-ach-like *handama* (two-colored gynura), which, being high in iron, reduces anemia; *Ryukyu yomogi* (Okinawan mugwort); and *fuchiba* (felon herb). Here there is *botanbofu* (Japanese peucedanum), which addresses high blood pressure, alleviates rheumatism, acts as an anti-sclerotic agent, and can work as a cough medicine; there, a sprig of *gekitsu* (orange jasmine, or cosmetic bark tree), which Lorimer claims is an instant cure for diarrhea. It soon becomes clear that we are not walking through a theoretical terrain but a tried and tested one, as Lorimer points out an herb known as *seronbenkei* (air plant), which he crushed, removed juices, made into a poultice, and used to great effect on his son's bruised arm after he complained that he could not sleep.

Lorimer uses herbs as cures for specific ailments and as preventive medicine. Since living in Okinawa, he has never resorted to Western medications. The second usage of herbs, connected to the maintenance of good health, is for everyday consumption in the dishes he prepares. He also makes his own herbal brews and mixtures of hibiscus flowers, mint, lemon grass, guava leaves, and *getto* (shell ginger) seeds. He even mixes his own potions for treating minor ailments like colds. He makes *habu* oil, derived from the venomous serpent of the same name, as a balm for grazes, cuts, and burns. *Nigana*, or bitter leaf, fires up the taste buds, but may also help, if Okinawan assertions are to be credited, in the treatment of stomach ulcers and fevers, for boosting blood supply, and for controlling body temperature. I recall this being effectively paired with *sashi-yagi* at a hole-in-the-wall restaurant in Naha, the herb offsetting powerfully odiferous slices of raw goat. These are among a sampling of the many herbal varietals that have passed from the pharmacopeia of Lorimer's garden onto his table, turning the simplest fare into a natural gourmet taste experience. Cognizant that much of the wisdom associated with the knowledge of herbs and their appreciation is vanishing with the passing of the elderly, Lorimer has translated a book into English, *Okinawa Yakuso Hyakuka* (*An Okinawan Natural Medicine Dictionary*), by Masako Ota.

Sitting on Lorimer's wooden deck, sipping turmeric tea, I reflect that, unlike mainland Japanese gardens, which, however beautiful, can seem like partitioned galleries or art installations, intended for hushed observation, Okinawan gardens are interactive spaces. Rather than contemplate nature, locals engage with it, sitting and chatting under the shade of trees, smelling nature, feeling it ripple over their skin. Casting an eye over Lorimer's half cultivated, half wild estate, I wonder how many of us, spellbound by the transcendent naturalism described in Henry D. Thoreau's *Walden*, or poet Janet Frame's account of her stay in the Iberian Islands before the advent of mass tourism, have dreamed of achieving maximum quality of life at minimum expense, by withdrawing to a corner of rural Japan like this? With a tinge of envy and pledges to visit again, I reluctantly make my farewell, tracing a fresh route along the coast.

A fixation on these independent land masses has led me to visit every inhabited island in Okinawa. The obsession with islands has a name: nesomania. Literature is full of island lore, narratives, and allegory — some of it magical (think *The Tempest*), some malign (*Lord of the Flies*). Mostly, the effect of islands on the human mind is benevolent. There is something hopeful, even redemptive, about the beauty and power of these semi-tropical islands on the periphery of Japan.

A little south of Lorimer's home, I park on high ground with an unimpeded view of the East China Sea. Out in the middle of this featureless ocean I had expected the sea to resemble a healing blue ointment, but thunderheads quickly sweep overhead, turning the water into indigo furrows, their spectral shadows passing into phantasmagoric depths far removed from the land.

About the Author

British-born Stephen Mansfield is a Japan-based author, journalist, and photographer with decades of experience covering Asia. His many books on Japan include multiple titles on its gardens and capital city, among them *Japanese Master Gardens* and *Tokyo: A Biography*.

3

On Tsushima

By Austin Gilkeson

Strategically located about halfway between Kyushu and the Korean Peninsula, Tsushima is one of Japan's best-kept travel secrets. My 2017 Lonely Planet Japan guidebook, for example — despite running over nine hundred pages — does not have a single mention of this picturesque, history-rich island. And that's not because it's a mere islet. Tsushima stretches about seventy kilometers, long enough and sufficiently important through the centuries to have had two canals built across it, the first in 1671 and a second in 1900. The island played a vital role in the peopling of Japan, regional trade and diplomacy, cultural exchange, and military struggles.

American Austin Gilkeson spent two years on Tsushima teaching English as an Assistant Language Teacher (ALT) in the JET Programme. He has two pieces about his time there, the first on an unlikely "friendship" with a student called Yuka, and another on exploring the island.

Yuka, My Enemy

SIXTH grade was the year I had no friends and — perhaps not coincidentally — the year I wore bright patterned sweatpants to school every day. My hair stuck out in cowlicks. In my backpack, along with my Trapper Keeper binder and textbooks, I carried well-thumbed fantasy books and a thick binder of Marvel super-hero trading cards. I wasn't bullied much, though; mostly I was left completely alone, wandering the middle school hallways like a terribly dressed ghost.

We moved twice in two years while I was in high school, which meant I got to leave behind any human being my age who remembered the Year of Sweatpants. I also started combing my hair. My sense of humor honed to a sarcastic edge, I learned that making friends is easier when you're "funny." By the time I started grad school at twenty-three, I'd learned to make friends quickly and easily. I wasn't that shy, lonely kid in sweatpants anymore; I was witty and charming (or so I liked to think). And then I went right back to middle school, only this time I found myself on the other side of the teacher's desk, and the other side of the earth.

When I took a job in 2004 as a middle and elementary school assistant English teacher on the Japanese island of Tsushima, I fancied myself as Frodo Baggins from *The Lord of the Rings*: bravely setting off on an adventure to a faraway land. When I arrived on the island, I quickly realized I was more like Frodo's foolish cousin Pippin Took: a naïve youth in way over his head.

Toyotama, the town I lived in, was composed of little farms and fishing villages. It had one stoplight. When I told a group of students at Kozuna Elementary School that my eyes were naturally blue (they thought I wore colored contacts), they backed away and whispered, "Scary." The first time I went to the grocery store, my appearance alone caused a small child to burst into tears.

Like most expats, I had bouts of culture shock, made worse by my linguistic and geographic isolation. I loved teaching, but outside the English classroom I felt like a poltergeist trying to communicate a message to the living, one who succeeded only in making weird noises no one could understand. Even after months of language study, my conversations in Japanese often amounted to little more than, "The weather is nice," or, on my more daring attempts, "I was stung by fried chicken while swimming in the sea," (the words for "fried chicken" and "jellyfish" sound similar in Japanese).

I remember sitting at a work party, trying to understand a funny story the art teacher was telling about his college roommate. "I had a weird roommate, too," I finally said in Japanese, recalling my freshman roommate and his habit of using our floor as his personal dumpster. The other teachers looked at me, waiting for more. "He was dirty. Trash ... a lot," I said. They gave me polite smiles, and the art teacher picked up his story again. I slumped back into silence.

I became friends with some of my Japanese co-workers and neighbors, but my poor language skills and the cultural barriers still created unwanted distance between us. My jokes fell flat, and I struggled to move beyond small talk and really connect with people. I didn't just feel out of place — I'd expected that, after all. I didn't feel like *me*. Or rather, on my lowest days, I felt like that older me I thought I'd left behind: the quiet, friendless kid in sweatpants.

* * *

During my second year in Toyotama, I began taking a calligraphy class after school with my Canadian friend Sylvia, at the invitation of our friend Asako. Asako was a star graduate of the class, and I envied the beauty of her writing, the way that, in her hands, words themselves could become works of art. I never got anywhere near that level, but it was a nice way to learn both a traditional Japanese art and practice my kanji writing. Most of the other attendees were my students from Toyotama Elementary School, sent to brush up their kanji skills. The calligraphy teacher was a grandmotherly woman called Oyama-sensei, who taught the class in a small studio next to her house. We sat on tatami floors at low tables and practiced writing the sample characters in black ink, then took them to Oyama-sensei, who corrected them with reddish-orange. My efforts usually came back bloodied.

Sylvia and I chatted and joked with Asako and the students — all but one, that is. A nine-year-old fourth grader with French braids, Yuka, studiously ignored us. She sat at the table in front of us and concentrated on her calligraphy.

But then one day, as I was talking with Sylvia before class started, Yuka dipped her brush deep into her ink, turned around, and stuck it straight into my mouth. I froze, shocked by the bitter, earthy taste of the ink. Yuka flashed me a toothy grin and then burst out laughing.

My tongue and teeth were stained black for a few days, and Yuka went from the quietest student in class to the most mischievous.

She hid my calligraphy supplies regularly. She stole my shoes from the entryway. And then the drawings started.

One day, Yuka gave me a piece of calligraphy paper with a crude pencil drawing of my smiling face and the words "*Osutein wa teki*": Austin is my enemy.

It was the first in a series, always delivered with a smile at the start of class: "Austin is Dracula," "Austin is the Devil," "Austin is a mummy," "Austin is dead." The drawings became more elaborate, with my pencil likenesses gaining horns and blood-dripping fangs. I decided to play along, and drew a picture of her and wrote, "*Yuka wa tomodachi*": Yuka is my friend. When I handed her the drawing, she said, "We're not friends. We're enemies," and returned it. I pretended to be distraught. She laughed.

Whenever I arrived at Toyotama Elementary School, Yuka would greet me with a wave and a smile. "Yuka is my friend!" I would say.

"Austin is my enemy," she'd reply.

After a few weeks of this routine, I showed up one day at Oyama-sensei's studio and found a drawing at my usual seat that read: "Austin is my friend." Though I'd enjoyed all the other drawings, this one touched me. The next time I saw Yuka, I thanked her.

"What?" she said, sounding offended. "I didn't draw that."

As it turned out, one of the other kids worried that Yuka had hurt my feelings and wanted to cheer me up. It was a sweet gesture but unnecessary. I adored Yuka's drawings. I also enjoyed her teasing. It was my kind of humor, sarcastic and a little morbid, and also the rare Japanese joke I understood — even though I myself was the butt of it.

Even though I couldn't yet express how I felt in Japanese, Yuka could. Consciously or not, she had taken my feelings of alienation and monstrousness and turned them into a hilarious joke we two

Osutein wa teki

shared. In her own innocent way, Yuka got me — in both senses of the word.

Eventually my contract ended and it was time to move back to the States. After my final lesson at Toyotama Elementary, I was in the hallway talking to a group of students when Yuka walked up and hugged me. She pointed to a poster on the wall of smiling children playing together.

"That's what we are," she said. "Friends."

"That's right," I replied, and blinked back tears.

A week later, as I was walking down the street to my last calligraphy class with Oyama-sensei, a gray van passed me going the other way. Yuka leaned out the window, and I saw her big, toothy smile. She waved to me. I waved back. Then I watched the van continue down the road until it reached the town's sole stoplight, where it turned and disappeared.

* * *

There are friends we keep for decades through shared experiences and intimacy, the Samwise Gamgees who remain with us on our journeys through life. And then there are the brief, peculiar friends we stumble upon on strange detours off the expected path. We may not know them well or for long, but they linger in our memories, like dreams of a far country.

While a few of my former students from Toyotama have found and friended me on Facebook — seeing them as grown-ups, with jobs and families, makes me feel both incredibly proud and utterly ancient — Yuka hasn't. Sometimes I wonder if she would remember me, but I also know that's beside the point. We all grow up and change, and if part of me is still that lonely little nerd in sweatpants, it's only a part. Whoever and wherever Yuka is now, she's no longer that little girl in French braids. I hope she is happy, and remembers some of the English I taught her.

Last fall, during a trip to my wife Ayako's hometown near Kobe, Japan, we visited the home of her old calligraphy teacher, Katayama-sensei. The teacher invited us into the studio on the first floor of her house. Our five-year-old son, Liam, sat at a low table and practiced writing the character for the new year on a calendar, which the teacher then kindly corrected with her reddish-orange ink. The smell of the ink transported me back to Oyama-sensei's studio, and those hot, quiet afternoons in my own calligraphy classes with Sylvia, Asako, Yuka, and the other kids.

We go back to Japan about once a year. Now that my Japanese has improved, I can usually keep up with the conversation at gatherings with my wife's family and friends. But sometimes, when I'm feeling a bit lost, I leave the adults and go outside where the kids are. Playing with Liam, my nieces Haruka and Hikaru, or Ayako's friends' kids, feels comfortable and familiar, like slipping into an old pair of shoes, or slipping into English. It's not just that I have an intimate knowledge of the rules of onigokko (tag) thanks to my time in Toyotama; like the children, I'm still learning how to navigate the adult Japanese world. Perhaps that's why Yuka got me so well: I might have been her teacher, but in that little studio near Oyama-sensei's house, we were both students — still learning our kanji and the rules of the world around us.

Sometimes I think of my old friend Yuka as I watch Liam grow up; as Ayako and I try to teach him Japanese and English, along with rules and manners. Like most five-year-olds, he makes a point to test his limits and what he can get away with. This often takes the form of teasing: he'll ask for a kiss and then playfully bite our noses. He'll burst into a room and shout "Boo!" trying to scare us.

He likes to run up and headbutt my stomach or smack it like a drum. The other day he told me I was, "the chubbiest adult in the world!"

Liam also loves to draw, and he especially loves to draw monsters. Our basement has a low table where he can sit on the carpeted floor and conjure all kinds of beasts from his imagination onto blank sheets of paper: vampires, zombies, skeletons, demons, and werewolves. One day a few months ago, we were at the table and he drew a picture of me as a giant monster from the Japanese TV show *Ultraman*. "You're the bad guy, Daddy!" Liam said and laughed. I laughed too. And I couldn't help but look up at the picture framed on the wall above his drawing table, Yuka's pencil drawing of my face and the words *"Osutein wa teki."*

The Shallow Sea

One night in October 2012, three South Korean men broke into a small Buddhist temple in the sleepy fishing village of Kozuna, on the remote Japanese island of Tsushima, and stole an ancient statue of the bodhisattva Kanzeon. When caught three months later, the men claimed they weren't stealing the statue at all but retaking it for Korea, centuries after it was plundered by pirates from Tsushima. Japan disputed the claim and demanded the statue be returned. A South Korean court ruled the statue belonged to Korea, and the matter remains unsettled.

Soon after the theft, I opened the *New York Times* website at my office in Chicago, and saw a photo of the little temple under the headline: "Japan-Korea Dispute Revived by Statue's Theft." I recognized the temple at once. I lived on Tsushima from 2004 to 2006, in the town of Toyotama, which includes Kozuna. I'd passed the temple dozens of times on my twice-monthly visits to teach English at Kozuna Elementary School. I couldn't believe I was seeing a picture of the village in the *New York Times*.

How had Kozuna, an isolated fishing village so small the school had only a dozen students with four surnames between them, ended up on the front page of the United States' preeminent newspaper? How had a theft from an unremarkable temple sparked an international incident? One reason is that both Japan and Korea claim the statue. The other is that Tsushima sits both at the end of the world, and at the heart of it.

The island is remote and rural, covered by forested mountains roamed by wild boars and subspecies of deer, martens, and leopard cats found nowhere else on earth. But Tsushima also sits within sight of a major metropolitan area. On a day trip to Tsushima's northern tip, I glimpsed the sun glinting off the skyscrapers of Busan, South Korea, fifty kilometers across the water. From Toyotama, where I lived, I sometimes saw the mountains of Korea looming like a blue wall on the edge of the ocean. Tsushima is the only place in Japan where you can see the Asian continent.

Living on Tsushima, I quickly came to understand how the island's geography defines its history and culture. Tsushima lies halfway between Kyushu and Korea. The East China Sea laps at its eastern shore. And Aso Bay, the great marine bite in the center of the island, faces the continent like an open door.

Aso Bay nearly bisects Tsushima, the island's northern and southern halves linked only by a tendril of land in Mitsushima town. The bay offers shelter and calm from the rough seas that surround the island. For countless centuries, it was a rest stop between Japan and the continent, the place where ambassadors, pirates, traders, scholars, and armies gathered before setting sail this way or that.

The standard kanji for Aso Bay are 浅茅湾, meaning "shallow reed bay." But I also encountered another set of kanji for Aso: 浅海 — "the shallow sea." I've always liked that version of the name more. It's more poetic, at least in English, and the bay has a sea's worth of historical sites scattered around its shores. But to reach them, I found I needed to strap on hiking boots or pick up a paddle.

In June of my second year on the island, my parents and younger sister came to visit me. I wanted to show them the island at its best, so I called up my friend Ueno-san, who spent his nights running an *izakaya* (a traditional Japanese pub) in the main port town of Izuhara and his days leading sea kayaking trips around Aso Bay and the rest of the island. He knew Tsushima's every cove and cranny.

My family and I met Ueno-san at a small inlet in Toyotama, where our kayaks were waiting. We pushed off and paddled out into Aso, past the islets and pearl farms studded across the bay. After lunch on one of the islets, we paddled to the other side of the bay, where a narrow pass flows between two high, rocky cliffs. The northern cliff, called Nokowaki Rock ("saw cut"), is a towering spire of stone dotted with trees. It looks like something out of a Chinese ink painting. Or, as my sister Jenna pointed out as we paddled beneath its vast stone feet, the colossal Argonath statues the Fellowship float by in *The Lord of the Rings*.

What lies beyond Nokowaki Rock is no less fantastical than Middle-earth. We paddled hard through the rushing waters of the narrow pass and into a calm inlet. Ueno-san guided us to a thin, muddy beach where we pulled in the kayaks. We extracted ourselves from our seats, and after a brief stretch of our legs, headed up the hill and into the woods. A broken stone staircase led to a seemingly abandoned Shinto shrine, its door broken, its bell silent, its stone lion-dogs furred with green lichen. Past the shrine, we hiked alongside a gurgling waterfall, and then over a small bridge. After a brief, steep scramble up a rocky incline, we came into a clearing. Looming over us was a high stone wall, its corner sharp as a ship's prow. The wall ran along the crest of the hill and then disappeared into the forest. We'd come to the ancient ruins of Kaneda Castle.

Ueno-san explained that the castle was built in AD 663, during an alliance between Japan and one of the three warring Korean kingdoms of the time. Japanese and allied Korean soldiers manned its walls, preparing for a possible invasion. It was Japan's first stone castle, the great-great-grandfather of Himeji-jo and the other samurai castles that rose in the feudal era. The invasion from Korea never came, and eventually the castle was abandoned. Nature quickly conquered it, and today all that remains is the wall, most of it little more than rubble, and the mountain's name: Joyama, "Castle Mountain." We walked among the ruins for a while, then hiked back to the beach and our kayaks, pushed off into the water, and headed home.

I returned to Joyama a few months later with my friends and fellow English teachers Aaron and our friend Sylvia. This time we came on foot, up a gentle hiking trail through the brown autumn forest. We weren't looking for Kaneda Castle but another fortification built on Joyama, twelve centuries later. After a short hike, we found it: vine-choked brick walls, algae-slicked wells, machine gun nests full of weeds and broken stones, and deep, dark bunkers carved into the hillside.

The bunkers were filled with leaves, mud, and animal droppings. When Aaron and I ventured into one, an enormous brown bat flew out, skimming our heads. The dim blue light of my cell phone showed more bats deeper inside, hanging from the ceiling like dark, quivering stalactites. We ran out as fast as we could.

Like their far ancestors at Kaneda Castle nearby, the Japanese soldiers who manned these bunkers were preparing for a potential invasion from the continent. This time not from a Korean kingdom but from Russia. The bunkers never saw combat, but the climactic battle of the Russo-Japanese War was fought in the rough waters just offshore at the end of May 1905. It was a decisive Japanese victory, one that shocked the world: an Asian nation had defeated a European power for the first time in modern history. The Battle of Tsushima marked the beginning of the Russian Empire's decline, and the rise of the Japanese Empire as a great power.

There are similar bunkers to Joyama's — many far larger and grander, built between the Sino-Japanese War and World War II — scattered across the island. Nature has reclaimed most of them, as it has Kaneda Castle, but they're a reminder that Tsushima is a borderland, and for all the island's pastoral quiet, the outside world is never far away.

Before I visited the bunkers with Aaron and Sylvia, I took a trip to the place where a foreign invasion did land on Tsushima. I drove over the island's serpentine mountain roads into Izuhara town, windows down to let in the breeze, as the engine of my little white car couldn't handle both air conditioning and going uphill at the same time. After an hour, I came out of the mountains and into a flat valley quilted with rice paddies.

The valley ended at Komodahama Beach, a narrow strip of sand and a concrete embankment, with a small shrine at one end. It was there, on October 5, 1274, that Kublai Khan's Mongol forces came ashore. The Mongols ravaged Tsushima before embarking on a failed invasion of Kyushu. Nearly seven years later, in April 1281, the Mongols returned, but that time the islanders managed to drive them off. In August, somewhere in the stormy seas off Tsushima, the great armada foundered in a typhoon that came to be called the divine wind: kamikaze. Japan remained unconquered and, in the view of its leaders, divinely protected.

I walked down Komodahama as the sun sank behind the green hills. I tried to imagine the scene all those years ago, of Mongol soldiers coming ashore and engaging the local samurai in a pitched, bloody battle. But my imagination wasn't up to the task. I couldn't get past the tranquility of that little beach, the calm of the dusk gathering around me. Tsushima's history isn't just hidden in coves and forests; it's also buried in the deep quiet of the centuries.

The more I read about the history of the island, the more the ruined wall of Kaneda Castle seemed like a border itself, marking the divide between history and myth. On this side of the wall, the well-recorded history of the island from the seventh century up to the present. On the far side: "Here Are Dragons." Quite literally.

My town, Toyotama, was named after a dragon goddess, Princess Toyotama, daughter of the sea god. Princess Toyotama is venerated at a number of shrines across the island, but none more beautiful than her namesake town's Watazumi Shrine. The shrine sits in a large cove of Aso Bay, its sanctuary tucked within a primeval forest. Five stone torii gates lead from the sanctuary to the sea. The last two stand out in the water, and seem to float at high tide.

I went to Watazumi Shrine often. It was a short drive, or long walk, from my apartment. In the spring, we held a *hanami* (flower-viewing) picnic beneath the shrine ground's fluttering cherry blossoms. My second summer, I helped my islander friend Tom (as he called himself) sell shaved ice from a stall on the shrine grounds during the summer festival. But more often I went alone, to read or relax in the tranquil grounds, after stopping at the sanctuary to pay my respects to the dragon goddess.

In the myth, a mountain deity named Hoori arrives at Watazumi Shrine looking for his brother's lost fish hook. He doesn't find the hook, but he does find Princess Toyotama. The two fall in love and marry. They live first in Toyotama's palace at the bottom of the sea but move to the land when she becomes pregnant with their son. Hoori builds a hut roofed with black cormorant feathers where Toyotama can give birth. She warns him not to look at her during her labor. But this is a myth, and in myths curiosity is never to be denied; and so like the French husband of Melusine, or the Scottish husbands of selkies, Hoori peeks. He sees Toyotama in her true form, a great dragon of the sea (or a shark or crocodile, depending on the version). Toyotama returns to the deep but sends her sister to care for her son. The son grows up and marries his aunt, and among their children is Jimmu Tenno, the legendary first emperor of Japan.

Many places in Japan claim to be the site of the Princess Toyotama myth, and the birth of the first emperor, but it's hard to deny the appropriateness of Tsushima's claim. After all, so much of what became Japanese culture flowed directly through the island from the Asian continent. The Yayoi people, who along with the Jomon comprise the ancient roots of the modern Japanese people, would have come through Tsushima with their bronze wares and rice-farming techniques.

During one hike on Tsushima, I came across an old burial mound on a hill. I later learned it's one of a number of ancient Yayoi tombs scattered around the island, many found to be full of pottery and goods from China and Korea. Later imports from the continent, like Buddhism and kanji, would have come to Tsushima before reaching Kyushu and the other mainland Japanese islands. Not far from Kaneda Castle and Joyama's bunkers, at the site of an ancient overland portage, sits a small Buddhist temple that claims to be Japan's oldest.

Even when Japan was closed to the outside world during the Edo era (1603–1867), Tsushima remained open to Korean merchants and emissaries. The Sou clan governed the island and grew rich from the trade with Korea. They did all they could to protect it, including fraud. At a small museum in Izuhara, not far from the remains of the Sou's castle, my friend Mayumi showed me old picture scrolls that tell how the Sou secretly forged messages between the Korean court and the shogun to ensure peace and continued trade. As much as Tsushima's history has been defined by war and conflict, it's also been defined by peace and cooperation.

After the Battle of Tsushima, when the islanders had literally bunkered down to fight, they took in Russian sailors who washed ashore from sunken ships, and gave them food, medicine, and shelter. That fact doesn't surprise me at all. When I arrived on the island a century after those waterlogged Russians, despite my ignorance of the Japanese language and culture, the islanders welcomed me warmly.

It's not that Tsushima is exempt from the usual prejudices. As a white American, I was mostly greeted with curiosity and patience rather than suspicion. But despite the island's economic dependence on Korean tourism, I saw a bar in Izuhara with a "No Koreans" sign on the door. But far more typical than that bar were the kids who eagerly studied Korean, and the islanders like Ueno-san who worked hard to create exchange programs and lasting connections between the people of Tsushima and South Korea.

Not long before I left the island to return to the United States, Tom and his girlfriend Yuka took me to the Arirang Festival, an annual celebration of Tsushima's ties to Korea. Tom was in a motorcycle gang in Fukuoka — his arms sleeved in dragon tattoos — but he drove like a grandpa, crawling over the island roads at ten miles an hour, a cigarette hanging from his lips and an open beer in his lap. When we reached Izuhara, we lined the streets to watch a parade recreate the arrival of Korean emissaries on the island in feudal times. Reenactors and performers in colorful traditional Korean costumes marched and danced in the street. The "emissary" was borne aloft in an ornate palanquin down the asphalt roads. The people of Tsushima took pictures, clapped, and cheered. Later that night at the festival, we bought *takoyaki* from the food stalls, listened to a Korean singer belting out K-pop to an excited crowd of Japanese and Koreans, and watched fireworks bloom over the dark water.

Tensions between the governments of Japan and Korea remain high. The issue of the stolen Buddhist statue is unresolved. But whenever these incidents occur, I think of the Arirang Festival and all that the people of Tsushima have done in those long centuries when history has ignored them, when the fortresses were left to the grass and bats: the slow, quiet work of peace and friendship, of facing the world outside and welcoming it with open arms.

About the Author

Austin Gilkeson worked for two years as an assistant English teacher on the Japanese island of Tsushima, and now lives with his wife and son just outside Chicago. His essays have appeared in *Tin House*, *Catapult*, *Foreign Policy*, *Vulture*, *The Toast*, and other publications.

4

Stone Hammer Mountain

By Brian Burke-Gaffney

Of Japan's four main islands, Shikoku is the least visited by foreigners. It's a good place to experience the beauty and laid-back charms of rural Japan, and it is now easily accessed with three separate networks of bridges across the Inland Sea connecting it to the island of Honshu. Shikoku was off the beaten path back in 1973 when Brian Burke-Gaffney took up residence at a temple in Ehime Prefecture. The young Canadian had arrived in Japan the year before, penniless and battered by his travels on Asia's hippie trails, yet determined to continue his search for spiritual knowledge. Frustrated with his religious experiences in India, he hoped the rigorous discipline of Zen Buddhism would be more fruitful. Buddhism came to Japan from mainland Asia in waves starting from the sixth century. It developed alongside Shinto, the indigenous religion marked by a reverence for nature and its rich pantheon of *kami* (deities). There are several Buddhist schools in Japan. Shikoku is most closely associated with Shingon Buddhism; it's the birthplace of the sect's founder and where eighty-eight of its temples make up Japan's longest pilgrimage. Unlike the esoteric Shingon school (the name derives from the Chinese word for "mantra"), Zen Buddhism emphasizes simplicity and meditation as a means to spiritual cultivation. There are three main Zen schools in Japanese Buddhism, among them the Renzai Sect, and it was to this demanding tradition that Brian Burke-Gaffney would devote nine years of his life, starting in the shadow of Stone Hammer Mountain in a small temple, under the tutelage of a strict Zen master, the only other resident of Busshin-ji.

* * *

NIGHT had fallen by the time I reached the port of Iyo on the northern coast of Shikoku Island. It was early March 1973. I engaged a taxi in front of the ferry terminal and asked the driver to go to Busshin-ji in the village of Komatsu, but the man had either never heard of the temple or mistook my stilted Japanese for an incantation in some impossible foreign language. I showed him a piece of paper with the address written in kanji, but he still had to call his dispatcher three times before finally pulling to a stop at a point in the darkness that he assured me, after getting out of the taxi to check, was the entrance to the temple.

Not a single lamp or house light provided guidance. I groped for invisible banisters and protected my head from hidden beams as I crossed a bridge spanning a creek and walked up a gravel path, passed under the portal of a large building, and cut across an enclosed compound to the sliding door at the front entrance. Inside, a single naked light bulb hung from the ceiling of a traditional vestibule, the yellow glow revealing a spotless earthen floor and deep brown woodwork all around.

"Gomen kudasai!" My call echoed in the dark recesses. A few seconds later, Yamagishi Zenrai Roshi appeared barefoot and knelt down to greet me in the corridor above the vestibule. My teacher-to-be was wearing a rough indigo-blue cotton robe mottled with patches, and his diminutive stature and smooth boyish face gave him the look not of an old teacher as suggested by the title *rōshi* but of a young training monk. I could hardly believe that he was forty-six years old. He ushered me into the temple with an order to put my shoes in the rack to the side and, as I stepped up onto the corridor, to take my socks off as well. The floor felt icy under my feet. He led me to a small room with paper screens on two sides and a large square wooden brazier serving as a table in the center, told me to sit down, and silently went about preparing tea. He ignored the letter I placed on the edge of the brazier — an introductory message penned by the Kyoto University professor who had kindly taken me under his wing and arranged for me to visit Busshin-ji.

"Why did you come?" he asked in English after putting a cup of tea in front of me.

"I want to know the truth of Zen," I answered.

"Fine. You learn Zen quitely."

I would realize later that *quitely* was his word for "exhaustively."

After I finished the tea, he led me along a corridor to the kitchen, switching lights on and off, then out a side door and across a courtyard to a small single-story building. A dome of stars and country silence stood around us. My room was a bare three-mat compartment with a small table, a light bulb dangling overhead, and a window facing what I would discover the next morning to be a bamboo thicket.

"Get up at five. Good night."

After turning off the light, I lay in the thick quilt provided for me and looked up at the dark ceiling boards. Here I was in a Zen temple in Japan, at the end of a long journey from Canada, across Europe and Asia overland to India and then Singapore to Kobe by cargo ship — all in search of the vision of truth and beauty conjured up by the Beatles, Alan Watts, Baba Ram Dass, and the other pied pipers of the sixties.

* * *

My first brief conversation with Yamagishi Zenrai Roshi set the tone for subsequent exchanges. After a day or two he started speaking entirely in Japanese. It was not hard to understand, though, because his utterances were limited to short sentences in the imperative, like "Sit down here" or "Do it this way." Not as much as a word was spoken about Buddhism or Zen, and any attempt on my part to strike up a conversation failed miserably. My ambition to become an ordained monk and to train in one of the ancient monasteries in Kyoto remained a dream as outlandish as it had been when I had conceived it in India, plodding along the back roads of Bihar and Uttar Pradesh wondering what to do with my life.

Busshin-ji is a temple of the Rinzai Zen sect located in the village of Komatsu. A dot on the map of northern Shikoku, the village is best known as the point of access to Ishizuchi-yama (Stone Hammer Mountain), the highest peak on the island. The commercial center has probably changed little since I was there:

a single street stretching for a few hundred meters from National Route 11, flanked by a disparate array of grocery stores, shops, and beauty salons and surrounded by a patchwork of farmland. Despite its proximity to the famous Shikoku Pilgrimage, Busshin-ji is a Zen temple and therefore has no connection to the iconic string of eighty-eight temples, all of which belong to the Shingon Sect.

Founded by the ruling Hitotsuyanagi family in 1650, Busshin-ji maintains a proud if inconspicuous position in the Myōshin-ji School of Rinzai Zen. The cluster of classic buildings nestles as if by mistake amid rice paddies and vegetable fields, hidden in the shade of tall trees and circumscribed by a forbidding earthen wall.

Despite Busshin-ji's remote location and paltry revenue, its small cadre of *danka* (parishioners) insist that the Myōshin-ji School dispatch an unmarried, certified dharma successor to serve as resident priest. Yamagishi Zenrai Roshi trained at Myōshin-ji *senmondōjō*, renowned as one of the strictest Zen monasteries in Japan, for seventeen years and emerged as one of only seven *hassu* (dharma successors) of the much-feared Zen master Kondo Bunko Roshi. He had taken up the post of resident priest at Busshin-ji as part of his traditional training, in Zen parlance a custom called *gogo no chōyō* (post-enlightenment cultivation). He did not have a television, radio, refrigerator, or any other electrical appliance I could see. He abstained from alcohol, tobacco, and non-vegetarian foods, including eggs and milk, and he followed the same schedule every single day regardless of weather, season, or social custom. "No holidays in the mountains," I once heard him say. I simply fell into the routine with him, rising in the predawn darkness to chant sutras in the main hall, going for a brisk walk on the country paths near the temple, then, after breakfast, sweeping the gardens and lanes while the sun broke through the trees. The rest of the morning was allotted for study, the afternoon for work, and the evening for sitting meditation, day after day without change.

At the sutra-chanting service, I was commanded to keep rhythm on a wooden drum and to hit bells at appropriate intervals. I quickly mastered the technique because the sutras were short, and I could help myself recite them by jotting down the sound of each character in the Roman alphabet. I had no idea what I was saying, but it did not seem to matter. Roshi's only advice was to "straighten your back and chant from your belly." The afternoon work was also exceedingly simple and monotonous, usually weed pulling in the gardens and vegetable patch, or floor wiping on rainy days. The only prerequisites were good health, patience, and the ability to distinguish a dandelion from a radish sprout.

Our three daily meals followed the traditional manners of Rinzai Zen. We recited short incantations before and after each meal and used a set of black lacquerware bowls that fit together like Russian matryoshka dolls. Every last morsel of food was consumed, using a piece of pickle to wipe away the remnants and rinsing the bowls with a last gulp of tea.

The menu was simple to the point of austerity, little more than miso soup, pickles, and barley cooked with a sprinkling of rice. Everything was either homegrown or donated by benevolent neighbors. The ingredients of the miso soup were slices of whatever happened to be growing in the vegetable patch or sprouting wild in the fields and hillsides. We even made our own tea, trimming the bushes along the temple lanes, steaming the sprigs over the kitchen fireplace and then kneading them on straw mats.

One day, Roshi announced that he had business in Matsuyama, the capital of Ehime Prefecture, and told me to join him. We walked to the highway and caught a bus into the city, then paid visits to the post office and bank. At the latter, we were invited up to the second floor, where I sat in silence while Roshi talked to the manager. In the middle of the discussion, the manager offered to order something for lunch. Roshi accepted with thanks. A few minutes later, one of the tellers brought up three bowls of ramen with side dishes of pressed rice and radish pickles. The noodles were garnished with strips of bamboo sprout and a slice of pork. I drank all the soup and ate everything except the slice of pork, dutifully leaving it at the bottom of the bowl.

Noticing the pork in my bowl, Roshi said, "Eat it."

I could hardly believe my ears. I looked at him, shocked that he was urging me to break my abstention, and further shocked to see that he had eaten his own slice of pork and swished his bowl with tea so thoroughly that it looked fresh from the dishwasher.

"Eat it!" He raised his voice this time, causing the manager to wave his hand and say, "Oh, please don't worry. If you don't care for it, just leave it."

But Roshi was adamant. I retrieved my chopsticks from their paper sheath and carried meat to my mouth for the first time since ingesting mutton shish kebab in Afghanistan.

"Wasting food prepared with sacrifice and offered with hospitality is more life-killing than eating a bit of pork," said Roshi, donning his priest's cap after we left the bank. "If you're trying to accumulate virtue, do it in private."

Another time, when someone asked him what he would do if he got a sudden urge to eat a steak, he said, "I'd go right out and eat it." Yet he never wavered from his simple vegetarian lifestyle.

I had little trouble emulating Roshi's diet, but adjusting physically to life in the temple was a different matter. My knees and ankles were in a state of chronic pain from having to sit constantly on the floor, and I repeatedly forgot to duck when passing through doorways and smashed my head on the beam. Anyone six feet tall trying to function in a traditional Japanese building is in danger of brain damage until he or she either develops a slouch or invests in a helmet.

Evening *zazen* (sitting meditation) also tended to be more of an endurance test than an opportunity for quiet reflection, let alone an outing to transcendent spiritual regions. Roshi showed me the correct way to sit: back straight, eyes half closed, legs folded in the full lotus position (both feet up on the thighs), and hands molded into a ball with the left thumb held in the right fist. I tried to maintain it, but after a few minutes the pain would become unbearable and I would guiltily slip back into the half lotus position. Concentration was just as impracticable. Roshi suggested that I adopt the breath-counting method — counting exhalations one to ten and then back to one — but I could rarely reach four or five before wandering off into the usual maze of worry and rumination.

One afternoon, Roshi and I set about cleaning the main hall, a large wooden building with a high ceiling and an altar surrounded by a tatami-matted space capable of accommodating at least a hundred people. He told me to sweep the tatami mats and wipe the corridors inside and out while he worked around the altar. We were pursuing our separate tasks in silence when he suddenly called my name. I answered "*hai*" in a loud voice and rushed to the side of the altar where he was standing. He stared at me for a few seconds and then shouted, "Ladder! Bring the ladder!" The tone was one of exasperation, as though he had expected me to know what he wanted beforehand.

I'm sorry, but I'm not telepathic, I grumbled to myself as I ran to get the ladder. It would take a few more years to understand that what Roshi wanted was not extrasensory perception but single-minded engagement in the job at hand. If I had had my wits about me — and if I had been one in spirit with Roshi — I would have noticed instantly from the inflection of his voice and the timing of the call that he needed the ladder. That afternoon, all I had on my mind was a pageant of wistful thoughts about the deep-fried sweet potatoes and chestnut rice and sesame tofu that the women of the neighborhood would probably prepare for the ceremony the following day.

Something similar happened a couple of months later, only with graver consequences.

Roshi handed me a letter that had been among the mail and asked me if it was from my parents in Canada.

"Yes, from my father," I answered, looking at it front and back.

Later that day, I went to the kitchen as usual to prepare tea before the work period. When we finished, Roshi told me to pick weeds in the garden behind the *shoin*, the building containing his quarters and the large main room for formal gatherings.

It was my favorite garden at Busshin-ji, an oasis of tranquility lying in an L-shape around the corner of the building, circumscribed by an earthen wall topped with mottled roof tiles. The ground was covered in a carpet of moss. A few bushes of varying size, well groomed but arranged as though growing naturally in a forest clearing, stood around an old cedar pointing straight up into the sky. Viewed from the open corridor of the building, the garden and the wall surrounding it seemed as old and perfect as the crest of Stone Hammer Mountain rising among the trees in the background.

I was coaxing weeds from the moss with a bamboo spatula when I heard Roshi approach. I barely had time to stand up and notice how angry he looked before he yelled, "Go home!" and started waving his hand in the air as though batting away a horsefly. "A heartless person like you has no business in a Zen temple. Leave at once!"

I was dumbfounded.

"The letter! Your father poured his heart into a letter and went to all the trouble to seal it and mail it," Roshi shouted, "and you leave it lying on the tatami mats where you walk, sit, and fart! Pack up and leave the temple at once!" With that he stomped out of the garden and disappeared into the temple.

My face was burning and my hands were trembling when I returned to my room. Roshi must have noticed the letter while fetching something from the adjacent storage space. It was now lying on the center of my desk. I packed up my things and put on a pair of socks and shoes for the first time since coming to Busshin-ji. A storm of anger and defiance raged in my chest. What a stupid, trivial thing to get so upset about! But I hesitated when I went outside. I put my bag in the doorway and got a broom from the work shed, then went out to the front entrance of the temple and began to sweep the path.

I continued moving my arms until every fallen leaf and pine needle was gone, then went back to start again. The sunlight drained away, sinking the buildings and bamboo groves into a twilight gloom. As the heat of rebellion subsided, I realized with stinging clarity how oblivious I had been to a whole set of human feelings. I had been like a callous dimwit trudging through a field, not even noticing the flowers and insects crushed under my feet.

Roshi appeared from the darkness behind the front gate and said, "Come in and get ready for dinner." It was his usual tone of voice. I returned my bag to my room, and we ate our simple meal in what can only be described as a profound silence. He said nothing more about the incident, and our life continued as before.

* * *

The hours allotted for study every morning opened a blank in my daily schedule, because, aside from the Japanese-language lessons that I had been giving myself since the previous autumn, I had nothing to study, and Roshi was certainly not encouraging me to read or to struggle to understand anything. One day, however, he handed me a book and ordered me to copy it. It was a pad of about two hundred sheets of thin paper hand-bound in the old-fashioned way with a cloth cover. Inside was column after column, page after page of Chinese characters handwritten in black ink.

"Copy it?" I asked back. My first impulse was to refuse. Zen is a teaching beyond words, right?

"Go to the store and buy a notebook," said Roshi, handing me a couple of hundred-yen coins and then turning and disappearing into his quarters. He did not utter a word about the content of the book or the purpose of copying it, nor did he raise the subject again — until one morning after breakfast the following week.

"Bring your notebook," he said.

I had purchased a notebook as instructed and started copying the cryptic characters as best I could with a ballpoint pen. I went to my room and fetched the notebook. Roshi told me to sit on the other side of his table and open it. By that time, I had completed little more than a page, and my renditions looked more like chicken footprints than characters. The only thing I could discern about the book was that it was a collection of phrases grouped according to length, that is, one character, two characters, three characters and so on up to twenty characters or more. Just as the meaning of the morning sutras was completely lost on me, I had no idea what I was writing.

"Read."

"I can't!"

"Then study the first row in the one-character section," said Roshi. With that, he pulled a tattered Chinese–Japanese dictionary up from under the table and put it in front of me with a matter-of-fact "Tomorrow morning we'll try again."

Thus began the painstaking task of searching for the characters and their pronunciations in the Chinese–Japanese dictionary and then trying to decipher the explanations using my little Japanese–English dictionary.

Every morning after that, I sat at Roshi's table, fighting pain and numbness in my legs while presenting my hard-won readings. Roshi corrected me if I made a mistake but eschewed lengthy explanations. When he saw me trying to jot something down, he said, "Don't take notes. They only give you an excuse not to remember."

The book was Roshi's personal compilation of *zengo* (Zen phrases). Despite my inexpert view to the contrary, knowledge of zengo is an essential prerequisite for *sanzen* interviews, the very heart of training in Rinzai Zen. He had been trying all along, wordlessly yet relentlessly, to wean me from my tendency to keep one eye on the work at hand and the other on some future goal.

One of the installments in the two-character section of Roshi's book succinctly expressed the foible: the term *ronen* (驢年). Meaning simply "year of the donkey," it points with a touch of humor to the fact that the year of a person's dreams — the year in the future when he or she expects to finally find happiness — never comes, just as the year of the donkey (unlike the year of the tiger, year of the dragon, or the other years that rotate in the twelve-year Chinese zodiac) never comes no matter how long you wait for it.

While working on the longer passages, Roshi showed me how to decipher the *kaeriten* punctuation marks inserted into Chinese prose to make it easier to read in Japanese. He also gave me blocks of text from ancient works and let me try to read them, again without any discussion as to meaning or historical background, as though, as the Canadian philosopher Marshall McLuhan suggested, the medium itself was the message.

It took about nine months to copy the book and more than a year to go through all the readings, but by the time we finished I had developed a working knowledge of zengo. Never before in my long career as a student had I worked so intensively or experienced such pleasure and satisfaction in the process. And never before had I felt such respect and gratitude toward a teacher.

* * *

The day of my ordination came and passed unremarkably about nine months after my arrival at Busshin-ji. There were no documents to sign, no declaration, no pledge of allegiance to the Buddha or anyone else. All I had to do was keep my head shaved, wear the uniforms of a Rinzai *unsui* (monk), and continue my studies and preparations for advancement to the monastery in Kyoto. There was, however, one unpleasant duty which I found myself compelled to fulfill after ordination, namely attendance at funerals and the services called *hōji* held to commemorate anniversaries of the death of ancestors. Busshin-ji had only a small number of parishioners and so did not see many of those rituals, but because of his high rank in the Rinzai Sect, Roshi was often asked to officiate at funerals held in other parts of Shikoku Island, and I would invariably have to accompany him and participate as drumbeater and incense-bearer.

It was not something that I had reckoned upon when I came to Japan. I had imagined the Zen temple to be an enclave of discipline and self-sufficiency, a timeless niche aloof from the business of the secular world and the hollow sacraments of established religions.

I had perceived Zen to be the one religion that rejected words and symbols in favor of direct insight, as in the maxim "One seeing is better than a hundred hearings."

I was appalled to discover that the majority of monks serving as resident priests at local temples made a living off funerals and hōji. I could hardly suppress a feeling of disgust and disillusionment as I sat in the ceremonies beating the drum and cymbals, with clouds of incense smoke choking the air, the priests wearing gaudy robes and mumbling sutras, and the country folk sitting to the side bowing and rolling *juzu* rosaries in their hands.

It was all just a game, the lay people hoodwinked into thinking that they somehow benefit from the mechanical recitation of sutras and the priests glibly taking advantage of their superstition. My skepticism increased when I learned that most of the priests had been born and brought up in the temples in which they served and that they had wives and children like any other Japanese *salaryman*. They had simply succeeded the positions of their fathers after a perfunctory two or three years of Zen training, just as the latter had taken over from their own fathers in the wake of the Rinzai sect's decision to sanction marriage in the early part of the twentieth century. Yamagishi Zenrai Roshi seemed to be the only real Zen monk this side of Kyoto.

That winter, a student named Koji came to stay at Busshin-ji for a few weeks, ostensibly to hone his powers of concentration for the Ehime University entrance examinations. One day, we were walking together on the narrow road beside the temple when an elderly Busshin-ji parishioner pulled up in his taxi, rolled down the window to say hello, then drove off and turned the corner onto the bridge at the temple entrance. He was a pious man who rang the temple bell every evening and participated in meditation sessions. He even called his company Manji Taxi and embellished the sides of his car with the *manji* character (卍), an ancient symbol of Buddhism and Buddhist temples.

"Manji Taxi?" snorted Koji with an incredulous laugh as the car drove away. "What an unlucky name! How does he find any passengers?"

"Do you mean because manji looks like the Nazi swastika?" I asked, not understanding his surprise and amusement.

"Swastika? No, no. Because manji is the symbol for a Buddhist temple. Riding in Manji Taxi would be like riding in a hearse. Ha, ha, ha!"

It was a shocking revelation. The common Japanese view of Buddhism, I saw for the first time, does not go beyond the scope of funerals and hōji, and the Buddhist temple holds little more significance in Japanese society than a funeral parlor. Now I knew why the young Japanese urbanites I had met after first arriving in Japan — especially the students at the English Conversation Center in Osaka where I worked for a few months — were so astonished to hear that I wanted to become a Zen monk. When they asked me what I planned to do, and I told them that I wanted to enter a Zen monastery, their jaws invariably dropped and their eyes widened in disbelief. Rudyard Kipling's famous comment that "East is East, and West is West, and never the twain shall meet" took on an ironic new meaning. In the huge unbroken metropolis encompassing Tokyo and Osaka, then as now, everything is geared to the pursuit of modernization and economic growth. Buddhist temples, Shinto shrines, and the other trappings of old Japan have been pushed to the fringe of all the noise and activity, just as religion and tradition seem to occupy only the peripheral regions of the national psyche.

A few weeks later, I joined Roshi in making the rounds of the homes of Busshin-ji parishioners during the mid-summer Urabone (Festival of the Dead). As always, it was an ordeal to participate in the theatrics of reciting sutras in front of the little family altars, reading off the posthumous Buddhist names of ancestors and pretending to have some special ability to communicate with the dead. The ancestral name tablets were so numerous in some of the family altars that they hid the figure of Buddha from sight, vividly symbolic, it seemed to me, of how ancestor worship has eclipsed the true message of Buddhism in Japan.

One of the families we visited was commemorating the first Urabone after the death of a grandfather. The altar was decorated with garish cloth curtains and plastic ornaments, and the floor in front of it was as crowded as the base of a Christmas tree with electrically powered revolving lanterns, artificial flowers, and cases of canned fruit, beer, and Coca-Cola. We had to compete throughout the service with the excited commentary of a baseball game because none of the family members thought to turn the television off. The whole thing was so far removed from my image of *The Way of Zen* that I nearly started laughing in the middle of the Heart Sutra.

And when we were walking down the street in single file after leaving the house, I could not hold back an outburst: "Cheap ornaments have nothing to do with the practice of Buddhism." I expected Roshi to agree with me at least in principle, but his response came like a bolt of lightning.

"The reason you find them cheap," he said without looking back or losing a step, as though he had been waiting for me to let it out, "is because *you* are cheap."

I almost fell over into the ditch.

* * *

The following year, Roshi declared me ready to go on to formal training, choosing his alma mater Myōshin-ji, the largest of the five great temples of the Rinzai sect in Kyoto, as my destination and equipping me with all the clothing and utensils that I would need. He did not mention it, but I knew that I would be the first foreigner in history to engage in formal training there.

I left Busshin-ji early one morning, decked out in Zen monk's travelling gear. When I finished tying up my straw sandals and turned to make a last bow, Roshi was sitting in the corridor above the vestibule, just as he had been the evening I arrived so many months earlier. It was all that I could do to hold back tears. I started to say thank you and goodbye, but Roshi stopped me mid-sentence with an order just to depart.

With that I was out the door and down the path to the temple gate, where the light of dawn threw an orange halo up over the summit of Stone Hammer Mountain and the last stubborn stars glinted in the sky.

About the Author

Brian Burke-Gaffney was born in Winnipeg, Canada, in 1950 and came to Japan in 1972, going on to train for nine years as an ordained monk of the Rinzai Zen Sect. He left the priesthood and moved to Nagasaki in 1982. He is currently professor of cultural history at the Nagasaki Institute of Applied Science and honorary director of Glover Garden. He was awarded the Nagasaki Shimbun Culture Award in 2016. He has published several books in Japanese and English, including *Starcrossed: A Biography of Madame Butterfly* (EastBridge, 2004), *Nagasaki. The British Experience, 1854–1945* (Global Oriental UK, 2009) and *The Glover House of Nagasaki: An Illustrated History* (Flying Crane Press, 2015). The present chapter is a revised excerpt from a travelogue entitled *Same Road Different Tracks* (Tellwell, 2016).

5

Falling and Rising on Burning Mountain

By Paul Barach

MY third day of hiking Shikoku Island's ancient Buddhist pilgrimage will be the hardest day of my life, but I don't know that yet. As I wake up on a small bus bench with violent cramps twisting from my palms through my soles, there are only three things that I do know about this journey.

1. Wild boar are terrifying in person and will charge you if they're with their babies.
2. It is the hottest summer in Japan's recorded history.
3. I am in way over my head.

I have plenty of time to reflect on these facts as I wait for the cramps to subside. Once they're gone, I unravel myself from the narrow bus bench and don the traditional white vest of Shikoku pilgrims, who are known as *henro*. After tying my sedge hat securely beneath my chin, I grip my walking staff, hoist my backpack onto bruised shoulders, and continue on a path that I'm praying leads me somewhere better.

At age twenty-eight I left an office job to hike this 1,500-year-old trail circling Shikoku Island, hoping to change a life that had stalled into a stable routine of waking up sighing every day and a future that looked pretty similar. I didn't know what exactly I was searching for out here, but I figured after hiking 1,200 kilometers and praying at 88 separate temples perched on mountaintops, hidden in forests, overlooking the crashing sea, and nestled in rice fields, I'd be closer to an answer than I would dealing with spreadsheets.

Having done almost no research, all I knew about the pilgrimage before my flight touched down in Japan was that it was basically a walking tour of the many feats of Kukai, Shikoku's famous eighth-century monk, temple founder, engineer, holy man, and monster fighter. Posthumously given the name Kōbō Daishi (Great Dharma Teacher), his presence permeates Shikoku in landmarks, legends, and the henro's apparel.

The kanji embossed down the back of my sweat-stained vest announces that I travel beside him; my conical sedge hat bears his name in Sanskrit to lead me on this path; and the staff making a metronome click against the highway shoulder embodies the great holy man as well (but in stick form). So far, Kukai's spirit and I have walked around forty kilometers, visiting a concentrated cluster of early temples, mostly on sidewalks and highway shoulders. Ahead of us today are temples eleven and twelve, the halfway point of the twenty-three temples of Tokushima, the "Land of Awakening Faith."

If you imagine a lion animal cracker that got real soggy (and also has mountains running across it), that's Shikoku Island. The smallest and most rural of Japan's four main islands is separated into four regions (*shi* = four, *koku* = region), each representing a different level of the pilgrim's spiritual journey.

Once I've completed the lion's mouth and throat, in the northeast of Tokushima, the route will take me clockwise alongside the Pacific Ocean and up and down the legs of Kōchi, the "Land of Ascetic Training," then across the rump and back of Ehime, the "Land of Enlightenment," and finally across the mane of Kagawa, the "Land of Nirvana," returning me to Temple 1, where I started.

In the early morning dawn here in the Land of Awakening Faith, the highway continues past a horizon of rice fields, with grain in every stage of processing. Rice harvesters like giant hair clippers trim the fields with a mechanical whine, and long tubes sticking out of wooden shacks spit out the chaff into tan piles. Even with all this mechanization, I'll sometimes still pass an old-fashioned rice-drying operation, the stalks hanging over bamboo racks looking like giant stick insects.

There are no henro walking the road with me this morning, which isn't a surprise statistically. As of 2010, an estimated five hundred thousand Japanese undertake the pilgrimage every year by bus, bike, or car. Their reasons vary. Some are seeking redemption from past mistakes or wisdom in avoiding future ones, giving thanks for business success or a loved one's recovery, or simply there to sightsee in a rural countryside so historically isolated that a bridge to the mainland didn't exist until the 1980s. Out of that half million, I am one of the few hundred devout and masochistic choosing to walk the entire 1,200-kilometer *o-henro* trail. And out of those few hundred I am one of maybe a dozen foreigners, a *gaijin*.

Even if there were henro on the road this morning, we wouldn't have much to say to each other, since my Japanese is limited to "*mizu*" (water), "*arigato*" (thank you), and two ways to express disbelief that a *kaiju* (giant monster) is attacking the city (*Masaka! Bakana!*). Since the island has remained *kaiju*-free, the only real conversation I've had with anyone is about where I am from, and I'm only understood because of one man: Ichiro Suzuki.

In 2010, Ichiro is a fan favorite on the Seattle Mariners baseball team: our right fielder and at times the only reason to watch disappointing season after disappointing season. He's even more famous in Japan, and this summer he's on every fan's mind both here and back home. Holding the single-season record for hits with 262 in 2004, he's on track to make history again by completing his tenth consecutive 200-hit season. His fame and my inability to pronounce the name of my home city leads to the following exchange, which repeats for the entire pilgrimage:

Japanese person: Where are you from?
Me: Seattle.
JP: Cee-ah-tu-ru?
Me: (slower) Seattle.
JP: Cee-ah-tu-ru?
Me: (Pantomime swinging bat.) Ichiro.
JP: Ah! Ichiro Suzuki! Cee-ah-tu-ru Ma-ri-nah!
Me: *Hai.* (Yes.)
JP: (Nods.)
(Awkward silence.)
Me: Bye.
JP: Bye-bye.

It's not much, and it's ninety percent of all conversations I'll have here.

Besides the lack of henro, the highway is also devoid of shops. Despite all the rice harvested in the fields, there's no breakfast to be found along the three-kilometer descent through paddies, orchards, and ramshackle farmhouses, which is fine. By the time I've reached the tree-shrouded valley floor of Fuji-Dera (Wisteria Temple, no. 11), the rising temperature has suppressed both my appetite and will to live.

Beneath the sloped roof of Fuji-Dera's gateway stand carved statues of red-skinned monsters with the muscular build of DC Comics villains. These are the *Niō*, heavenly kings whose fearsome visage guards the temple against demons and thieves. Flanking the entrance in twin alcoves, this forms the *niōmon*.

As the last twisting wisps of mist disappear from the courtyard with the morning chill, I crack open the sweat-stained pages of my map book. This palm-sized paperback contains the only information I have about the entire pilgrimage, including the routes, the rituals, and local tourist attractions.

For the eleventh time since arriving on Shikoku I begin the ritual, bowing at the niōmon to show reverence and also ward off evil spirits. Once humbled and de-ghosted, I enter the complex, then check my book again for the next step in the twenty-minute ritual of bows, bell ringing, hand washing, prayer chanting, and stamp collecting. As robotic as it feels, I'm committed to performing the entire thing at each temple. Thanks to my years attending synagogue, I'm used to repetitive rituals and arcane prayers.

Various offices and outbuildings flank the two large halls that front onto the courtyard, the main and Daishi shrines. At the free-standing belfry, I swing the log clapper into the iron bell to announce my presence to the gods, then wash my hands and mouth out with a tin dipper at the ritual basin.

I scrawl my signature down the side, slip the paper prayer strips known as *osamefuda* into a slotted tin box at the main shrine, and drop an offering of coins into a second box. Then I bow three times to the carved deity and thumb over to the list of seven phonetic Buddhist prayers in my map book. This should be the easy part, but the heat and the unfamiliar vowels rob me of oxygen.

Midway through chanting the Heart Sutra, a weight grows in my chest. For the past two days I've sunk to my knees while reciting the prayers, gasping out the rest of them from the ground while surrounding henro cast sideways glances. I'd be more concerned about it, because it never happened in synagogue, but that temple has air-conditioning.

Salvaging some pride today, I finish the prayers braced against a pillar on wobbly legs. Then I cross the courtyard and repeat the same prayers to a statue of Kukai at the Daishi shrine.

With the prayers complete, the next step is getting the temple's signature in my stamp book. A sort of spiritual passport, each of the stamp book's eighty-eight blank pages will eventually be filled with a calligraphy of each temple's name and three red stamps at a cost of 300 yen each.

The temple priest dunks a horsehair brush in ink, then gracefully conducts a series of soft loops and sharp angles across the page before applying three red-ink stamps onto the page. I slide it carefully into its ziplock bag to protect it from the sweat already eating through my map book and pass over the yen. With a final bow at the niōmon while facing the shrines, the ritual is complete.

I beam with pride. I didn't collapse once.

* * *

Damp shirt pasted to my chest, I glance around for a soda machine, ubiquitous even here in rural Japan, to buy a Pocari Sweat sports drink. No such luck. Bland, zero-calorie water it is.

Construction scaffolding surrounds the temple's residential complex. Shaded beneath the rustling blue tarps, I guzzle and refill my water bottles from an outdoor spigot until a half-gallon sloshes in my empty gut. Wiping my hands dry, I crack open the map book I still can't read. From here, the thirteen-kilometer route of red dots meanders down the page to Temple 12 across blobby mountains, the elevations ranging from greenish-tan to less-greenish-tan to tannish-green. Seems easy enough. At least it's not another day spent along that frying pan of asphalt.

Pondering whether this mountain hike will take two or three hours, I don't notice the priest standing over me.

"*Atsui, desu ne?*" he asks, using the ubiquitous summer greeting for "Hot, ain't it?"

"*Hai, atsui,*" I reply to the only non-Ichiro conversation I'll have in these first muggy weeks.

We nod through the awkward silence and I return to the map book. The priest remains.

"Do you need help?" he asks, using the "Please leave now, gaijin" tone.

Taking the hint, I stow the map book.

* * *

The dirt steps wind into the woods past stone Buddha shrines. Dug into the crumbly mountainside, their sloped roofs are lightly dusted with moss. Had I read further into the map book, I'd know that the next temple is the first *nansho* (dangerous place). This would explain the offerings from previous henro piled at the Buddha's feet, asking for protection on the arduous journey ahead. Oblivious to their reasonable concern, I hike into the forest as the islands of

Japan continue tilting toward the sun. The gurgling stream running through the valley floor grows fainter and fainter.

* * *

Thirteen centuries ago, Kukai climbed through a roaring inferno to Shōzan-ji (Burning Mountain Temple, no. 12), where he battled the dragon that had set the slopes alight. Following in his footsteps in 2010, I have a hard time believing that story. There's no way this mountain could get any hotter. By the time the steep path levels off into an open clearing, I've already sweated out my first beer from high school.

Chest heaving, I drop onto a bench across from a red shrine and ask whichever god's inside for strength. I've never done well with regular heat, but over the past two days I've drained both 32-ounce water bottles on an hourly basis and still haven't peed while the sun was up. Although I didn't make it far in Boy Scouts, I remember that being a bad thing.

A couple of meters away the path disappears up into the bamboo, where another series of switchbacks awaits. At the foot of the path stands a statue of Jizo, the holy, monk-like guardian of travelers. He extends an upturned palm full of coins offered by previous henro in exchange for safe passage. I glance over the map book again and have no idea where I am on the page. It's too early in the pilgrimage to gauge how far I've actually walked versus how far it feels like I've walked versus how far I hope I've walked. All I know is that it's been over an hour since I left Temple 11 and I'm already as drained as I was by the end of my first day of hiking, so I must be halfway done. I finish off my first water bottle.

A wizened, gray-haired henro passes the bench.

"*Atsui, desu ne?*" he comments, which is an understatement. Clearly we've angered the sun.

"*Hai, atsui,*" I gasp back as he vanishes into the bamboo without breaking stride or a sweat.

And with that, the gauntlet is thrown down.

I may be tired, but I'm not about to let a senior citizen beat me to the top. Having yet to learn that no amount of fitness matches the Japanese hiking ability, regardless of age or packs per day habit, I charge off the bench. Racing past the Jizo's outstretched hand, I attack the slope and soon overtake the old man, but it's a struggle to stay ahead. Breathing in shallow gasps, I stab my staff into the soil with each step, hoping to somehow deflate this mountain. By the time the trail levels off again, each heartbeat rams against my ribcage in a desperate attempt to escape and a rapidly depleting reservoir patters to the ground behind me. Half of my second water bottle is swallowed in one gulp.

The trail is empty for a while, gently undulating along the ridgeline through a dense wall of pines. I'm starting to worry. It's been hours since I left Temple 11, my last water bottle is a quarter full, and I have no idea how far it is to the temple. The wood posts along the path display arrows and distance figures seemingly at random. One says "3 km," but after a long hike up, then down, the next reads "4.6 km." The hikers and henro along the path are even more inscrutable. When asked the distance to Burning Mountain Temple, everyone replies with "five, six kilometers," no matter how far I've gone, always followed by a reassuring "*chotto*" (short). Unable to ask follow-up questions, I nod and keep going. The posts have to run out of numbers at some point.

I know I'm not lost thanks to tablets hanging from the branches with the kanji for henro in red paint. Eventually, the path descends along a stone stairway. A small temple comes into view and I let out a whoop. They were right, it was "chotto." In celebration I finish off the last of my water.

Setting my backpack on the bench facing the temple, I drop my coins and name slips into the slotted box then pray at a small, outdoor Daishi shrine. Hoisting myself onto the veranda circling the main shrine, the sliding doors reveal an atrium containing a simple shrine to the temple's main deity, where I complete the ritual. After an unsuccessful search of the empty, silent grounds for the stamp office, I shrug and give up. It'll be a blank page, which irks me.

But I don't need ink; I need water.

Sitting on the veranda, I tip the last drips from the bottle into my mouth. Since no one is around, I'll pull a very respectable Goldilocks. Shoes off, I bow and enter, calling out with no answer. The calendar hanging from the yellowing wallpaper is out of date, but there are shoes beside the staircase and the shrine is swept and maintained. The monks must have escaped to someplace cooler.

In the kitchen I twist the squeaking faucet handle. With a shudder and a groan, water pours into my first bottle. Through the dirt-caked window is a shallow cave, which must be where Kukai confined the dragon. I place the second bottle under the sputtering stream and tip the first to my lips. Just as I taste something musty, the thrumming faucet vomits rust-brown liquid into the bottle. Spewing my mouthful into the sink, I can feel protozoa crawling past my tongue toward my intestines. I keep spitting as I dump the water bottles down the drain.

Passing the damp shadow of my lower half soaking into the veranda, I return to my backpack to stare blankly at my map again. It can't be much farther to the town below Temple 12.

A henro tablet dangles above the bench.

Oh no.

There's a bright red flash of panic. Another tablet twists in the breeze above a steep path, sloping into the forest: "3.1 km" says the distance marker.

You can make three kilometers, no problem, I lie to myself, sweat streaming off my chin. *It'll be easy, especially without all this extra liquid weighing you down.*

Ever since I was a chubby thirteen-year-old who decided to turn off the TV and start jogging, I've been an athlete, competing in karate tournaments, bicycling century rides, and running marathons. So it's really confusing when the blurry ground rushes to my face. This has never happened on any hike, ride, run, or game. I've thrown up on the field and played through. Rolling to my knees I wipe the smear of mud off my forehead, snatch the hat wobbling beside me, and rise to my feet.

When my legs buckle halfway up the switchback, panic alarms begin strobing. Once my eyes refocus, it's finally clear how dangerously unprepared I am for this journey. However, I'm even less prepared to explain to everyone back home why I quit three days in, so I'll continue despite the growing dehydration and my newly malfunctioning legs. Eyes shut, I draw deep inside to the will that years of karate training has instilled: The thousands of push-ups and sit-ups, the hours of drills, the intense rush of tournaments, sprinting barefoot across the snow-covered dunes to spar in the frigid ocean. Rising against the pressing weight of my backpack, I pound my staff into the soil.

I will not stop again.

Fifty steps later I'm back in the dirt, curled on my side and glaring jealously at the millipedes' extra legs as they crawl by. A passing hiker places the last of his plastic water bottle in my hand. Chugging gratefully, I watch in disbelief as he speeds up the trail.

The sixth time I crumple into the dirt, the panic alarms are flashing extra bright. When my stomach stops looking for something to throw up I raise my head again. Light filters through the oak and maple branches. I'm near the peak. Thank the gods.

With long rests and short hikes I force myself up the switchbacks until I sprawl across the foot of a stone staircase. The benevolent iron visage of Kukai peers down at me. Behind him I hear a soda machine thrumming.

I made it.

In celebration, I gulp the last of the gifted water bottle, which sieves through me to puddle onto the steps. It's finally over.

Catching my breath, I charge to the top. Past the Kukai statue is another empty clearing. No temple, no water faucet, no soda machine. Somewhere between terror and disbelief lies the noise I make. A lady henro rests on the bench, fanning the dewy perspiration from her plump cheeks. She must have passed by me unnoticed on one of my frequent trips to the ground.

"*Mizu?*" I ask, pointing around the clearing.

She shrugs.

"*Mizu?*" I ask, pointing to her water.

She shakes her head apologetically.

"*Shozanji?*"

She points further down the path.

I turn to the statue and yell "You lied to me Daishi," getting partway through "lied" before my vision goes to static and I fall at his feet. A klaxon joins the panic alarms blaring through my skull. For the first time since a childhood prank ended with me getting chased down by a truck, I'm sure I'm going to die.

Since I can't pantomime "emergency medical evacuation" to the lady on the bench, I collect myself and think. The obvious solution is ditching my large backpack for my small daypack crammed in

the bottom, which would carry only my essentials. After struggling under the weight for two and a half days, the urge to leave
it behind leads to rationalizations like *Do you really need the tent,
the sleeping bag, and all the clothes? After all, isn't a sleeping bag just
a tent without scaffolding? And aren't pants just a thinner sleeping
bag with legs? And who really needs pants, when you think about it?*

Sadly, the only thing keeping my belongings from tumbling
down the mountainside is how much I paid for them. I look back
at the henro, who smiles and points away from the clearing again.

"*Shozanji.* Five, six kilometer," she reassures me. "Chotto."

With a whimper I push off the ground and stand at the edge
of the clearing. A cool breeze of no comfort flutters the branches.
It's clear what's ahead on this path slithering through the forest.
With no end in sight I'll collapse in the dirt, rise, bargain with my
legs for fifty more steps, then fall again with air igniting my lungs
and burning through my limbs. Each time will hurt more than
the last until I either reach Temple 12, get rescued incapacitated,
or die somewhere between these distance markers and assurances
of "chotto."

In that moment, I accept it.

Until one of those three outcomes happens, I'll live in the awful
now, resigned to the weakness, fear, and pain of the upslopes while
appreciating the less grueling descents.

With one step into the forest, then another, my pack thudding
down on bruised and blistered soles, I ascend to Burning Mountain Temple.

Of course, this revelation doesn't stop me from praying to find
the temple or water at the next peak, around the next bend, or
when I walk far, far down into a ravine.

* * *

Kiyotakiji, temple 35 of the 88 temples on the Shikoku pilgrimage

At the bottom there's a small pasture with three horses that I may have hallucinated and a dry trough with no spigot. Groaning, I drop onto the concrete. Ants scatter from the biblical torrent gushing from my face, repenting their sins with tiny waving antennae. I wonder if I have it in me to make another climb, and if it's possible to drink sweat from my shorts. After a long rest I decide that yes, I can, and no, I shouldn't, marshal whatever is left inside me, and trudge up another steep path.

When the trees open for a vista, all I see is a ring of green peaks blocking any hope of escape. I stop asking for water and begin begging from the dirt as hikers pass by in their sweat-wicking technical shirts and tiny backpacks, out for a rousing stroll up a mountain. Some give me what they have left. Others politely decline. I can't blame them as I curl on my side, trying to convince myself that you can't die of dehydration in seven hours.

Back on my feet I breathe through ragged coughs, electricity crackling through my skin. With each shaky step up the path I promise myself there will be a soda machine at the temple or, if I don't make it, in heaven if they haven't been watching me too closely. In a vision as clear as a commercial, a blue-striped can of Pocari Sweat sports drink tumbles from the soda machine. The tab compresses with a metallic tear and pop, mist escapes in a spiraling burst. I raise the can to my lips, the refrigerated liquid cooling me for the first time today. It will be heaven.

Cresting another plateau, the overhanging branches part to reveal blue sky and another empty clearing. There's no energy left for hope or disappointment. I lay on a trailside bench. Across from me a distance marker claims "1 km."

Liar sign.

My sedge hat covering my face, I dream of cold aluminum cans and wake only to beg hikers for water. A jogger in a green technical shirt shakes his empty bottle, then points down the path.

"*Shozanji.*"

I ask how far.

"One km. Chotto." He motions that I should follow.

Liar jogger.

But I lug my pack onto my shoulders and trudge behind him. The dirt trail soon becomes gravel, curving between Buddhas meditating in their lotus thrones and a granite railing of stone lanterns bordering mountainside's sheer drop. I refuse to believe it until we've passed through the niōmon and stand beneath eight gargantuan cedar columns rising from the courtyard's bleach-white gravel. Up a small staircase stands Burning Mountain Temple.

And, more important to my survival, a soda machine.

The refrigerator motor hums an angel's chorus. My pack drops to the ground. I lunge up the stairs, remove my dripping wallet from my pocket, and push the sweat-soaked bill into the machine.

It whirs for a moment and returns the bill.

I insert it again.

Rejected.

"Nooooooo!"

Slamming my fists against the machine, a desperate panic sets in. I'm scanning through the pebbles at my feet for something large enough to smash the front panel when a meek woman approaches to offer the crazy man a dry bill. I gasp out sounds resembling thanks and the slot swallows the money.

With no ceremony, three Pocari Sweat evaporate in my throat.

Attached to the Stamp Office is a cozy restaurant, where I slump onto a bench, my head resting motionless on the wood picnic table. A waitress with red-dyed hair appears over me.

"*Atsui, desu ne?*"

"*Hai, atsui,*" oozes out.

I point in the menu's direction until she understands "food." She returns from the kitchen with a paper fan and places it on the table. With no energy to waft it, the fan remains beside my head as I wait for my first meal in twenty hours. An energized table of hikers beside me chatters cheerfully, their small packs filled with whatever they need between here and their car.

"Where are you from?" one of them asks.

"Ichiro," I mumble, weakly swinging my chopsticks.

Nodding, she rejoins the group's conversation. The moment the waitress sets the noodles and salty soy broth on the table it vanishes into my gut.

It's getting dark and the town below is far away. The courtyard bell announces my presence with a soft ping and I preemptively fall to my knees before reciting the sutras to the main shrine and to Kukai. I bow again at the niōmon, mostly in reverence to the soda machine, and depart.

The mountain pathway becomes roadway, then driveways, and I take shelter at a former elementary school at the edge of town. An ominous silence permeates the abandoned playfield. Shadows gather in the pocked dirt, torn up by students long since gone. A frozen clock hangs from a wall of chipped paint and shattered windows.

This place is definitely haunted, but walking any further is laughable.

Setting up my tent beside the remains of desks and toys crusted with dirt and spiderwebs, I beg any spirits still hanging around to let me rest in peace. I'm scared enough already. To leave this valley ringed by steep mountains means the same struggle awaits me at sunrise, and I may not survive another day like today. It's not as if it's unheard of here. In henro tradition, the staff doubles as a gravestone and the white vests are considered funeral shrouds, reminding pilgrims that death can come at any time.

No day of the Shikoku Pilgrimage, or my life afterward, will be physically harder than Burning Mountain; but there is even more to come than I could have imagined. Over the next thirty-nine days, I'll hide from guards in a toilet stall, deal with a leg infection, and challenge a priest to a karate match in a mountaintop temple courtyard.

However, at the end of my third day on this ancient Buddhist pilgrimage circling Shikoku Island, there are four things that I know for certain:

1. Wild boar are terrifying in person and will charge you if they're with their babies.
2. It is the hottest summer in Japan's recorded history.
3. I am in way over my head.
4. I will not quit.

About the Author

Paul Barach is a writer, author, and storyteller based in Tacoma, Washington. In his off time, he is an avid runner, cyclist, and hiker who recently completed the entire Pacific Crest Trail. His first book, *Fighting Monks and Burning Mountains: Misadventures on a Buddhist Pilgrimage*, is available on Amazon in ebook, audiobook, and print. You can find more of his photos and writing at PaulBarach.com.

6

A Dyeing Tradition

By Suzanne Kamata

My father has blue hands. Or at least that's what Mom tells me — one of the few facts I've been able to wring out of her. See, he's the eldest son of one of the last indigo producers in his village on the Japanese island of Shikoku. His family has been growing indigo for generations — centuries even — since back in the time of the shoguns.

"You were named after that plant," Mom told me. "*Ai* means indigo. *Ko* means child."

Indigo is my destiny.

The color begins with a seed planted in early spring. After the first green sprigs pop up through the earth, the seedlings are transplanted to fields. The leaves are still green then. Later, in the hot, sticky days of summer, the plants are harvested and dried out. Then the leaves are tossed into a vat with wood ash, lye, and wheat bran and fermented.

"It's very stinky," Mom told me, "but it produces the most beautiful hue — the color of a storm-bruised sky."
—from *Gadget Girl: The Art of Being Invisible*

THERE are certain things that almost everyone living in Tokushima has tried at least once. Most likely, at one point or another, they have moved rhythmically around a room or a playground, arms in the air, in some approximation of Awa Odori, a folk dance performed at the annual summer Obon festival, and also at weddings, school sports festivals, cultural events, and any other large gathering. They have probably dug up sweet potatoes. (This is a favorite activity on autumn school outings, which is followed by roasting said sweet potatoes, preferably in a fire out of doors, and then peeling off the slightly charred skin and eating the yellow insides.) Also, denizens of and even visitors to this prefecture on the island of Shikoku have probably dipped a cloth into a vat of indigo dye.

Having lived in Tokushima Prefecture for more than thirty years, I have done all of these things more times that I can remember. Although I started out in Naruto, a town famed for its gigantic natural whirlpools and tasty seaweed, I have settled in nearby Aizumi. The town's name is written with the characters for *ai* (indigo) and *sumi* (dwelling). Thus, I live in the dwelling place of indigo, a low-lying plant with long, pointed green leaves.

As you might imagine, locals make the most of this motif. Buildings, such as the brand-new school that my daughter attended, are often trimmed with indigo. Tokushima's minor league baseball team is called the Indigo Socks. A recently opened restaurant in my town serves pasta and bread flecked with dried indigo plants. In my own home, I settle my coffee cups on coasters dyed in indigo by my daughter. I sometimes wrap a deep-blue scarf around my neck or sip tea made from the leaves of the plant. I have written two novels about the daughter of an indigo farmer from Tokushima. Indigo is everywhere.

* * *

Indigo-dyed textiles have been around for millennia, the oldest find, from coastal Peru, dating to around 4200 BC. In the ancient trans-Saharan trade, camels conveyed indigo, as well as gold, salt, and slaves to Mediterranean markets. Around this time, indigo leaves were crushed and rolled into balls and dried for export from Asia to Europe. Because the leaves arrived in the form of blue cakes, for a long time, until explorer Marco Polo found out the truth, there was a misconception that indigo was a mineral. Later, when sea travel became more common and it was possible to import greater quantities of indigo from India, the leaves presented a threat to local woad production. In some regions of Europe, laws were introduced to prohibit the use of indigo in order to protect the woad industry. Those who broke the law were sometimes punished by death. Ferdinand III of Hungary (1608–1657) nicknamed it "the devil's dye."

In addition to being used to dye textiles, indigo was used as a hair dye and in cosmetics in Europe. Meanwhile, in West Africa, women burned it to ward off evil spirits. It was also used in scarification and tattooing, as medication, and for birth control. Western African women acquired power and wealth through indigo dyeing and trading.

In South Carolina, where I am most recently from, indigo grew wild along the coast. In the mid-1700s, Eliza Lucas, a sixteen-year-old left in charge of her father's plantation, learned to cultivate and produce indigo dye from her family's African slaves. As a crop, indigo, it turned out, was better than rice, partly due to its ability to repel insects. The plants kept the mosquitoes at bay, thus staving off malaria and yellow fever. Lucas ultimately started a trend, and in 1775, South Carolina planters exported a record 1.1 million pounds of indigo to England.

It is believed that the plant that we know of as Japanese indigo (*Persicaria tinctoria*), aka dyer's knotweed, was first exported from southern China to Japan around AD 500. The cultivation of indigo began in Japan during the Muromachi period (1338–1593). During that era, farmers in Tokushima Prefecture on the island of Shikoku suffered many failed harvests due to the typhoons that blew in off the Seto Inland Sea. After two consecutive years of failed rice crops, Lord Hachisuka Iemasa encouraged the production of indigo, which could be harvested in summer before the typhoon season and could be used to dye textiles.

Throughout most of the Meiji Era (1868–1911), indigo production was one of the main industries in Tokushima, and there were once at least a thousand indigo producers here. In 1886, however, German scientists discovered a chemical process for making the dye; the natural indigo industry then went into decline. In Tokushima today, only five families still process indigo commercially.

* * *

Last winter I visited Bunka no Mori (literally "Culture Forest"), a cultural center at the edge of Tokushima City, to check out "*Ai no Keshiki* — Indigo Views," an installation directed by American fiber artist Rowland Ricketts III. I entered a dark, hushed room. At the center, there was a tent-like structure made of hundreds of handkerchiefs individually dyed in indigo. Each small length of cloth had been dyed with Awa indigo in workshops and studios in

Tokushima. The cloths were then sent to "live with" 451 participants in ten countries for five months.

As Ricketts says, "The indigo that has been grown and processed here in Tokushima for centuries doesn't belong to one person. It's something that belongs to everybody. I wanted to involve people who aren't dyers, who aren't involved in growing the indigo, to create an opportunity for them to have Awa indigo in their lives for a few months and then be involved in a project."

In January 2018, the cloths were brought back together, suspended in a kind of cloth dome. Because they were connected via thread, light seeped through the spaces between them. Some squares were darker than others, reflecting the way that indigo-dyed fabrics alter after exposure to light or frequent washing. Ambient music, created by sound artist Norbert Herber of Indiana University, added to the experience. Sounds came from forty-eight small speakers, loud and soft, strong, then fading like indigo-dyed textiles.

Ricketts himself had traveled from the University of Indiana in Bloomington, where he teaches, to oversee the event. I was happy to bump into him, to exchange news of our families (we both have twins) and to give him a copy of my recent novel, *Gadget Girl*. The book began with the line "My father has blue hands." This beginning had been inspired by the sight of the artist's indigo-tinged hands the first time we met.

Now he is a world-renowned artist; but nineteen years ago, when we first met, he had been only dreaming of such things.

* * *

Ricketts was an anomaly in the small Japanese town of Hirose, where he farmed and dyed with his wife, Chinami. For one thing, at the age of thirty, he was not old. "There are not many young people around here," he said at that time. His landlord, a paper-maker, was in his sixties. Ricketts' appearance back then, too, attracted notice. He wore a beard in a close-shaven country, and unruly brown curls spilled from his knit cap.

He'd first become interested in indigo when he was working as an assistant English teacher on the Japan Exchange and Teaching (JET) program, the same government-sponsored scheme that had brought me to Tokushima. Ricketts had been stationed in Gojo, Nara Prefecture. He'd had plenty of free time for other pursuits after explaining American idioms to Japanese high school students. "I dabbled in woodblock printing for a while, but was never satisfied with the colors I produced," he said.

He later became acquainted with some dyers who used only colors available in nature. After a life-changing weekend with these artisans, during which he learned the basics of vegetal dyeing, he set out to find an old house in a rural area where he could wander, and gather plants and boil them to extract their colors.

"I did my first dyeing at the end of my first year on JET," Ricketts recalled. "After that, almost every weekend was filled with dyeing experiments of some sort, but I noticed that I was mostly able to produce yellows and browns, and most of the colors faded rather quickly."

Then he began learning about indigo and a passion bloomed. "The color of traditionally dyed Japanese indigo surpasses colors I have seen elsewhere," he said. "The process of couching [composting] the indigo leaves into *sukumo* [dye-stuff made of dried leaves] is very similar to the process in Europe. The same can be said for the vatting process, yet these techniques died out in the West almost one hundred years ago. This connection with our past has been lost, but it is still alive in Japan, barely. Using these techniques somehow connects me to the past and a shared human knowledge, a shared human experience that simply isn't part of modern chemical dyes."

Next, the young American sought an apprenticeship. With the help of his former boss, Ricketts was introduced to one of Tokushima's remaining indigo producers, the Nii family. At first, Osamu Nii refused to take him on as a student. Ricketts, who'd spent his junior year studying Japanese at Doshisha University, was not about to give up easily. He eventually won the farmer over with a letter-writing campaign. In October 1996, he began an apprenticeship with Nii in the rural Tokushima town of Kamiita.

What should have been a hopeful beginning was marred by tragedy. Shortly after Ricketts' arrival, Nii's wife and co-worker died from injuries sustained in a car accident.

"It was a quiet, difficult, painful year," Ricketts remembered. He and the other workers helped with preparations for memorial services for Nii's wife, but most of the labor was in the field.

"On the farm I learned about making *sukumo*, the dye-stuff. It's a long process that begins with planting the seeds in early March. The seedlings are transplanted to the fields and harvested during the summer months. The summer months, late June through late September, were the most tiring ones. Work began at seven every morning and ended about eight in the evening. Each day involved chopping the indigo plants harvested the previous evening, separating the leaves from the stems and spreading the leaves out in the sun to dry. The afternoon involved emptying the dryers that were filled with the leaves from the day before. In late afternoon, the drying leaves were then gathered and placed in the dryers for the night, and we all set out either to cut Mr. Nii's fields or to pick up indigo grown by one of the twenty-some farmers Mr. Nii contracted out to."

According to 1997 prefectural statistics, eighty-eight families were growing indigo on contract for the big five producers at that time; but the farmers were aging and younger generations were not stepping in to take over. "It's unbelievably hard work," Ricketts explained. "No one wants to do it."

Although the demand for indigo was increasing, the supply was decreasing. Ricketts was concerned about the future of natural indigo dyeing in Japan. "It's important to raise people's conscious-ness about natural indigo, to make them aware of just what's involved in producing the dyestuff," he said. "It's not just the dyeing — it's these farmers who are behind the scenes. Without them, this tradition is going to disappear. No matter how many Intangible Cultural Assets [an honorary title bestowed upon traditions that have contributed greatly to the nation's culture] the government gives out, without the farmers who grow the indigo plants, dyers can't make a single thing."

After a year of farming with Nii, Ricketts moved on to study the dyeing process with Riichiro Furusho, a designated Intangible Cultural Asset himself. From Furusho, Ricketts learned the value of *sukumo*, which is used to make vats of pungent dye. "I believe that he saw it as a living thing to be treated with respect and used very wisely."

Furusho was well-known for his *chu-zen* dyeing ("pour-dye") technique, but his son, Toshiharu, who often taught Ricketts during his apprenticeship, specialized in the *shibori* method. Although some refer to this process as "tie-dye," Ricketts said that this definition is too simple. Before dyeing, fabric is handstitched in a desired pattern, drawn tight and bound so that no dye can get into the bound areas.

In addition to the actual dyeing, Ricketts learned to make tradi-tional wood-ash lye, a liquid made by adding ash from leafy trees to water. This liquid is used to extract alkaline substances from the dye and increase the pH value in an indigo vat. A high pH and an oxygen-free environment are necessary to reduce the indigo, making the solution more concentrated. Ricketts also learned to prepare the natural fermentation indigo vat using *sukumo*, wood-ash lye, slaked lime, and wheat bran. "I spent a good portion of the year watching how Toshiharu started and cared for the indigo vats, and I took a lot of notes," he said. "It's a bit of a process and simply requires experience over time to master."

Ricketts met his wife, Chinami, who was also an apprentice, while working with the Furusho family. He finished his second apprenticeship in November 1998. After spending some time back in Nara, the couple moved to Shimane Prefecture, where Ricketts endeavored to grow as much indigo as he could manage while dyeing. Meanwhile, his wife studied *kasuri* weaving. At the time, he was using fabrics bought on a trip through Laos, China, India, Myanmar, and Thailand to create indigo-dyed tapestries, scarves, *noren* (a short curtain used in an entryway in Japan) and *obi* (the sash used to tie a kimono). He now collaborates with Chinami, dyeing fabrics that she has woven herself.

* * *

Like Ricketts, Hungarian textile artist Hanga Yoshihara Horvath was lured to Tokushima by indigo. Although I had met her before at various international gatherings, we had never discussed her work. To talk about indigo, I made a special trip to the house she and her husband rent When she met me at the door, I couldn't help but think that the blue of her eyes matched the indigo-dyed scarf around her neck.

She showed me into her living/dining room and proceeded to make tea while I had a look around. A child-sized cotton shirt, dyed partially blue, hung from the curtain rod. A pillow with an indigo-dyed cover was nestled into the corner of the sofa. On a table, there was a cloth featuring a bird embroidered with indigo-dyed thread. Horvath explained that she had just finished a private embroidery lesson with a Japanese student. After the tea was ready, we sat down at the table and she told me her story.

Horvath was born in Mor, a small town in Hungary. She studied textiles at Moholy-Nagy University in Budapest, specializing in machine knitting. As an undergraduate, she spent a semester studying dyeing in Finland. Even at that time, she was most interested in plant dyeing, though she did not yet work with indigo. In 2004, she came to Japan on a Japan Foundation Fellowship, spending ten months in Osaka learning Japanese, and how to write a dissertation in the language. While in Osaka, she also researched plant dyeing in Japan. One of her teachers recommended that she come to Tokushima to learn about indigo.

"I wanted to study indigo because when I was an au pair and learned patchwork and quilting, I saw a book about *sashiko*. I was amazed by the running stitch, and blue and white — nothing more."

Sashiko refers to an embroidery technique used to mend or stitch together one or more layers of fabric. According to tradition, white thread is used on blue fabric. This dates back to eighteenth-century Japan, when a law came into effect prohibiting farmers and fishermen from wearing colorful clothes or clothing made from cotton. They weren't allowed to embroider their garments with stitches larger than a grain of rice. However, seamstresses found ways to be creative even with such limitations. Special patterns and approaches such as embroidered lines which represent hemp leaves and persimmon leaves were developed.

After Horvath's sojourn in Osaka, she decided to return to Japan, this time going to Tokushima for a year and a half as a research student sponsored by the Japanese government, to learn more about indigo for her doctoral work. When her time was up, she realized that she wanted to learn more. She extended her stay by becoming a graduate student of Human Sciences at Shikoku University, studying a variety of subjects such as food and psychology. Most importantly, being at Shikoku University gave her a chance to work with indigo in the college's Indigo House, an on-campus workshop with a recessed vat of *sukumo*.

At the start of her second stay in Japan, she met the man who would become her husband. "His work is also related to indigo," she explained. He is a public servant, working at an agricultural research center in Ishii, a nearby town patchworked with rice paddies. As part of his job, he experiments with different ways of making *sukumo* and dyeing, aiming to find cheaper ways of producing indigo from plants, and to make it more accessible. One of Yoshihara's team's recent innovations is the indigo crayon.

They are also researching the production of purple dye, which may also be derived from the indigo plant, though some local devotees to indigo are against the idea. Indigo, after all, has become the signature color of Tokushima, nay Japan. The practice of using *sukumo* is unique to this area.

Even so, it's a struggle to keep the dyeing tradition alive. Although there are many who are interested in traditional dyeing techniques, *sukumo* is prohibitively expensive. A local vendor sells it for 8,000 yen (US$75) per kilogram. (The same vendor sells a spool of indigo dyed thread for 1,000 yen.) Also, as Ricketts previously pointed out, growing indigo and producing *sukumo* is hard work. The workload might be lessened with more machines. Indigo purists are aghast at such a suggestion and insist upon sticking to traditional methods.

Yet when Horvath shows me photos that she took for her doctoral thesis, I see that even the venerable Nii, with whom Ricketts apprenticed, uses a tractor during the harvest.

Horvath gives private lessons in Hungarian embroidery using thread that she has dyed herself with indigo. She also teaches art at an international preschool and sees great potential in creating a curriculum for children based on indigo. "They can start from seed, make *sukumo*, make dye — it's good for educating kids about many things."

As for her own creative endeavors, Horvath uses a knitting machine, which resembles a loom, to make scarves, hats, and other pieces of clothing. She frequently exhibits her work and is an active member of the Indigo Association in Tokushima.

* * *

While indigo has attracted many foreigners with an interest in traditional Japanese crafts, efforts at rejuvenation of rural areas have also brought more young Japanese to Tokushima Prefecture. Yamagata native Kenta Watanabe, who'd been working at a trading company, arrived in Kamiita Town as a regional revitalization volunteer, part of a Japanese government initiative to counteract the problems of rural depopulation and overcrowding in urban areas such as Tokyo. He met fellow volunteer Kakuo Kaji, an Aomori native who'd studied dyeing and textiles at art college. They wound up staying to form Buaisou in 2012, making it the sixth commercial indigo producer in Tokushima. Buaisou, conceived of as a "farm to closet" project, is now made up of a group of six members: Kakuo Kaji; tailor Yuya Muira; Yuki Ken, a former banker; business manager Kyoko Nishimoto; and newcomers Kazuma Osuka and Tadashi Kozono. (Watanabe left the group in 2018.) Like Ricketts and Horvath, they have learned from sixth-generation indigo farmer Osamu Nii.

"I really like indigo dyeing," Ken says. "I love the indigo color. That's why I do everything from leaf farming to dyeing. I don't have this sense that I'm preserving our traditional culture. Such pride may come after, but at this point in my life I'm just doing it because I sincerely enjoy it. In my earlier days, I was just so happy seeing my hands turn blue. It was like a confirmation of what I do."

With their earrings, scraggly facial hair, and stunning Instagram feed, Buaisou is a decidedly modern bunch. Not content to limit themselves to the remote fields of inner Tokushima Prefecture, they have conducted workshops in Singapore, France, Mexico, and India. Buaisou also now has an outpost in Brooklyn — Buaisou Brooklyn Lab — which is overseen by director Sayaka Toyama. As another sign of their twenty-first century success, Buiasou has collaborated with the well-known American label Tory Burch and has hosted superstar Kanye West at their Tokushima workshop. But the point of their work is the indigo itself.

A large part of their income is derived from dyeing textiles for other people, including small businesses in Japan and abroad. On an average day, they dye six kilograms of fiber in each of their three nine-hundred-liter vats. Individuals can dip, say, a handkerchief or a T-shirt into the vat at a rate of thirty-five to forty yen per gram of cloth. But they dye other things too, such as pottery and a traditional Japanese wooden toy known as a *kendama*. An indigo-dyed cow skull adorns the wall of Buaisou Brooklyn Lab.

One of Buaisou's original goals was to produce a pair of naturally indigo-dyed jeans. "Jeans are an enormous part of my life," Kaji says. "Dyeing them with Japanese indigo was previously unheard of." The color "resonates with the heart." It can also be seen as a symbol of strength. For samurai, the strongest, darkest shades of indigo were the color of victory. Jeans were originally work clothes for coal miners in North America. The garment was meant to be tough and virtually indestructible. Buaisou has achieved its dream. Its website now features a custom-made pair of indigo-dyed jeans selling for the hefty price of three hundred thousand yen, which is somewhere between the cost of a silk kimono and a Chanel suit.

In addition to their more utilitarian pursuits, Buaisou also creates artwork, such as wooden panels covered with indigo-dyed cloth.

Thanks to Buaisou's outreach, more and more people are coming to Tokushima to try indigo dyeing. But if those with an interest don't have the chance to travel to Japan, they might be able to catch a workshop in another country. One hopes that some will even be inspired to begin the hard work of farming and producing *sukumo*.

* * *

Indigo blue is Japan blue. It can be found in noren, the traditional split curtains in Japanese doorways, and on hundred-year-old fishermen's coats. It can be found on runways at fashion shows, and in the shoelaces threaded through a pair of sneakers. It's the color of the Japan national soccer team's uniforms, and also that of the logos of the now-postponed 2020 Tokyo Olympic and Paralympic Games. But remember this: it started from Awa indigo grown in Tokushima Prefecture.

About the Author

American Suzanne Kamata has lived in Tokushima Prefecture for over thirty years. She is the editor of three anthologies and the author of eleven books, including the award-winning novel *Indigo Girl* (GemmaMedia, 2019); a memoir, *Squeaky Wheels: Travels with My Daughter by Train, Plane, Metro, Tuk-tuk and Wheelchair* (Wyatt-Mackenzie Publishing, 2019); and *The Spy* (Gemma Open Door), a novella for literacy learners. She is an associate professor in Global Studies at Naruto University of Education.

7

An Unexpected Retreat

By Sarah Coomber

In the far west of Honshu Island lies Yamaguchi. The prefecture's wild, sparsely populated northern coast looks out to the Sea of Japan, while its more developed southern shores face the placid, island-studded Seto Inland Sea. Sarah Coomber lived in the rural interior of Yamaguchi Prefecture for two years in the mid-1990s. Her posting was the small town of Shuho-cho, where she was the lone foreigner and the local schools' very first participant in the JET Programme. When the twenty-four-year-old Minnesotan learned of her assignment there, despite some familiarity with the prefecture from a summer high school stay in the old castle town of Hagi, she had trouble finding Shuho-cho on a map. Doing so is not that much easier today as the town has disappeared in part, absorbed into the rather incongruously named Mine City.

Over recent decades, several waves of territorial mergers have reduced the number of municipalities across Japan from 3,232 in 1999 to about half that number today. The amalgamation has been driven by urban sprawl and a desire for administrative efficiency, but above all by rural demographic shifts and the difficulty of maintaining services for shrinking, aging populations.

* * *

PORING over maps of Japan in a university library reference room, I struggled to find a town named Shuho-cho in Yamaguchi Prefecture.

Months earlier I had written in my teaching application that I was open to living in a rural area, so I knew I might be looking for a dot closer to the size of a pin's point than its head. (And in 1994 who knew how to search for such a place on the World Wide Web?)

Now clutching the letter that said I had been hired to teach English in Shuho-cho, an opportunity that would deliver me from my wrecked life in Minnesota, I scanned Yamaguchi Prefecture, going dot by dot by dot, until at last I found Shuho-cho beside one of the tiniest. *How could such a small dot be home to much of anything or anyone?* I wondered. But no matter. All I needed was a place to live and some income. I would teach junior high school students during the day and spend the rest of my time in solitude.

In my mind, I was signing on for a yearlong retreat.

To describe a place as a retreat can imply moving back or withdrawing to somewhere one has already been, and that was almost true here. I had visited Yamaguchi as a high school student, spending a summer with a Japanese host family, their seaside city an hour's drive away from Shuho-cho. I had arrived at their home a tabula rasa, my comprehension limited to black and white: this I understand, that I do not; this I like, that I do not. Over eight weeks, they instilled in me such a love for their culture — their food, their aesthetic sensitivities, their manners, their language — that when I faced stressful situations after returning to Minnesota I would call up five-sense memories of their city's white-sand beach, imagining myself floating in the sun, held in the embrace of the aquamarine sea. A psychological retreat.

I had retreated there physically once as well, both to the seaside city and to the plateau and caves near Shuho-cho, to recover health and heart on the way home from a college semester spent losing my idealism in India. I had encountered squalor the likes of which I had never imagined: families rolled in tattered blankets sleeping on streets, tangle-haired children carrying babies begging for food, men missing fingers and limbs imploring us for rupees through train windows, young girls in sweatshops swiftly stuffing matches into purple boxes that fit their tiny hands.

That first return to Japan soothed my body and mind. I inhaled bowls of rice and teriyaki beef, chicken and fish, soaked in a deep tub until ash and dust floated out of my pores and formed a scum on the water, climbed into a crisply sheeted futon and slept a whole day, recovering a measure of hopefulness that the world, in some places, was still okay.

Four years later, it only made sense that I was looking again to Yamaguchi for reprieve. I was twenty-four and freshly divorced, having abandoned a marriage that involved buckets of tears but only thimbles of laughter. Lacking a single dramatic event or issue that would have made our marriage's collapse easy to explain to stunned friends and family, I pawned my wedding ring, shoved most of my belongings into a Minnesota storage locker, and disappeared to Shuho-cho, that tiny dot in the middle of Yamaguchi Prefecture.

When I arrived, I found my post to be a sparsely populated district of hamlets, rice paddies, and pear orchards tucked among soft pine and bamboo-covered mountains — the perfect escape. When I heard it referred to as "Yamaguchi's Tibet," I assumed the moniker was a reference to the topography of the nearby plateau, Akiyoshidai, where wildflower-blooming hills were pierced by gray boulders, as if the earth were teething molars. Or perhaps the label had to do with Shuho-cho's isolation, for it lacked a railway line, and few buses served the road that wound its way out to my neighborhood, making it almost as hard to leave as it was to reach.

The latter explanation seemed promising, for my goal that year was simple: to form no new attachments, especially with men. I was so serious on this point that I set myself one solid rule: I would not kiss anyone unless I thought I might actually die if I did not.

* * *

Perhaps if I had studied English literature instead of biology and journalism I would have taken to heart the meditation of John Donne, the English cleric: "No man is an island, entire of itself; every man is a piece of the continent, a part of the main; if a clod be washed away by the sea, Europe is the less...."

I come from English stock, but I suspect my Japanese neighbors understood Donne's notions of interconnectedness and community far better than I did. I wanted to be an island and thought I could be, at least for a little while. Chalk it up to the naïveté of a young woman who grew up deep inland on the prairies of the northern Great Plains, a place where an embarrassment of space implies there is always more — more resources, more places to explore, more places to hide.

Donne and the good people of Shuho-cho shared an island-nation heritage — a descriptor often trotted out in Japan. "We are an island nation," people would tell me, as if that in itself would explain a surprising tradition, behavior, or outlook, tying it back to Japan's lack of land, lack of privacy, or lack of resources and its resulting need for harmony and community.

My Great Plains neighbors and I also considered community indispensable, whether for pulling one another's vehicles out of deep, snowy ditches or for celebrating the long-awaited arrival of a short summer. We throw weddings with enthusiasm. We share hotdish with newcomers and those facing cancer ... and those having babies ... and those losing loved ones. But there is always room — geographically and psychologically — to be alone. To be left alone.

Shuho-cho would not be such a place.

* * *

I imagine my new colleagues at the Shuho-cho Board of Education office could see where I was headed, this inclination toward solitude. Sitting at my desk, waiting for the school term and my responsibilities to begin, I shared a ready smile with all who stopped by to say hello, but I also was quick to return to my reading, my studies, my writing, or to go for a solo walk around the neighborhood. Did my self-containment worry them?

One day my first week there, my new boss, Kashima-*kachō*, rose from his chair at the head of our bank of desks, where five of us were clustered together in the stuffy, smoky office — phones and faxes ringing, file folders and ashtrays cluttering, people clattering by — and invited me to follow him out to the lobby and up the stairs to a world I had not thought to explore, assuming it to be more of the same.

However, the upper floor revealed a quiet hallway lined with wooden doors, art on the walls. A sanctuary.

Kashima-kachō approached and opened one of the doors. Inside was a room full of people in various stages of setting up musical instruments, now frozen in place looking out at us. An older woman, her back to the door, turned, saw me, and beamed.

This was my introduction to Shuho-cho's koto club and its members, who were preparing for their weekly group lesson on six-foot-long, thirteen-stringed zithers.

The beaming woman was their sensei, and she possessed a level of twinkle few could match. Her lined face and long, pinned-up hair were accented by finely detailed clothing and delicate jewelry, all offset by the energy of a young woman, even a girl, albeit one with wise, friendly eyes. She locked those eyes on mine. "Hallo," she said in a bubbly voice. "Howareyou? Hahaha!"

The other members were an assortment of townspeople: Kashima-kachō's wife, who worked at the post office; the wife of a local Buddhist priest; a brightly smiling town employee who farmed with her husband; a demure high school student; and a junior high school teacher, the group's token male, who played the bass koto, a broader instrument with seventeen strings.

The koto sensei quickly brought me down to the tatami mat, on my knees, *seiza*, in front of a koto, which, supported on one end by an orange wooden stand, hovered a couple of inches off the floor. This became my first koto lesson, my lower legs soon prickling and falling asleep, committing me to the spot, where, all but trapped, the sensei placed leather rings on the tips of the first two fingers and thumb of my right hand. Embedded with long ivory rectangles, these rings — called *tsume*, meaning fingernails

Sarah (second from the left) with her koto club

or claws — fit well enough. Seeing that, she introduced me to the koto. *Go on*, she nodded, encouraging me to make an overture, to pluck a few notes, which I did.

When asked to describe the koto's song, I say it is the stringed instrument heard over sound systems in Japanese restaurants. But often they feature the music of the three-stringed shamisen, a fretless banjo-like instrument, which is plucked with one corner of a plectrum the size and shape of a windshield ice scraper. The shamisen has a jauntiness, like a bouquet-carrying man bounding up the stairs to meet a new girlfriend, whereas the koto sounds more serious, like dinner parties, grocery shopping, small-scale debates that grind on for days, seasons passing....

That koto afternoon, the sensei pointed from her music book to the koto's strings, giving me my first lesson in tablature, where the character for one (一) corresponds to the first string and so on, up to thirteen (巾). The notations were written in boxes stacked top to bottom, right to left — beautiful but mostly indecipherable to me — and, like traditional Japanese books, the pages were turned with the left hand. This sensei seemed incapable, or perhaps unwilling, to believe I could not read what was right in front of me.

By the end of that first meeting, after I had successfully plucked a few notes, she secured a commitment from me: I signed up for the koto club and left the room with my own rings and *tsume*, plus an orange brocade folder of illegible music.

It was like going on a blind date and returning home engaged. But this was likely a not-so-blind date, for surely Kashima-kachō had seen my teaching application and knew that I was a recently lapsed pianist. Had he assumed I would be unable to resist connecting with the koto, and that would bring me, keep me, out of my shell?

I would later learn that the art of arranging marriages was alive and well in Shuho-cho, where families shared sons' and daughters' resumes with hired matchmakers — *nakōdo* — who would pass them along to other eligible singles, arranging initial meetings at fancy hotels with the most-interested parties in attendance: parents, potential bride and groom, and matchmaker.

In this case, Kashima-kachō had handed me off to this *sensei-na-kōdo*, who introduced me to the koto club family, certain that the koto and I were meant for each other.

As if I had not agreed to enough for one day, Sensei also exacted my vow to perform with the koto group at Shuho-cho's quickly approaching international contemporary music festival.

It was like an anxiety dream come to life, the one where you find yourself dressed in white, grasping an unexpectedly heavy cascade of roses, lilies, and ivy, walking down an aisle toward a man in a black suit, someone you've never seen before, someone you know nothing about, while hundreds of friends and family members smile and snap photos, expecting you to marry him, to start a new life together, right then.

I had first protested: *"Hontō-ni, Sensei, dekimasen!"* — "Really, Sensei, I cannot!" My new sensei's response? "If you get lost, just *po-zu!*" — "pose." She twinkled and giggled in the back of her throat. Even in that small, sun-warmed room, with just a few in attendance, the momentum felt overwhelming. It seemed I had no choice but to take the next step. And the next. The head-spinning pace felt familiar.

But this time I was agreeing to what surely was someone's wishful thinking. An international music festival in the hinterland of Shuho-cho? Perhaps the Japanese word I knew for "international" had more nuances than I knew. Maybe it could be used to describe people in nearby communities. I could not imagine performers arriving from faraway lands.

Whatever will be, will be, I thought. Soon, Sensei's loaner koto moved in with me, and I accepted my new companion, the new music in my head and my expanding community of acquaintances.

I hardly noticed my hard-won freedom slipping away.

* * *

The week I fell in with the koto club was also the week of my twenty-fifth birthday, and my new neighbors staged a combined birthday/welcome-to-Shuho-cho party in the apartment building we shared.

Everyone else in the three-story building was an employee of the multinational cement company that owned it, all transferred in from other parts of Japan with family members while climbing the career ladder. In a sense, all of us were outsiders in Shuho-cho.

I was added to the mix because Shuho-cho was small, and this was the only available rental with a Western toilet. Every other option came with an Asian squat toilet. My hosts wanted me to feel at home.

Not only was I housed in a company building but in a spacious three-bedroom apartment located on the second floor, right next door to the *shachō* — the branch head — and his wife. The rest of our floor and the third floor were home to other couples and families, and single men in managerial positions. Downstairs was a dormitory with several young men living in single rooms off a community area and nurtured by a sweet *obasan* who cooked for them, did their laundry, listened to their troubles, and enabled them to focus on their careers and extracurricular pursuits.

The night of my party, we gathered on the first floor in the company party room, decked out with bouquets and a fruit-covered cake, for introductions, toasts, and well wishes. I was seated next to one of the first-floor residents, also twenty-five and a geologist for the cement company. He patiently helped me negotiate the swirl of Japanese words around me and even smoothed over my first big gaffe, when I was asked my thoughts on rural Shuho-cho and replied, "I like it so much better than Tokyo with all its horrible cement." He spun my words so my hardworking cement company neighbors heard a sassy quip that made everyone laugh.

Later, as I retreated to the outdoor staircase that led to my apartment, my new ally dashed out the front door and placed books in my hands, one of which was titled *Beyond Polite Japanese*. A birthday gift.

Soon I was using my thirteen-stringed roommate to attract his attention, setting it up in an extra bedroom that faced the building's parking lot. I cracked the window, slipped the *tsume* on my fingers, and kneeled before the koto to play, listening for his car returning from work and hoping he would hear me, hoping he would remember me and pay me a visit. I felt like a character in some old Japanese novel, where the koto's song relayed messages, where men fell in love with unseen women playing koto.

Wait, not that. I was not looking for love, but it turns out going on retreat can get a bit lonely. I started looking for company. And indeed he did venture up to the executive floor to visit me.

Meanwhile, my Board of Education supervisors noted how passionate I was becoming about helping people converse in my native tongue, so they introduced me to more of their town, loaning me out to the six elementary schools, to the retirement home, to the adult education class, and to the Cultural Exchange group, which needed help corresponding with artists who, seeking that elusive commodity of solitude, came to stay and create art in an old refurbished farmhouse.

I learned little Shuho-cho inside and out, the town opening like a slow-blooming flower, introducing me to nearly every demographic and venue, from a well-hidden sake distillery, to a waterfall where visitors use chopsticks to grab swift-flowing noodles, to the plateau, where one can spend a happy day seeking out the Seven Grasses of Autumn with a new friend.

* * *

If I had had the wisdom to connect the dots, I might have realized on day one that Shuho-cho was not a place to find quiet seclusion, despite its sparse population.

I had awakened early my first morning there, quickly popped out of bed and pulled open the drapes, amazed by the sunshine and serenity, such a contrast to the gritty cacophony of big-city life in Minnesota, where my previous months had involved negotiating my withdrawal from graduate school and pleading with my ex to sign divorce papers.

I dressed quickly and left my apartment before 5:30, quietly descending the outdoor staircase. In a matter of steps, I reached a narrow asphalt road that led me along the rice paddies, their leaves dancing as dragonflies arced and dipped, red wings, blue wings, and double-decker black wings vibrating in the moist, sun-saturated air. Here and there farm wives wearing aprons and galoshes walked curly-tailed dogs. Traditional-style homes with tile roofs dotted the landscape. The odd rooster crowed.

As I wandered through the idyllic scene, its tranquility soothed both my eyes and my ears.

Until, out of nowhere, the song "Edelweiss" burst across the fields, bouncing against the nearby mountains. My heart skipped. I looked at my watch. Exactly six o'clock. But that was just the beginning. An air-raid siren wailed at noon, and a tinkly piece of classical music serenaded us at five o'clock. During school vacations, extra alarms sounded at ten a.m. and six p.m., all of this noise generated by a speaker atop the village's public building.

My immediate supervisor, Sasaki-san, explained that these alerts were a relic of the postwar days, when wristwatches were rare and people needed a way to keep time. Each alarm had its own meaning: "Edelweiss," he said, was for "waking the townspeople;" the noon siren told everyone to take a lunch break; the music at five said, "You did a good job today." The alarms during school vacations encouraged children to stop studying and go outside to play, and later reminded them to return home to help out around the house.

This communitywide timekeeping felt like a relic of history that could very well be abandoned now that we all had wristwatches. But as the weeks and months passed, I watched and listened with interest as the alerts and other agreed-upon times triggered predictable reactions around me: colleagues started the workday together with an invigorating round of *rajio taisō* — "radio exercises" — three minutes of stretches and jumps set to recorded plinkety-plunk piano music, a tradition since its first broadcast in 1928. Then at ten, noon, and three, people set work aside for tea (and smoke) breaks and lunch; and at five many of my coworkers packed up their work and headed home for time with their families — and, for some, more work in their rice paddies and pear orchards.

I felt rebellious as I learned to sleep through Edelweiss's daily assaults, although there seemed little choice but to fall in with the community-wide schedule in other ways, joining in *rajio taisō* and helping the women serve tea to our male coworkers, although it went against my notions of gender equity. (The real reason Shuho-cho was called Yamaguchi's Tibet, I learned, was its reputation as the prefecture's least-progressive area.) Predictability, it seemed, built community … or was it the other way around?

Still, as I watched my new neighbors and colleagues whirl through busy days of family, work, and hobbies, I imagined myself apart from all that — except for that newfound koto habit … and the nice young company employee, Hideo, who would come to my apartment to visit and laugh, listen to music, and drink tea. I let myself believe I was an independent operator, allowing the wreckage of my previous life fade into the background.

* * *

Had I been more knowledgeable about Japan's past, I might have been less naïve.

In the early seventeenth century, the beginning of the Tokugawa period, Japan's primary means of social control was the *goningumi*, literally the "five-person group," units of five to ten families that created a formidable network of social responsibility. Being part of a *goningumi* had its benefits: it promoted collaboration and created a ready labor pool for rice farming. But this was not a club or even a co-op; it was compulsory, and group members were responsible for one another's behavior, including obedience to local and national law, from paying taxes to enforcing the shogunate's ban on Christianity.

Goningumi requirements were abolished in the late nineteenth century with the Meiji Restoration, but we all know traditions die hard. The cement company apartment building where I lived was approximately goningumi size, and, I realized too late, watchful tendencies remained. There came a day when Hideo's supervisor told him that the *shachō*, my next-door neighbor, did not want him visiting me anymore. I had never realized we were under surveillance.

Perhaps it was verboten for a dormitory resident to visit the executive floor without permission from a superior. And maybe misbehavior, perceived or actual, could result in a reprimand or sanctions against everyone. I will never know. But what I learned that day was that while I still considered Shuho-cho my retreat, it was one hundred percent real-life to everyone around me.

Embarrassed, I told Hideo not to come back.

* * *

Meanwhile, I also tried to keep the koto at arm's length.

Soon after I entered my sensei's world, she started working on me to purchase my own instrument and get my license. Much as martial artists train to attain different colored belts, koto musicians study to reach ever-higher levels and then earn licensure for teaching. But I refused to engage in this. The whole intent of my escape to Japan had been to regroup in one discrete, deletable year. "What would I do with a koto in America?" I asked her, imagining the burden of hauling and storing this instrument that I would have the rarest of opportunities to perform upon and no one with whom to practice or consult.

No, I was in Shuho-cho to detach, and it made no sense to bring that creature home. I had taken a survival-based approach to both my Japanese language and my koto studies. In the realm of language, that meant focusing on conversation over reading and writing, which left me mostly illiterate but able to communicate in day-to-day life. With the koto, my goal had been to keep up with the other students and my sensei, which meant learning songs loosely and theory flimsily, never considering the music's pentatonic nature or how it compared to and contrasted with Western music. I accepted the koto as part of my life in Japan mainly because of the benefits I could reap: to mollify my employers and enjoy the company of a club.

Besides, to my ear the first time playing through any koto song sounded grisly, not only because of my errors but because my Western ears told me the composer had written intervals and lines of deliberately bad-sounding music in willful disobedience to common rules of good taste. Progressions made no sense, intervals seemed random.

But in the koto tradition, at least in this lineage, sensei and student play together almost all the time. Unlike my piano lessons, where I was expected to play for my teacher, demonstrating what I had learned and how far I had yet to go, koto lessons were collaborative. Listening carefully and watching Sensei from the corner of my eye, I mimicked her in sound and movement as best I could, and because she played with me, I knew the dissonance I produced was intentional, because she created it too.

Once I began to play a song with some confidence, though, Sensei would switch to another part — because apparently one line of melodic mayhem is insufficient — and my brain would insist we were playing two different pieces of equally grating music that were never meant to meet. The emperor had no clothes.

Over time, though, out of the fog of sound, sense began to emerge. And after more time, I would anticipate and even look forward to the next phrase and the next, until the discordant piece became like a friend with quirks. I became eager for each upcoming thematic element and, when it arrived, relished it and found that somehow the dissonance, in my ear, had become consonance, and the song, the instrument, my own.

*　*　*

The evolution of my feelings toward the koto and its strange songs was not so unlike the way I settled into that different — and, to me, sometimes strange — culture of Shuho-cho. My preconceived notions of how life was to be lived were disrupted in many ways: by fellow teachers, some of whom wanted me not to teach but to serve as a human tape player, reading English textbooks aloud to students; by cultural norms, like women serving tea to their male colleagues; by expectations of whom I would and wouldn't spend time with ... and when ... and where — all of these inputs (both requests and admonishments) needling me until I decided to rebel against some but find ways to accept others as terms of my adopted culture. I came to anticipate these challenges to my expectations and enjoy their predictability, watching them play out as expected and feeling a growing sense of belonging, of acceptance. Making peace.

As for my koto experiences, they included much more than weekly lessons and the rather harrowing international music festival, which actually did include musicians from all over the world and where I, the only foreigner in my koto group, wrapped in lavender *yukata* — summer kimono — while the rest were cloaked in somber indigo, lost my place in our performance and for some terrible seconds did need to "*po-zu.*" We went on to play at various koto gatherings and concerts for which we were wrapped and bound in multi-layered kimono and belts by professional dressers, and sent forth to kneel on stages, I all the while worrying that my sleeping legs would betray me, forcing me to crawl away, dragging my koto behind.

Koto lessons with Sensei sometimes involved as much visiting as playing, she arriving with seasonal treats wrapped in soft, exquisite papers, I arriving with questions about Japanese society and culture, expectations of work, of friendship, and of love, sometimes in tears.

But this koto club, and the music, performances, and people it brought into my life, including Hideo, who I finally decided it would indeed kill me not to kiss, became part of what lured me into extending my one year in the not-so-quiet *inaka* of Japan to two.

Toward the end of my second year, I began preparing to return to Minnesota. One day, I climbed the steps to the second floor of the Board of Education building for my koto lesson and entered the music room. There, my teacher greeted me with a surprise gift: a koto.

I was astounded. "No," I demurred, "I cannot take your koto."

"Yes," she insisted, "you will." Besides, she added, it was just her old koto.

Looking at my strong-willed sensei, I realized I had no choice. *"Domo arigato gozaimasu!"* I said, bowing low, using the most formal, deepest "thank you" I knew. And then she set out her conditions: before sending the koto home, I needed to get it restrung and refurbished for a few hundred dollars. *"Hai, Sensei,"* I said. Then, once home in Minnesota, I must introduce the koto's music to people there. *"Hai."*

There was nothing to negotiate. It was like receiving my own Great Commission.

So, focused on my notion of living like an island amid the Shuho-cho townspeople, I had failed to consider my sensei's desires and plans. Despite my effort to remain detached, she was attaching part of Japan to me forever. I tried to imagine hauling that cumbersome instrument — along with all my other memorabilia, clothing, and housewares — from place to place to place in my as-yet-blurry future.

Some weeks later, I double-wrapped my refurbished koto in my work colleagues' farewell gifts — an orange brocade koto cover, cranes flying across it, a sober black case over that — and tucked it into a long, narrow, specially made cardboard box. I sent it via airmail, the only way the postal service would accept such a strangely shaped object, and it beat me back to Minnesota, where my parents opened their door to welcome it into our family home.

What I could not envision at the time was that nearly a decade in the future, I would move to Washington, on the West Coast of the United States, and find another koto club and another strong sensei. For the next ten years, nearly every week I would descend the spiral staircase to her studio, where we would speak Japanese and play koto together, those lessons providing an unexpected retreat, respite from the gale-force challenges I encountered parenting a child whose hours-long tantrums and remarkable defiance nearly drained me of all patience and hope, a far weightier trial than the one that had launched my flight to Shuho-cho.

An hour with my old sensei's koto and my new sensei's instruction would refresh my mind, still my heart, and, week after week, give me the strength to leave the studio and drive home to my real life.

About the Author

Sarah Coomber is the author of *The Same Moon* (Camphor Press, 2020), a memoir about what happened when she abandoned her wrecked Minnesota life to spend two years teaching English in Yamaguchi, Japan. A career communicator, she has since worked in public relations, journalism, science writing and advocacy, and has taught English at the university level. Sarah has an MFA in creative nonfiction from Eastern Washington University and a master's in mass communication from the University of Minnesota. Currently she lives in Washington state, where she achieved her level four certification in the Seiha School of koto and teaches yoga.

8

Fishermen of the Seto Inland Sea

By Amy Chavez

SHIRAISHI ISLAND, population 450, is one of a collection of small islands in the Kasaoka chain in Okayama Prefecture. The Seto Inland Sea boasts over two thousand islands, although not all are inhabited. The populations that still exist are dwindling.

The port is the hub of life on any small Japanese island. In the old days this center of arrival and departure was called *machi*, indicating "town center," although there isn't — and never has been — a downtown on Shiraishi Island. But the lofty designation is indicative of the hustle and bustle of goods being delivered and distributed, ferry passengers coming and going, and residents clamoring about their daily activities. The Shiraishi harbor was constructed over four hundred years ago by local laborers who mined the island's granite. They chiseled the rock by hand into blocks and fitted them to form two jetties on each side of the entrance. These two lobster claws leave just enough space between them for one ferry to pass through, or two small fishing boats — one coming in while the other is going out.

The port is indeed small, the length from claws to tail being 391 meters, and the width less than half that, or equal to the distance a professional archer could sling an arrow. I don't know how deep the port is, but twice a year during the lowest tide, the island's half-dozen sailboats lean on their keels waiting for the high tide to right their masts. Cargo ships, at all times, are left swinging on their anchors outside the port when their captains come home to spend the weekend with their families.

For me, moving into a house by the port was a chance to get up close and personal with island traditions, superstitions, and folklore. Over the years, more than twenty now, I began to realize that island living is a small niche under the wider genre of Japanese countryside living. Here, each season gives way to the preparations for a festival, ceremony, planting, or harvest, just like anywhere else in the countryside; what sets it apart is isolation. The briny borders have preserved this islet like a jar of pickles, keeping the island traditions protected for decades longer than their mainland village counterparts.

Here, the living past carries on via the elders, who orally hand down their stories to those who will listen. But when these children of the Taishō and Shōwa eras pass on, they will not be replaced by sons, daughters, or grandchildren, because the young people have all moved away. When the last of the elders dies, only these boulders and mountains will be witness to what once was.

Last year, I decided to interview islanders and collect their stories in an attempt to create an oral history of Shiraishi Island and its people.

The Golden Era of Fishing

Mr. Nakatsuka (born 1927, Shōwa 2)
and his wife, Namiyo (born 1936, Shōwa 11)

"Sorry, the two of us are old; we're not much good," says Namiyo in deft Japanese-style modesty as I enter their pristine house located next door to the post office. Stepping up from the floor of the entryway into the tatami mat room, I am surrounded by a veritable museum of artifacts and family memorabilia — hand-carved wooden statues, certificates in gold-plated frames, and fancy calligraphy scrolls — every artifact dusted or polished to gleaming. Soon the Nakatsukas would introduce me to these items as if they were members of their family.

"That used to be a dirt floor," says Mr. Nakatsuka standing in his *jinbei* (traditional lounging clothes) and pointing to the concrete entryway I had just stepped up from. "We had an old wood-burning stove there, where we boiled rice and pounded it into *mochi* rice cakes. We'd use a stone mortar to put the rice in and pound it among four family members, all at once."

Namiyo sweeps a hand in the air toward the treasures of the room. "All this was passed down to us because my husband's oldest brother didn't have any children. Since my husband was the second in line, we inherited everything from the family in the hopes we would pass it down to our children."

"We have two children and two grandchildren. All boys. One is in Tokyo. He won't come back. The other comes back occasionally to visit," says Mr. Nakatsuka. "Everyone moves so far away these days. It's lonely." I consider for a moment what it must be like to live alone in a house of memories but no one else to share them with.

Namiyo chimes in again, "People say they want to preserve the old things, but we're too old to worry about preserving anything. And no one else is here to carry on with them.

"This certificate is from the Red Cross," says Namiyo indicating to one of the many frames filled with fancy calligraphy. "My husband has done a lot of things in different places. Even though he can't go places to help anymore because of his age, he still sends help." I walk slowly down the length of the room in my stocking feet while peering up at the ceiling. Japanese portrait frames are hung from a cornice board near the top of the wall, making them tilt out as if they were looking down at you. The next one that catches my eye is a certificate in a gilded frame that bears the Japanese imperial crest.

"I was the head of the island post office for thirty-three years," explains Nakatsuka. "Before that, I worked in the telephone office in Okayama City, because in those days the telephone and mail were based out of the same office. So all together, I worked seventy-something years for the mails. That's why I got that certificate from the emperor. For my long service."

"Only because he worked so hard," adds his wife. "But he got stomach cancer when he was eighty-eight and lost a lot of weight. He's fifty kilos now, but he's not that healthy anymore. Until he was eighty-eight he was very healthy, and he did everything for me.

"We have no interesting stories," she says. "We worked too hard to do anything else!"

"We've had a lot of nice things done for us," says her husband, referring humbly to his accolades.

"Who's that in this photo?" I ask.

"That's my husband's great grandfather. It's a sketch, not a photo. He drew that calligraphy over there." She points to a scroll hanging vertically in the alcove of the living room reserved for displaying the traditional Japanese arts. "It says 'tenchi moromoro no okami' [golden kami of the universe]. "Tenchi means everyone's god. It's a Shinto saying."

I comment on their lofty *kamidana* god shelf, a staple in traditional Japanese houses. Theirs is maintained with a fresh sprig of the sacred *sakaki* branch (gathered from the mountain nearby), its shiny green leaves sprouting decoratively out of two small white vases. Between the vases is a miniature wooden Shinto shrine. "From long ago we always made requests to the gods because we humans can't do everything on our own," says Mr. Nakatsuka, who gives his age as ninety-three and a half.

"I was born on Shiraishi at the very beginning of the Shōwa period," he continued. "I have two brothers and five sisters — seven siblings in all. That was normal then. There were 2,300 people living on Shiraishi at that time. My father was a fisherman and my mother sold vegetables. In those days, they fished for *sawara*, red snapper, puffer fish, squid, and *yosogi.*"

Up until the mid-twentieth century, Japan's lakes and other bodies of water were home to itinerant fishermen who rowed from cove to cove living on their boats. They fished to feed their families and to earn a meager existence.

But people who lived in the Seto Inland Sea had an advantage. The briny borders of the islands delivered an abundance of fish straight to the islanders' doorstep. Whereas an itinerate fisherman on the mainland might take up fishing because it was one of the few jobs available to an unskilled laborer, in the Seto Inland Sea generations of fishermen had refined their avocation into an art form. This area of the Inland Sea is especially good for trapping red snapper, called *tai*, which gave rise to a method of catching red snapper called *tai-ami*, a type of net fishing that involved more than fifty workers per catch.

Over 350 years ago, fishermen in Hiroshima and Okayama prefectures formed co-operatives to carry out tai-ami. The mainland port town of Tomonoura, which can be seen from Shiraishi, re-enacts the event every May for the Tai-ami Festival.

Mr. Nakatsuka and I are now sitting on the tatami mats. Namiyo brings in hot tea and rice cracker snacks on a tray and sets it on the low table in front of us before retiring to a seat on the other side of the room.

"Although tai-ami is famous in Tomonoura, this entire area of Hiroshima and Okayama used the technique. Fishermen worked on their boats near Sanagi Island in Kagawa Prefecture and sold their catches in Shikoku. That was the best place to fish at the time. And we'd catch sardines to bag and sell."

In those days fishermen were not limited by fishing boundaries like they are today and they often crossed prefectural borders.

The Inland Sea is fed by waters from the Pacific Ocean through two openings: the Kii Channel near Osaka, and the Bungo Channel between Kyushu and Shikoku. In addition, the Kanmon Strait, located between Honshu and Kyushu, brings water in from the Japan Sea. With three straits from which the current rushes in and out, the resulting tide rises and falls up to four meters twice a day.

"This area is the exact middle of the Inland Sea, where the waters from the east and west meet," Nakatsuka says, referring to the town of Tomonoura just over the border in Hiroshima Prefecture. This area is considered especially fertile as fish seek more somnolent waters to lay their eggs. This abundance of fish is what kept the tai-ami tradition fruitful for so long.

The fishing people of Shiraishi, celebrating a record catch of niboshi
(small sardines), 1944

"Of course, it involved a lot of people, but there were around 2,500 people living here in those days, and many of them fished for a living."

The tai-ami method employs two large boats of twenty or so rowers on each. A large net is floated between the two tandem vessels, with each securing one side of the net. The net, dropped deep into the water, is then lifted to form a scoop while the boats are rowed forward. The men relied on their collective brawn to cinch up the net full of trapped fish.

With the advent of motorized boats in the 1930s, tai-ami was replaced by *kinchaku ami* (referring to the shape of the net: gathered at the top and pulled tight with a cord like a cotton coin purse). "The way we fished was like this," explains Nakatsuka. He put the tips of both index fingers next to each other on the table, then dragged each finger down in an arc on to show how each vessel created a half circle that joined up again at the 180 degree mark. With engines, the boats could quickly surround a school of fish. Once the fish were entrapped, the men would heave the contraption full of fish onto the deck.

The kinchaku-ami nets were passed among different groups of fishermen. This marked a very competitive and lively time, a golden era of fishing. So successful were the Shiraishi fishermen that they often appeared in newspapers in the 1950s showing off their record catches of small sardines, which are used in the making of *dashi*, the base for Japanese soups and sauces.

"Did you just drop the nets anywhere?" I ask Nakatsuka.

"Of course not!" he says in a rather endearing, husky old-man voice. "We had people looking for fish from the top of Takayama, on the southwest side of the island."

"From the top of the mountain?!"

Nakatasuka was only too eager to demonstrate. "One guy would stand on top of Takayama Mountain with a telescope." He stands up and, like the child he was at the time, forms his two hands into a circle in a make-believe telescope. The fishermen were waiting on their boats below. "From up there the observer could look far out and see the movements of fish. He was looking for a change in the color or surface of the water, a disturbance," he says, his eyes boring through the walls of the house towards the sea. "The watcher had a pair of white flags, one in each hand, and when he spotted a school of fish, he'd signal to the boats by waving the flags." Nakatsuka shoots his hands above his head, holding imaginary flags, and leans to one side while yelling, "To the left!" He thrusts his arms up again in a semaphoric gesture and hollers, "To the right!" And the chase would begin as the boats headed to that area, constantly looking back to consult their cicerone.

The silvery sardines were transferred from the net, flopping and shimmering in the sunlight, into round wooden casks, which were passed to a smaller third boat to be taken back to shore while the huntsmen continued fishing. The fishermen's wives transported the heavy casks from the smaller boats and carried them up the beach to be boiled in vats then laid out to dry in the sun.

Each house was awarded a portion of fish based on how many people they had helping with the catch. "I remember my family always got six casks," Nakatsuka-san told me rather proudly. "Yes, six. I know because my father was a fisherman and when I was a kid, I used to go out and help."

I suddenly hear the trill of the cicadas outside get louder, and it occurs to me that while fishing is all fine and well in the warm months of summer, what did the fishermen do in the colder months? I turn to Nakatsuka-san. "Did they fish in the wintertime?"

"Of course," he says. "They wore *donza*," the local name for the fishing jackets that I was told were used by the men on the island until at least 1955. When one is brought out to show me, I marvel at the thickness of these handmade fishermen's coats sewn with layers of cloth.

"They didn't have rubber fishing boots then either, so they fished barefoot or in straw sandals," adds Nakatsuka.

"My father was tough. My family worked very hard. But things aren't easy now either. Now the boats are mostly trawlers and fishermen go out alone at night. There's no one to help you if something goes wrong."

A Modern Fisherman

Kazuyoshi Nakano (born 1981, Shōwa 56)

At sunrise, a young skinny guy in scuffed white rubber boots and turquoise waterproof bibs arrives at the port with a cigarette hanging from his mouth, looking like the fisherman's version of the Marlboro Man. This is Kazuyoshi, or "Kazu," getting ready to head out in his boat to check his octopus traps.

At thirty-nine, Kazu is the youngest fisherman on Shiraishi Island. His father runs a seafood restaurant on the beach where old glass fishing floats hang from the eaves of the building and terracotta octopus pots serve as nostalgic decorations. "All the octopus pots are durable plastic now because they are lighter and don't break easily," Kazu explains to me as we talk in front of the restaurant. They're also weighted on the bottom so the fishermen can lay the pots — tied at intervals along a rope, like a string of pearls — on the seabed. The unsuspecting octopuses snuggle into these newfound abodes at night, only to be surprised by Kazu, who evicts them the next morning.

"These blue glass floats were used in *sashi-ami* (gill net fishing)," Kazu tells me, referring to the glass balls hanging from the eaves. Glass floats are no longer used either and have been replaced by the black plastic ones that can be seen bobbing on the sunlit surface of the Inland Sea these days.

Kazu is a third-generation fisherman. His father, seventy, still dives for abalone and turban shells for his customers, who expect only the freshest seafood. A live fish tank holds fish, sea slugs, abalone, and mollusks until they are ordered.

The octopus is considered the most efficient seafood because there is no waste: every part of the octopus is eaten, including the head. In this country they are served raw, boiled, grilled, and as a festival food, when the tentacles are dropped into batter to make fried octopus balls.

Approximately forty-five thousand tons of octopus are caught every year in Japan. The most common method for catching them in the Seto Inland Sea is with octopus pots called *takotsubo*. These pots can be seen stacked up next to fishing ports all over Japan.

"I moved away from the island in elementary school, when my parents divorced. My father stayed here, and my mother moved to Tokyo, taking both me and my older brother with her. When my mother remarried, she had another son, my younger brother.

"I never came back to the island, and my parents didn't have any contact. Then in 2003 my older brother, who was twenty-two at the time, decided to come visit my father for the summer and help out at the restaurant. One night, he and some of his friends visiting from Tokyo decided to go to Kasaoka to the bars. My brother didn't have a boat license, but one of the other young guys did, so they borrowed a fishing boat to go to the mainland. It was already dark when they left. When they got to the place between Konoshima and Takashima islands, my brother realized he had forgotten his cell phone. So they decided to turn around and return to Shiraishi Island to get it. It must have been low tide then, because when the driver turned the boat in a big semicircle, he ran it up onto some rocks. The passengers were all thrown from the boat. The driver, who suffered a broken arm, swam around for a while in the dark and ended up on the shore of Takashima. The other friend also found his way to a beach. But my brother was nowhere to be found. My father is a diver, so he spent the next several days looking for him on the bottom of the sea but turned up nothing.

"I was in Osaka at the time, working at a restaurant, but came back with my mother when we heard my brother was missing. It was the first time I had been back to the island since elementary school. To tell the truth, I didn't remember that much of the island, but it was so different from the city. It was so small. It seemed insignificant: just a lump of sand in the middle of the Inland Sea. I remember I took off my shirt and laid out in the sun on the deck and just got lost in my thoughts about my older brother. My brother couldn't have just been swallowed up by the sea like that."

I remember the events in Kazu's story like they were yesterday, even Kazu taking off his shirt and lying in the sun. Someone had given me the news that the restaurant owner's eldest son was missing when I boarded the first ferry one morning to go to work on the mainland. When the ferry stopped to pick up passengers at Takashima, there was the father standing in his wetsuit on the dock. He was dripping wet and was apparently taking a break from searching for his son. He looked up at the ferry just as the last person got on. I was standing in the door. We made eye contact, and I gave him a deep bow. He looked down at the dock. He was so helpless.

"My mother stayed in an accommodation next door to my father's restaurant. I stayed at my father's house with his new wife and their two small children. My father and I hadn't seen each other since my mother left him because she was pregnant with another man's child: my younger brother.

"Anyway, after three days, we got a call early in the morning. A fisherman found my brother's body floating near Takashima.

"The funeral was in Tokyo, but my father didn't come. I guess I understand, since it would have been awkward with my little brother and my stepfather there, who were after all, the reason my mother had left my father. But I brought the urn back to the island that autumn, and we scattered the ashes at sea."

I had barely met Kazu when we all boarded that fishing boat weeks later, everyone clutching bouquets of flowers. The seas were mournfully calm, and the sun reflected off the water, making us squint. Near Takashima, the site of the accident, his father slowed to a stop and cut the engine. While drifting in the vast silence, Kazu slowly shook out the ashes from the urn. The lighter particles sparkled in the sun like fairy dust and settled into a line on top of the water. In silence, we tossed the flowers into the floating line of powder. Some of the bouquets pirouetted in the eddies, while others rested peacefully, rising and falling in the natural breath of the waves. All the flowers remained huddled in their bunches, their stems refusing to separate. We drifted for some moments, watching the fragile remnants of a life begin to lose form. The captain cranked on the motor and steered the boat homeward. We watched as our offerings shrank in the distance until they had disappeared from view and we were convinced that body and soul were absorbed into the renewing waters of the sea.

Kazu's trip to Shiraishi Island must have stirred something deep inside his past, because a few years later, he came back. Still single at thirty-three and tired of working in restaurants in the cities, he opted to become a fulltime fisherman.

Now the former short-order cook specializes in capturing octopus. He is one of just a handful of fishermen left on Shiraishi Island. Four trawlers, a few octopus hunters, and a couple net fishermen now service the entire island. Kazu admits it's a lonely job these days, and a far cry from the community with whom his ancestors combined their forces to produce a fortune. Perhaps because octopus hunting is easy to get into without the huge layout for a trawling boat and nets, Kazu made hunting octopi his destiny. He has a modest hand-me-down fishing boat and borrows octopus pots from the fishermen's co-op.

One day, in late summer but before the jellyfish arrived, Kazu invited me to go out hunting octopi with him, and I eagerly accepted. We left Shiraishi Port before sunrise one morning at 4:30 a.m. and motored out beyond the flashing red light of the port marker and into the Inland Sea. There wasn't a breath of wind; the sea was like glass. No other boats were out, but we were not alone: Nature was all around us. A seagull was perched in morning meditation upon a Styrofoam buoy, and a starfish jumped out of a spray of waves and landed on the gunwale of the boat. We slipped past the Shinto *torii* gate on tiny Benten Island, home to the shrine of the goddess of the sea.

When we arrived at the octopus-hunting grounds, the sun was appearing in pink streaks of cloud across the sky. The earth was awakening, but the octopi were still fast asleep. Everything was ready to arouse the mollusk residents: the net, the reel, and the hunter. The boat approached a buoy indicating where the octopus pots had been previously laid. Kazu lifted the buoy out of the water with a boat hook and pulled up a rock attached to the line to anchor the entire strand of pots on the sea floor. Then he draped the rope over the automatic winch and flipped a switch; the reel whirred into action.

Up came the octopus pots — *clunk-clunk* — attached to the rope. Each was quickly inspected; if there was a squatter inside, Kazu turned the pot upside down, tapped the side with a piece of wood — *tock-tock-tock* — until the cephalopod fell splashing into the boat's holding tank. After all the pots were pulled up, the sun was hot on the backs of our necks and the tank was full of eight-legged creatures. Already, a tentacle was sticking out of the hold, feeling around for an escape. Kazu prized the legs from the side of the hold and stuffed the creature unceremoniously into a net bag. The octopus writhed, turning bright red with rage. Kazu bagged the rest of them, leaving them afloat in the tank as he locked down the hatch.

That morning was an especially good catch. With over a dozen mollusks in the holds, we headed back to Shiraishi Island. Once the boat was tied up at port, Kazu transferred the bagged octopi from the hold into a larger net that hangs over the side of the boat in the fresh seawater. He would sell them to restaurants and accommodations on the island that day. Some individuals would also buy one to serve to relatives visiting from the cities.

Kazu works only part-time on the island these days because he also helps farm seaweed and oysters on Takashima. He has a house here with his wife and two small children. But the island's kindergarten and elementary school closed last year due to an insufficient number of students, so Kazu's wife and the little ones had to move to a relative's house on the mainland, where the kids could go to school. The island's junior high is still in session but will close in two more years after the three currently matriculated students graduate.

With the current population of the island at just 450, Kazu's children will likely be the last ever born on Shiraishi Island.

About the Author

Amy Chavez has been a columnist with the *Japan Times* since 1997. Her books include *Japan, Funny Side Up*; *Running the Shikoku Pilgrimage*; and *Amy's Guide to Best Behavior in Japan*. She is currently writing a book on the oral history of Shiraishi Island, in the Seto Inland Sea, where she has lived for the past twenty-five years. She is founder and editor of the Books on Asia website.

9

ONara

By Paul Vickory

Nara is a mountainous and heavily forested prefecture, and landlocked despite being located in the Kii Peninsula. The prefectural capital and largest city — also called Nara and with a population of about 367,000 — boasts a cultural heritage second only to Kyoto, which is forty kilometers to the north. Nara was Japan's first permanent capital (during the Nara period, 710–784) and was modeled after the Chinese capital of Chang'an of the Tang dynasty.

American Paul Vickory taught English for four years, 2008–2012, in Shimoichi, a small town set among gently rolling forest-clad hills about an hour's drive south of Nara City.

* * *

SURROUNDED by greatness, I make my own literary offering with not a little humility. Those entries before and after these ramblings will doubtlessly educate and enthrall the reader with their authors' keen insights. I, however, merely served as an Assistant Language Teacher (ALT) to the kindergartens and elementary schools of the rural town of Shimoichi, and so lack any such piercing acumen. Marooned as I was on this metaphorical island in the otherwise endless sea of rice paddies, wooded hills, and winding rivers that is the Japanese countryside, my tour of Japan was hardly scholarly. My mind wrestled instead with the baser task of how best to amicably coexist with my aged neighbors as a blond, blue-eyed white guy. I trust, then, that what I have simplified or misunderstood entirely in this passage might at least be accepted by the reader as pragmatic, if flawed, wisdom. I may also harp on the rustic nature of my second home; but, for all its faults, nowhere else better displays Japan's earnest hospitality and quiet stoicism than the countryside. As a shining example of these bucolic merits, the sparsely populated prefecture of Nara enjoys my deepest respect. In Japanese, one might indicate such reverence by placing an "O" before the inspirational object: so does "kyaku-san" (guest) become "okyaku-san" (honored guest). I would honor Nara thusly, but, as the locals were quick to point out, "onara" already means "fart." Now, having led with a fart joke, I believe the tone has been sufficiently lowered. Let us continue.

* * *

I, of course, hadn't planned on teaching in rural Nara. Nobody would. With stars in my eyes I confidently entered "Osaka" into the "requested placement" field of my JET application. The Japan Exchange and Teaching (JET) program is tasked with sending foreign teachers to those secluded regions that would otherwise be left foreignerless. Osaka, the country's second-largest city, has no shortage of expats willing to lecture on the finer points of English grammar in universities or, indeed, on the nuances of "Head, Shoulders, Knees, and Toes" in preschools. In fact, no major city struggles in that regard. So JET HQ shovels all those applications requesting cities the reader has heard of into a bin and scatters them over a giant map of Japan, and thus are placements assigned. I assume those applicants with appropriately obscure requests are given preference, but it's probably easier to just throw both such applications in the bin with the rest.

When it came time for my sentencing I received a curt missive informing me that my services were eagerly awaited in the town of Shimoichi in Nara Prefecture. Shimoichi's three-line Wikipedia article afforded me two facts: it had a population of 7,404 and was known for growing persimmons. My first thought was, "What the hell is a persimmon?" It turns out this is a fruit that looks like a cross between a tomato and a miniature pumpkin and, when in season, is given to foreign teachers by the bucketful. However, man cannot live by persimmon alone; if unable to keep up with the fruity tidal wave (delicious though it may be), a teacher might have to dispose of overripe fruit in a train station trash can so as not to offend the persimmon benefactors.

* * *

But I was not to be delivered to that land of persimmon bounty directly. The aforementioned JET Programme is run by the national government and is therefore permitted to put on airs at the taxpayer's expense. Accordingly, I passed my first nights at Tokyo's luxurious Keio Plaza Hotel among my cohort of hundreds of fellow incoming teachers. For days we were lectured on our duties in and out of the classroom and on life in Japan more broadly. Of course, every situation is different, and, in an effort to apply to every incoming teacher, information had to be so generalized or be delivered in such an equivocal manner as to be useless. Peanut butter, for example, cannot be found, unless it can, but even then it might not really be peanut butter, excepting, of course, those times when it is. Tokyo Orientation at least succeeded in setting the scene for Japan: here were the lights, crowds, singing toilets, and towering skyscrapers among which I would make my home. Oh, wait....

With this initial indoctrination complete, I traveled to Nara City (capital of Nara Prefecture) and received a much more intimate crash course on survival with a dozen other local newcomers. In contrast to Tokyo orientation's hand-wringing indecision, Nara orientation's content was alarmingly relevant, direct, and absent from the recruitment literature. "This is a *mukade*," our instructor stated matter-of-factly, gesturing to the image of a giant black segmented hellbeast with a blood-red head and a thousand sickeningly yellow legs. "It's a giant venomous centipede that likes to hide under furniture and in shoes. If you crush it, the pheromones will attract its vengeful mate, so it's best to catch it with some tongs and drown it in a jar of oil ... which is about as difficult as it sounds. Alright, moving on, this thumb-sized hornet is an *oosuzumibachi*...." I was then introduced to my Shimoichi Board of Education handler and whisked off on an awkward two-hour drive to my new home.

* * *

Throughout its hundreds of years of history, Shimoichi has been central to Nara Prefecture only geographically and has been largely ignored and left to its own devices. Centuries of spontaneous growth have produced a rat's nest of jumbled side streets, here too narrow for all but the most steady of cyclists, now a six-way intersection, now a dead end in a rice field. Like in so many rural communities, the youth have migrated to the glamor and jobs of the urban centers, leaving behind the more venerable demographic, who tend to vacant storefronts peddling the wares of those few surviving local industries, namely temple ornaments, *konnyaku* (a gel-like food made from the root of the ominously named Devil's Tongue), bath salts, those world-renowned persimmons, and high-end disposable chopsticks. Signs of stagnation creep in around the edges, but the street is otherwise orderly and dignified, much like the town's citizenry.

The community's somnolence suits its idyllic pastoral setting. At Shimoichi's center, the cheerful Aki River adds the finishing touches on its narrow valley in the surrounding monkey-infested Yoshino mountains. The lush hills mark the seasons with dramatic shifts, and at the time of my midsummer arrival were buried beneath an impenetrable green cloak. Fall would bring a brief explosion of flaming reds and yellows and then quickly fizzle into winter, which dulled the bare trunks to the same frigid gray hue of the cloudy sky. Finally, before the more impatient foliage can charge once again into summer, the gnarled sakura trees burst into bloom, coloring the year's first warm breezes with cascades of delicate pink petals. Though the community faces lean times, Shimoichi's backdrop remains the stuff of haiku.

* * *

Shimoichi's sleepy small town charm and verdant borders might well have inspired the works of Japanese animation legend

Miyazaki, though depending on the mood of the local wildlife it might tend more toward *Princess Mononoke* than *My Neighbor Totoro.* Indeed, while unrolling my futon on my first night the steady hum of cicadas was punctuated with cries that could only be those of women being stabbed repeatedly in a dark alley. But there were no sirens, no commotion, nothing but the resumption of the chorus of frogs and insects, resentful for the interruption. Was the town's peaceful agrarian facade masking some dark conspiracy, possibly involving virgin sacrifices? I avoided lonely backroads for fear of stumbling upon groups of hooded figures, which is difficult when every street is a lonely backroad. Cowardly though it may have been, it was too early in my stay to be entangled in a web of cultists and intrigue. After a week of eluding shadowy conspirators, I raised my concerns to a veteran English teacher from the next town over and learned that, rather than tortured screams of pain and terror, the screeches were just the local deer trying to get laid. I had not encountered any of the ruminants because, unlike the asshole deer of Nara Park, the mountain herds are almost invisible; contrary to popular belief, there *are* guns in Japan, and they are used to shoot tasty mountain deer.

But Nara does love its deer. As alluded to before, Nara City's central Nara Park is swarming with asshole deer. Once thought to be the sacred messengers of the Shinto gods, they are afforded special do-not-eat status. Tourists are encouraged to feed them. This has cultivated in the herds a brash disregard for humans as anything but finicky *senbei* (deer treat) dispensers. Children are knocked down easily enough, the pilfered senbei seasoned with their juvenile tears of pain and betrayal. Bigger tourists are swarmed or nipped on the butt until they drop their senbei from either panic or exasperation. And when there is no senbei to be had, a deer will just stand in the middle of the road because screw you and your car. That the uninitiated reader may have a favorable opinion of the Nara deer is a testament to the skill and efforts of the Nara Board of Tourism.

* * *

The Board of Tourism had been working especially hard in the year leading up to my arrival. It was the prefectural capital's thirteen-hundred-year anniversary, you see, and Nara was finally to be granted a mascot. By some shameful oversight Nara Prefecture had managed its first thirteen centuries without a mascot, an astounding feat in a nation where a mascot clause is standard in most municipalities' founding charter. Nara Park's giant bronze Buddha, the Daibutsu (big Buddha), had served as a kind of stand-in mascot, but it is a poor candidate: first, the Buddhist religion has arguably greater claim to Buddha, and, second (and more importantly), he's not especially cute.

Mascots are a staple of Japanese culture, affixed to everything from individual skyscrapers to instant noodles, and all of them are drenched in that unique Japanese brand of "cute" known as "*kawaii*." Many products — such as ground beef, train companies, and bug spray — lack any inherent cuteness, but much can be done with a large pair of eyes. I'm not proud to admit it, but when facing the quandary of comparably priced brands of toilet bowl cleaner I based my decision entirely on whether I felt more strongly toward the wide-eyed toilet brush with a trail of sparkles or the excited flower-belching toilet. Long neglected, Nara would finally get its own delightful character to stand beside disinterested politicians at all manner of tedious ceremonies.

Elected officials understood the gravity of selecting a mascot, and so employed the services of a mascot expert (which is an actual profession). This Michelangelo, however, did not come cheap: the going rate for a visionary mascot amounts to one dump truck full of taxpayers' money. A true professional, he did exactly no research, not even scrolling all the way down the first page of his Google image search for "Nara." There's this giant Buddha thing, so slap some big ol' eyes on him. I see some of those asshole deer too, so we'll stick some antlers on his head. Let's call him Sento-kun and take an early lunch.

This product of grafting asshole deer antlers onto the Beanie Baby reincarnation of the regional holy man was received by the public with horror and disbelief. Nara's citizens had stoically endured thirteen hundred mascotless years, and, for their patience, some elected officials had spent money on Sento-kun that could have gone to schools and hospitals. The outcry was deafening, and for months the mob, rallied by the merchants charged with the daunting task of selling Sento-kun towels to tourists, called for his misshapen head.

After months of joining the rest of the country in mocking the disfigured sage, the Nara citizenry eventually grew to appreciate that Sento-kun was easily the most unique prefectural mascot in the nation. Of course Sento-kun is ugly, but what of the mascot of Chiba, or Nagano, or Gunma? All those conventional mascots are judged by their cuteness relative to that of all others. In this kawaii arms race, all depth is sacrificed for more kawaii until all that remains is flavorless monochrome shell, a character with no character. Sento-kun boldly refuses to play this game, and stands defiant, a hideous horned middle-aged Cabbage Patch Kid beset by a legion of adorable Disney caricatures, revealing the petty quibbling of the kawaii mascots for what it is. "What good is it to be cute?" Sento-kun challenges. "Is there really nothing greater to which a prefecture might aspire?" Thus, the enlightened Sento-kun is unconcerned with becoming one-dimensionally kawaii and is free, instead, to be one-dimensionally creepy. This is the true brilliance of that mercenary mascot messiah; anyone can draw tarsier eyes on a furry critter, but only a true master could instigate a paradigm shift by uniting a prefecture under the banner of a borderline blasphemous image. He was worth every yen.

Paul (right) with friends Nate and Momoka and, of course, Sento-kun

I was an early adopter of Sento-kun. His initial pariah status ensured that even with my pitiful Japanese I could break the ice with the rehearsed phrase, "So what's up with Sento-kun?" Had he been kawaii the conversation would have concluded with an indifferent "He's cute, isn't he?" But nothing inflames passions and unites disparate peoples like a common enemy. My new conversational partner was always happy to enumerate Sento-kun's failings with little additional input (or understanding) from me. Out of gratitude I curated a small collection of Sento-kun merchandise in my humble apartment; he could have done little to lower the rooms' appeal anyway.

A person of standards may have found my aged and dingy accommodations lacking. Fortunately, I am no such person; furthermore, this was my first roommate-free abode. To me my new home was a *gaijin* (foreigner) penthouse, perched atop a worn four-story brick facade that held the title of tallest building in Shimoichi.

The ground floor was suitably nondescript: a few parking spaces, an entry vestibule, and a stairwell. There was also a small corner storefront abandoned, crumbling, and empty save for a telephone placed prominently in the middle of the floor, presumably awaiting a call from Morpheus. Prior to the unavoidable climb (elevators are for soft city-folk) shoes were removed and exchanged for those ubiquitous green slippers, freely provided to guests the whole nation over and designed with a far daintier foot in mind.

The building's only three apartments were on the fourth floor. My quarters were at the end of a dark corridor, pitifully illuminated by a flickering exit sign that burned a little dimmer each day. A revolving door of middle school JETs occupied the middle unit. The apartment adjacent to the stairs was uninhabited, a fact that distressed me on those evenings when the distinct sound of feet shuffling across tatami drifted through the steel door as I hurried by.

My pace through the dark hallway quickened as each new middle school JET independently confided that similar nocturnal sounds were audible through their adjoining wall. If I shared my perch atop the town with a restless soul condemned to wander the earth for eternity, it was content to confine its unholy ramblings to its own rooms, or at least to keep things civil when venturing further. An alternative speculation is that my landlord, my only interactions with whom were two chance encounters in the stairwell, recognized that Shimoichi's lack of official love hotels presented a prime business opportunity and leased it out on a nightly basis. Supporting such speculation are those occasions when I stumbled home very late to find my shoe locker occupied by various pairs of provocative heels from which tiny green plastic slippers would be a welcome relief. However, having never encountered the scandalous footwears' owner I readily concede that the mystery heels may have belonged to a specter of the damned; the ways of both errant spirits and women are closed books to me.

* * *

Upon entering my abode one would pass through a wide hallway — with a sink, tiny stove, and minifridge — that might generously be called a "kitchen." Ahead lay the bathroom, toilet room, and laundry room, disproportionately representing how much cleaning went on while I was in residence. To the left were the two comparatively spacious tatami rooms. Matt, with whom I spent many hours sitting on the floor of an *izakaya*, observed quite poetically that Japanese homes are "made of paper and dreams," which wonderfully summarized my quarters. The only solid walls were those on the narrow north and south extremes and those encompassing the bathroom and toilet. Of the remaining "walls," those interior were *shouji* (sliding paper doors) and those exterior were glass.

The box of glass and paper in which I lived made me depressingly in tune with nature and the changing seasons. Summer Japan is hotter and more humid than any island has a right to be, and my west-facing wall of windows ensured my apartment was as hellacious an inferno as Dante ever saw. Despite fearing my tatami might catch alight, I threw open my windows, mildly preferring to fight Japan's oppressive insect hordes to fires.

If Dante had been familiar with the summer climate, the winter months would have elicited from him a nostalgic sigh for the ninth circle. Japan's frigid winters wear at the human spirit by virtue of being completely inescapable. My schools' classrooms were mere stacks of unheated and uninsulated cement cubes, comprised as much of poorly sealed windows as concrete. These ice-cube trays of the gods offered as little opposition to the pervasive cold as the paper and dreams of my apartment. Many Japanese homes cope with the lack of insulation and central heating by employing carbon-monoxide-spewing kerosene heaters (which I was not provided with) and a wonderful little table/blanket/heater combo called a *kotatsu* (which also I was not provided with). Looting the neighboring apartment between the departure of the old middle school ALT and the arrival of their successor was one of my dearest traditions. After one frostbitten winter I pillaged my neighbor's coveted kotatsu. This ill-gotten heated table proved to be a gilded cage; as the nights grew colder, the prospect of leaving to feed and relieve myself became a disheartening chore that even Tenzing would have undertaken only begrudgingly. Too many evenings were spent sitting before the blank screen of my laptop, watching the clouds of my breath and mustering the nerve to emerge from my stinky cocoon to search for the charger. As long and brutal as the summers and winters might be, I put it to the reader to find a more pleasant setting than the Japanese mountains in spring and autumn. They are the most perfect two weeks likely to be seen in this life.

* * *

It could be argued that the primary function of a residence is affording the tenant a comfortable place to sleep. My rooms failed on this front. Upon cresting the mountains and bursting through my generous "kitchen" window, the sun, like a celestial Mona Lisa, invariably focused on my face no matter where I positioned my futon, entirely unimpeded by the tissue paper and supporting dreams of my bedroom "wall." After years of searching for a haven from dawn's brilliance I found respite in the closet, which enjoyed shouji made of heavier paper and stouter dreams.

This, however, put me directly next to the air raid sirens afforded every country town. Suspended about four stories above the street, the nearest speaker stood so close to my residence that I could have slid down its pole were it not for one wall of glass, and I could come no closer to that damnable noise box than my closet. While proximity to air raid sirens may seem irrelevant in an age when Japan's risk from American bombers is at an all-time low, they were repurposed to announce what the puritanical administration thought was a good time to wake up. Each morning I was shaken awake with a two-minute banshee scream.

I came to flourish despite the many rigors of Japanese habitation. The bugs established their own robust ecosystem that self-limited their numbers. I reduced my arctic expeditions by scooting the kotatsu around my room while still seated. The blaring siren at least ensured I never overslept. One element of domestic life, however, I never reached a harmonious understanding with; the device responsible for heating my shower was, perhaps, the first commercial attempt to bring the miracle of on-demand hot water into Japanese homes since the game-changing invention of fire. The colossal machination featured levers, knobs, and cranks (*cranks!*) comparable to the steam engines of the Old West, to which I suspect it was a close cousin. The twelve-step process of animating the beast required a dexterous pair of hands, sometimes a foot, and an ear attuned to the clicking and popping in which it spoke its current state of mind. My earliest experiments often yielded a dark smoke, adding to my fear that this anachronistic time-bomb would finally detonate, leaving baffled authorities to find me days later, dead and naked in my cold shower. All my efforts culminated in me choosing either a deluge of liquid nitrogen or a pathetic trickle piped up from Earth's molten core. Not a morning passed in which I didn't curse that contraption and its strident chattering.

These many faults ultimately served to endear my residence to me; it was all part of the great adventure that was rural Japan. With familiar modern accommodations in a cosmopolitan city I might have fashioned my flat into a little American oasis, an escape from Japan. But even when shuttered in my room, those paper walls and their faded dreams challenged my Western sensibilities. I could conform or adapt but not escape, and I grew comfortable with the ever-present challenge of engaging with "Japanese cul-ture," whatever that might be, a state I would come to understand as Stage Three.

* * *

I was enlightened to the framework for staging culture shock (or "culture fatigue" if you're feeling pretentious) in the Tokyo orientation, of all places, when an errant presentation with actual applicable information on the topic seems to have slipped the net. Though usually understood to be unpleasant, the initial high of culture shock (Stage One) is that first hit that gets a new resident hooked on the country. Newcomers are flying higher than the plane they arrived on, and find the whole island nation resting at their eager feet. Similarities leap to their starry eyes from every banal corner, arrayed in the technicolor garb of the exotic. How sweet is this ambrosia brewed of giddy naïveté! In Japan there are no wrongs, only endearing cultural quirks. Wait, the Japanese love beer too?! And it's sold in vending machines?! O brave new world, that has such people in it!

When the ephemeral bubble of euphoria inevitably bursts that airplane high comes crashing down, and like the opening of *Lost*, the new JET finds herself stranded on a mysterious island with strange people, few comforts of home, and a smoke monster. Perhaps the reality of being alone in this foreign country finally sinks in. Maybe some jarring encounter precipitates the fall. Even the simple attrition of illiteracy and inability to express oneself can tear open the Stage Two abyss. Like in a Murakami novel, everyone finds themselves at the bottom of this well at some point. Those previously endearing quirks become personal affronts. Every curious glance from passersby becomes a xenophobic stare of seething racism. Suddenly everything from back home takes on a rosy shine. Why did I ever leave? What am I doing with my life on this godforsaken rock? And why is this slice of bread as thick as *four* slices would be in the civilized world?!

But then, finally, that dark tempest recedes into the pleasant calm of Stage Three. This is a good place to be: life in Japan feels natural. Day-to-day tasks are navigated with familiarity, and although one may still be aware of differences, they are not an emotional focus. An afternoon in Osaka is enjoyed, not because of the bustle of Shinsaibashi but because it's a beautiful day to sit by the river and share a beer with friends. Likewise, when a lesson goes awry an ALT blames poor planning or disruptive students rather than condemning the entire country and wishing it were swallowed by the sea. This might be integration.

* * *

I must stress to the reader that this is not a linear progression, but a cycle with Stage One ups and Stage Two downs, though Stage Three should be the norm for a well-adjusted gaijin like myself. Unexpectedly, as the years passed the most frequent source of Stage Two regression was my job. I passed many a long hour of my final year in the collective staff office of Shimoichi Elementary (my largest elementary school), my thoughts floating unmoored, with only the beacon of the day's delicious school lunch to prevent my sinking beneath the waves of ennui. My musings often drifted to a one terabyte USB hard drive that had never once migrated from its perch atop the back bookshelf. There was nothing remarkable about the hardware except that it was in the office at all. Acquiring funding for this basic piece of equipment would have demanded a Herculean campaign from some driven technological prophet set on dragging Shimoichi a little nearer the rest of us in 2012. After what must have been an epic twelve bureaucratic labors he secured his prize and then abruptly faded into legend. And here the real existential tragedy begins: while that champion of digital progress had won his funding, he had done nothing to win any hearts and minds. The teachers and administrators eyed the unfamiliar box with suspicion and continued backing up the school's flickering computers, which ran on Windows 95, on *floppy disks*.

Thousands of those plastic squares crowded the back bookcases, growing each year like a mosaic tumor around the neglected hard drive. Indeed, like so many Americans, I had imagined Japan was poised on the cutting edge, rife with robots (some even giant) and gadgetry. But in my corner of the country, at least, that fanciful spirit of progress was conspicuously absent: more faxes were sent than email, smartphones were met with resistance due to their lack of clips for dangling charms, and one acquaintance confided that she was considering upgrading from VHS to DVD. It turns out all that science fiction anime is still fiction.

I can only imagine the labyrinth of red tape faced by the champion founder of my position: I was far more expensive than a computer peripheral, not to mention all the responsibilities that come with maintaining a clueless foreigner. But my bureaucratic Theseus vanished before the finer points could be hammered out, which is exactly what is expected of Assistant Language Teachers at schools with no English teachers to assist. English in elementary schools was entirely optional, you see, and the homeroom teachers with whom I taught, though friendly, were quick to cut my classes in favor of nationally tested subjects. And so the hard drive and I collected dust among the floppies.

I wasn't always akin to neglected hardware. In my first year I was charged with three elementary schools and associated kindergartens, meaning I had six schools at which to draw up curricula, design materials, and build rapport with staff and students. Shomoichi, however, was hemorrhaging young adults/potential parents into the far-off Osaka and not-too-bad-of-a-commute Kashihara City. This, combined with Japan's birthrate trending toward that of a nation of migraine-prone pandas, meant that only a trickle of new students toddled into kindergartens each year. To the surprise of no one, Minami Elementary, averaging less than five pupils per class, was shut down midway through my tenure, Minami Elementary was shut down. The real mystery was why Minami had existed at all: it was less than a decade old and Aki Elementary (closed for low enrollment just prior to Minami's founding) was visible from the school's roof. Years later, as I prepared for my repatriation, I heard whispers of plans to refit the shuttered Minami Elementary School as a senior center for the town's burgeoning pensioner population. I can't think of a more poetic summary of the state of rural Japan.

What transformed my attitude toward Shimoichi Elementary from apathy to angst was the loss of my first love the following year. Achiga Elementary was a brilliant beacon of bilingual aspirations, with enthusiastic teachers and a student body of linguistic savants masquerading as seven-year-olds. Every lesson was a resounding success, propelling my pedagogical ambitions ever higher. But suddenly and without warning Achiga was taken from me. I know of no plans for retrofitting Achiga for use as a bingo hall and denture emporium; I suppose its closure was ordered solely out of malice. The part of me with professional aspirations closed with Achiga. With only a third of my original class load, I sat at my desk full of premade lesson plans and waited for lunch.

* * *

Even with my professional woes, my departures from culture shock Stage Three equilibrium were typically brief and minor affairs most often affected by the changing seasons. Winter's polar temperatures plunged me back into Stage Two. While patiently awaiting Ragnarök, I staved off hypothermia with my burning hatred for a country that can have the world's third-largest GDP and still make houses out of paper. But as the numbness crept in, the Stage Two despair lost its edge and eventually, with a few *tokkuri* of hot sake, a kotatsu, and a sympathetic English ear, faded back into a frosty Stage Three.

After many frigid months I would emerge from my flat one morning to find the street almost warm (though, perplexingly, my apartment would remain chilly for several more weeks). Oh, the rapture of spring! My rugby and Ultimate Frisbee teams kicked into gear. March wrapped up with graduation ceremonies, which whisked my angsty preteen sixth graders away to middle school, while early April welcomed their pliable doe-eyed first-year replacements. Soon after, the sakura exploded, sometimes violently, bringing *hanami* (cherry blossom viewing), a return to Stage One, and a resolve to never ever leave this mystical magical utopia.

Summer was a confusing time. Provoking not a few "fuck Japan" days were the despair of rediscovering that humidity can actually surpass 100 percent, the terror of bird-sized insects, and a cultural reluctance for public institutions (like, say, schools) to waste money on air-conditioning. But to restore balance were the big sports tournaments, summer break work hours, and riverside BBQs. The fleeting hot milk tea disappeared from vending machines, but pineapple *chūhai* could again be found in every convenience store. Summer could be rocky, but it was certainly better than winter.

* * *

I have thus far shied away from discussing the fourth stage, that dark and sinister side of living abroad nobody likes to talk about. After fighting to integrate and battling the cycle of culture shock to emerge after each encounter better adjusted, the saying "you can never really go back" is realized. Repatriation brings with it the very same waves of euphoric crests and dismal troughs, which settle down but never disappear. Living abroad changes how one thinks, and even years after returning I find I don't quite fit in either country. Each nation has its own stronger and weaker points, better and worse ways of doing things, and having to do things the "wrong" way is frustrating. While one expects not to fit in while abroad, it is much more depressing to feel so disconnected at "home." But, at the same time, knowing there is a better way is preferable to contented ignorance, and having two homes at least shifts one a bit closer toward cultural objectivity. As the reader can see, I deal with Stage Four by feeding myself unsubstantiated moral platitudes and reminiscing with patient readers about angry deer, ugly mascots, and haunted apartments.

About the Author

Born in Oregon, educated in Colorado, and now living in California, Paul Vickory has worn a variety of hats since leaving Japan, including caring for injured raptors and working as a SCUBA dive master. He currently works as an RN at a hospital in Long Beach. Paul has returned to Japan to play in the Tajima ultimate Frisbee tournament, continues to study the Japanese language, and is planning to move to the country with his wife and two-year-old son. Paul's time in Nara is the subject of his affectionate and funny memoir *ONara: Four Years of Misadventures in Rural Japan.*

10

The Oiwa Mystery

By John Dougill

"The Oiwa Mystery" is something of an outlier in this anthology because of the near-city setting of its subject: an abandoned shrine hidden among overgrown vegetation on a hilly green oasis just six kilometers southeast of central Kyoto. This chapter is included because it involves several rural themes. There are millions of abandoned homes across Japan (government statistics for 2019 revealed a record high of 8.46 million, representing 13.6 percent of the housing stock), and this problem is especially pronounced in the countryside. Other kinds of buildings face a similar dilemma; rather soberly, many — even those of cultural importance, and within the orbit of a prosperous, heritage-oriented Kyoto no less — are not as safe as you would assume. On a happier note, John Dougill's investigations show that undiscovered

treasures and intriguing stories lie a mere stone's throw
from busy city streets.

* * *

It's not often you get to play Indiana Jones, but that's how it felt
when I came across an overgrown Shinto shrine near Kyoto with
something of the feel of a miniature Angkor Wat. My adventure
had started with a picture a friend sent me that showed a most
unusual *torii* with square pillars covered in decorative motifs like
some ancient Greek doorway. He'd stumbled upon it while walking
the Kyoto Trail, which runs around the hilly fringes of the city. All
he knew was that the carved gateway was by local artist Dōmoto
Inshō (1891–1975) and it belonged to Oiwa Jinja (Big Rock Shrine).
Mysteriously, the shrine had been abandoned; but when and why
he didn't know. Curious, I decided to investigate.

And so one late spring day, I set out with a Japanese companion
in quest of the shrine. Strangely, neither my companion nor her
friends, all born and raised in the city, had ever heard of it. We
managed to locate it on a map, however, and found that it stood
just to the southeast of the city, in rural surrounds. As we drove
up to the site, we saw a plain torii straddling a track open only to
pedestrians. After parking the car, we walked through woods into a
lush bamboo forest. There was not a single sign or any indication of
where the path might be leading, but since it was a pleasant spring
day and dappled sunlight filtered through the delicate branches,
we followed it uphill to a small pond of green water, where notices
gave ominous warnings of *mamushi* (venomous snakes).

Rounding a bend in the path, we suddenly came upon an aston-
ishing sight. There in the clearing before us stood the Greek-style
torii, fronting a bizarre scene of dilapidated wooden buildings

half-buried by fallen trees. In one corner a huge trunk lay trium-
phantly atop a crushed roof, the supporting walls having been
eaten up by the forces of nature. Stone lanterns, rock shrines,
and guardian statues spoke of a once-flourishing shrine. Now,
however, neglect and decay were everywhere evident. Clearly
the precincts had been abandoned.

Despite the devastation of the scene, it was the torii that
commanded attention with its swirling lines and stylised images.
Along the top was a frieze in which birds and rabbits were prominent. The birds made sense, for torii literally means "bird's roost"
and the creatures are thought to be intermediaries between this
world and the next. But what of the rabbits? And who could the
human figures represent? One had no lower legs, indicative in
Japan of the way the deceased float like ghostly spirits.

Among the collapsed buildings was a narrow opening through
which was visible a trickle of water dripping from the hillside
behind. From out of the darkening recess peered a grim-faced
Fudō Myō-ō, a Buddhist Wisdom King and the solitary sentinel
of the disused facility. The deity is often found at places used for
ascetic practice, as this uninviting spot must once have been.
Practitioners would have come here for cold-water purification;
now the dank air hung heavy with moths, mosquitoes, and the
stench of rotting vegetation.

Just beyond the crumbling buildings stood stone altars typical
of the Inari faith, a branch of Shinto characterised by fox statues
that serve as guardians of the deity. Indeed, the area looked very
similar to parts of the head shrine at Fushimi not far to the north,
though inscriptions spoke of donors from distant Osaka. Further
revelations lay in store, for the path continued uphill past sub-
shrines to another group of abandoned buildings, which turned

out to include the shrine's main object of worship: the eponymous Big Rock (Oiwa), partnered by a Little Rock (Koiwa). They served as "spirit-bodies" into which *kami* (Japanese deities) descend to the material world. In this way the formless takes on form, and the rocks are charged with animist power. Such rocks are usually festooned with a twisted rice rope to denote their sacred status, though these appeared desolate and neglected, deprived of the sustenance of daily worship.

Nearby was another carved torii, similar in design though less ornate than its partner below. Behind it stood the shrine offices, shuttered and left to rot. Someone had thought to post a handwritten notice on the front door stating that due to the retirement of its long-serving priest in November 2014 the shrine had ceased to function. Yet all around were signs that suggested that until recently it had been a flourishing operation. A bright-red lacquered torii was dated 1999; and one of several splendid stone lanterns was marked 2014, the year of closure.

It seemed we had come up via the rear of the shrine, for the stone lanterns lined the formal approach, which led from an apparently disused road. Eager to learn more, we walked down the road to where an elementary school stood at the bottom of the hill. It was the end of the school day, and a small group of teachers in the forecourt were taking their leave of each other. We took the opportunity to enquire about the shrine, but no one knew much about it (one teacher wasn't even aware there was a shrine). However, they helpfully unearthed a leaflet about the area that contained a short paragraph saying the shrine had been founded in ancient times by the Kii clan, who had settled around Oiwa Hill.

The information sparked my imagination, for early clans in Japan had tended to adopt the nearest hill as the seat of their kami. Reaching up toward the Upper World, mountains were seen

Huge cedar trees have crushed the roof of an altar building at Oiwa Shrine

as sacred "landing spots" for spirits, and big rocks in prominent positions served as a symbol for the hill as a whole. It was into such rocks that spirits descended, as often as not the ancestral spirit of a clan leader who watched over his followers on the plain below. In this case I supposed Oiwa Hill had served as the focal point for a clan from the Kii Peninsula. In prehistoric times the Yamato and other immigrant clans had entered into Honshu via the peninsula, and no doubt they had brought with them the rock worship that characterised Korean shamanism.

According to the leaflet, Oiwa Jinja had been destroyed during the Onin War (1467–1477), as had most of Kyoto, and it was not until after the Meiji Restoration of 1868 that it had been revived by a local citizen. In former times it had acquired a reputation for healing dangerous diseases such as tuberculosis, and those who had come to pray at the shrine included the mother of Kyoto artist Dōmoto Inshō. Aha! This helped explain the two carved torii, as they would have been offerings to the deity. The leaflet also clarified another mystery, for it said that Dōmoto's mother was born in a Year of the Rabbit, which explained the inclusion of the animal in the carved decoration. (Later I learned that Dōmoto was seriously ill as a child and brought to the shrine by his mother. In 1962, at the age of seventy-one, he had donated the sculpted torii, honouring her memory in the legless figure depicting the deceased.)

This was all very interesting, but now I was even more intrigued. How and why had such a remarkable shrine been left to rot? What lay behind the abandonment? The name of the author of the leaflet was written at the bottom, so I called him and learnt that he knew little more but had obtained information from the shrine's last priest, who had retired due to illness. Perhaps I could get his phone number? Unfortunately, the aged priest was bedridden, barely alive, and unable to talk.

Thwarted in my pursuit of the priest, I tried another tack. In northwestern Kyoto, not far from the Golden Pavilion, stands the former house of Dōmoto Inshō, now converted to a museum housing his works. Surely the curator would be able to shed light on the matter. However, this too proved disappointing, for although he was aware of the torii there was no information about them and they were the private property of the shrine. I turned instead to the local ward office, situated not far from Oiwa Hill, which my partner thought would carry information about the property. The staff on duty were helpful but unfamiliar with the shrine and had to pull out a map to confirm the location. And that apparently was as much as they could do. Instead they suggested we visit the Land Deeds Office, where the shrine would be registered with the name of the owner. That was unnecessary, however, since the name and address of the "legally responsible person" had been given on the notice posted on the door of the shrine office.

There had been no phone number on the handwritten notice, and NTT, the national telephone corporation, could not provide one. Though it might be against Japanese etiquette to make an uninvited visit, we had no plan B and so set about tracking down the address. It was in a residential area about ten minutes by car from the shrine. The house was spacious by Japanese standards, modern in design, and detached from its neighbours by a narrow gap on both sides. There was a front garden and gate, where we pressed the bell and stood waiting in the drizzle. After a while the front door opened tentatively and a middle-aged lady appeared, clearly puzzled by the appearance of two bedraggled strangers. I explained that we were curious about the shrine, and though she identified herself as the owner, she reacted with suspicion, stonewalling my enquiries. It was clear that she was unwilling to disclose information. Seeing that we were getting wet, however, she relented and invited us in from the rain.

For the next half hour conversation took place in the neutral area of the *genkan* (entrance space). As guests we stood in the paved porch, water dripping from our clothes, while as hostess she knelt on the raised wooden floor before us. During the initial courtesies she reacted in the Kyoto manner, brushing aside questions with pleasantries and soliciting information about my country of origin, my status, and my interest in Japan. I produced a name card, which reassured her, and slowly the barrier of distrust began to dissolve. As she opened up, a tragic story emerged.

In her youth, she told us, she had married into the Kubo family, whose ancestor had been responsible for reviving the shrine in Meiji times (1868–1912). Being preoccupied with her three children, and not particularly religious, she had given it little thought. The custom after all was for males to manage the shrine, and the succession seemed secure with the eldest son training as a priest. However, her husband had died unexpectedly at the age of fifty, joined not long afterward by her oldest son. Of the two other children, the daughter had married and gone to live in England, while the younger son had become a company "salaryman." With a family to support, he had little interest in taking over a shrine that was little more than a financial burden.

Thus, against all expectations, and against her own inclinations, she had found herself in middle age responsible for a substantial shrine. Once it had been prosperous, sustained by supporting groups (mainly in Osaka). There had been many worshippers, and donations flowed to the shrine. But this had changed with the Second World War, after which it had never fully recovered. The shrine had chosen independence rather than join the Association of Shinto Shrines, and for many long years it was kept going by a part-time priest to whom a small honorarium was paid. With the passage of time, however, shrine income had fallen while the cost of maintaining the property had risen. (Being wooden, traditional buildings in Japan are constantly deteriorating and need periodic renewal. The average house lasts only sixty years.)

At one time it had been hoped that the son of the priest would take over his father's role, but though he had studied for a priest's qualification, he had chosen a secure job with the well-established Yasaka Shrine in the heart of Kyoto. As the health of the elderly priest declined, Oiwa Shrine too had deteriorated. In addition, the volunteer gardener had retired without a replacement being found. The falling birthrate and aging population meant a shortage of labour in general, on top of which the young were no longer minded to maintain the traditions of the past. There were constant outgoings for property repairs, but there was little money coming in, so when the priest reached the end of his physical limits the shrine ceased to function.

In response I tossed out random suggestions. Could the *ujiko* (parishioners) not help? There was no *ujiko*; it was a family shrine. Had she considered selling the shrine? No, it would be a betrayal of her husband and his ancestors. How about the National Association of Shrines? She had telephoned, but the shrine was not a member and the fees were too high. Would it not suit a young enterprising priest? There were no youngsters willing to take on such a project for little money. How about volunteers? No one had come forward, though ironically there was a Conservation Group for the pond of green water where the venomous snakes loitered.

Aware of my nationality, she likened her position to that of the impoverished aristocracy in Britain. Many had inherited large country houses and estates, the upkeep of which was way beyond their means. Some had opened up their houses to the public; some had turned the estate into a theme park; some had had to sell up, thus ending centuries of tradition. They were fortunate to have buildings made of brick and stone, she pointed out, but what could she do with dilapidated wooden shacks?

Afterward, as I digested what she had told me, the crumbling buildings of Oiwa seemed symptomatic of a wider trend in Japan. Secularisation, modernisation, and depopulation meant that whole aspects of the culture were under threat. Buddhist temples too, particularly in rural areas, were suffering falling membership and dwindling income. But the changes were by no means confined to religion, for crisis point had been reached in all kinds of traditional practices. Hereditary occupations in arts and crafts, sometimes stretching back centuries, were facing the end of the line.

As we drove back into the city with its department stores and ugly high rises, I couldn't help but feel downhearted. The animist soul of Japan was withering away in the collapsed Oiwa buildings, but the new gods of consumerism were very much in the ascendant. People had once gone into the woods to revere the spiritual; now they made pilgrimages to shopping malls, and the depletion of natural resources was leading humanity into a dead end of waste and pollution. It was a gloomy outlook, yet as I reached home a warming thought struck me. The real mystery of Oiwa — the enigma of the spirit-containing rock — would continue to hold people in thrall long after the concrete buildings and department stores were gone. As a symbol of durability, the rock embodied the power of the human spirit to transcend limitations. After all, the kami of Japan had existed long before any kind of sanctuary was put up to house them, and though the shrine buildings might rot, the Big Rock would surely live on.

About the Author

Originally from Yorkshire, John Dougill moved to Japan in 1986. He is a professor of British Culture at Ryukoku University in Kyoto. Among his many books on Japan are *Kyoto: A Cultural History*, *In Search of Japan's Hidden Christians*, *Shinto Shrines*, and *Japan's World Heritage Sites*. His most recent project, *Kyoto: A Literary Guide*, is an anthology compiled by a poetry in translation discussion group he organizes. He is also the founder and coordinator of Writers in Kyoto, and runs the *Green Shinto* blog.

11

Changes I've Seen in Forty Years in My Rural Community

By Rebecca Otowa

In a small village, about an hour's drive east of Kyoto, stands a much-loved farmhouse that has weathered three and a half centuries of work and life and is now immortalized as the subject of the memoir *At Home in Japan.* When American Rebecca Otowa married into a Japanese family in the 1980s, the groom didn't just come with in-laws but with the farmhouse as a member of the family. From this old home, Rebecca has observed the currents of change in rural Japan.

* * *

A FEW months ago, I participated in a local town meeting where members of the town council were asking citizens to identify problems in our community and suggest possible solutions. Participants were divided into random groups of five or six for discussion purposes, and I ended up in a group consisting mostly of elderly men. When the question "How can we improve our community?" came up, one old guy blurted out, "Put things back the way they were!" He was roundly seconded by the others.

I felt the emotion, and the desperation, in their voices. Most elderly people operate on the premise that things used to be better than they are. I'm sure these old guys were remembering a time when wives and children offered respect and weren't always yammering about equality and free choice or looking to the big city for satisfaction; a time when food flowed unceasingly from the fields and the weather could be predicted with useful accuracy; a time when people at bank and post office windows did their jobs instead of saying "You know, you can do that online;" a time when people knew how to use their hands to deal with their physical surroundings. They don't remember the food shortages; the smiles they had to keep fixed on their faces when the government demanded yet more war sacrifices; the bad roads, the lack of sewage, the disease, the uncontrollable bugs; the slaps and shakes they got from their own parents when they were slow about helping with the unending chores; the lockstep society and the tyranny of the Eye of the World (*seken no me*, the all-seeing and all-judging eye of Japanese society, which is trained on individuals).

Yes, there's no doubt there have been enormous changes in rural life, in Japan as in many other places in the world. And we who live here are all scrambling to catch up to them.

I live in one of a chain of villages stretching eastward from the main part of our township, located southeast of Lake Biwa in central

Honshu. This village, consisting of one hundred houses, is a place with a very long history, situated as it is near Kyoto, and I married into a family that has been here for over four hundred years — my son is the twentieth generation. At the time of my wedding in 1981, in this very house, the place was still quite traditional. My mother-in-law, with whom we lived, was determined to make me into a proper Japanese wife. I'm sure she had a hard time with this, but at least I was a *tabula rasa* — I didn't know anything compared to a Japanese daughter-in-law, who would have come with lots of habits that needed correcting. I also had the advantage of loving the house — even though it was (and is) old, drafty, and dark — and being willing to continue the traditions that remained.

The situation, from my point of view, was that I, a modern woman, was making huge efforts to fit into a traditional lifestyle, while all around me, women of my generation were eagerly embracing modernization. There is good in both; and one does not wish to throw out the baby with the bathwater. In essence, traditional Japanese life means thriftiness, endurance, selflessness; working with the hands, and being proud of what one has made; fitting into the rhythms of nature; putting up with a little inconvenience for the sake of doing honor to objects and thought patterns that have survived from long ago — essentially, grounding, deepening one's viewpoint. Modernity means ever-increasing freedom from physical and psychological pain; freedom to question long-held beliefs to see if they hold up to the test of time; opportunities to exercise one's individual identity and choice, and to develop one's unique gifts; the chance to learn about the big world out there, and to experience it if one wants to — essentially, flying, widening one's viewpoint. It's easy to see the attractions of both, and to be tempted to find a balance between them.

Where to begin describing the changes I have seen in the almost forty years I have lived here? I guess I should just recount my observations, in ever-widening circles of life. Reader, please bear in mind that these may not be accurate reflections of reality, colored as they are by my pesky refusal to quit being a *gaijin*. I could never completely shed the persistent voices of my Western past; and now they have reclaimed their place in my soul, side by side with the Japanese-ness I made such an effort to acquire.

The House

When I came to live in this village things were already changing fast. My husband being the eldest son, his mother (his father had already passed) considered it a foregone conclusion that we would live with her in the ancestral house, as tradition dictated. Elder sons inherited the houses, and younger sons got money to set up their own households — that was the way things had been done for centuries. However, when I married, it was already considered something of a coup for older people to convince their children to live with them in an extended family situation.

Nowadays it is even harder to persuade the younger generation to take over the ancestral home and land. This is partly due to the difficulty of getting a job in this area and the expense of keeping up a traditional house with its constant need of repairs; but even more, it is no longer a social imperative. Parents try to sweeten the deal by building a new house on their land or renovating part of the original house, to satisfy daughters-in-law who demand white walls, sufficient heating and air conditioning, and no bugs; but the success of this strategy is variable. Some years ago, neighbors built an extravagant new house for their son, whose wife promptly turned around and refused to live there. I remember thinking "You mean it's okay to say no?" No one had ever told me that! Choices that my generation already considered natural were not presented to me as an option, so I didn't think they applied to me. What did I know? I had only my mother-in-law's word for it. So what kept me here? Partly it was love of the house. I also felt the challenges would be good for my soul, in the Buddhist sense of making my life my practice. Agreeing to live here, in my inmost heart, amounted to a vow of entry into a monastery. That kind of vow is not easily broken.

Since I became the lady of the house with my mother-in-law's passing in 1999, I have made some surface changes, but the house has not been altered that much. To me, traditions, to survive into the present, must have an energy that keeps them going, and I feel that energy as a background to my life, and I'm happy to ride along on it.

My house is an embodiment of that energy. It's steeped in the old virtues of thrift, hard work, and gratitude. In the usual design of farmhouses four hundred years ago, four large rooms form the center, with removable sliding doors instead of walls; from this core, succeeding generations have built other rooms, storehouses, gardens, and so on. There are now about fourteen spaces used as rooms, flanked by corridors, breezeways, and courtyards. Before my time, my father-in-law decided that the old kitchen with its wood-burning stove and earthen floor was too outmoded, so he put in a "modern" kitchen in 1973, complete with a propane stovetop, "wood" paneling that later turned out to be cardboard, and particleboard lowered ceilings (*keshu tenjo*) that masked the original old beams blackened with centuries of soot. One of the biggest changes I myself made in the house, about twelve years ago, was to rip out all that fake stuff and restore the kitchen (with mod cons) so it fits in with the look of the house. The big old beams and sooty bamboo ceiling are once again visible.

Other changes in our house that I have participated in include the bath (which used to have a firepit underneath for heating but is now the usual automatic model connected to an electric boiler) and toilets (when I first came here they were the old earth type, but now we are connected to the town sewer system; also they are now Western style instead of the earlier floor-squat models). The house is still a dark space where you have to burn lights even at midday; cool in the summer, air-conditioning provided by the breeze and greenery all around; and cold in the winter, heating (inadequately) provided by space heaters. But it has a deep peace that is very hard to find in an urban setting; and I have always felt its large, welcoming heart.

We have done our part to make other improvements on the house, as each succeeding generation has done. The roof, made of approximately thirteen thousand ceramic tiles, is repaired and rejuvenated bit by bit. My husband has also done various extra tasks, such as replacing the rain gutters, pruning the hedge that runs for almost 150 meters around the property, repairing the wall around the garden, making improvements in the vegetable patch, and re-roofing the garage.

Our house is one of only two or three very old traditional ones left in the village. Almost all of the other old houses have been razed to make room for more recent structures. For me this is another reason to keep it the way it is, as much as possible — because this kind of structure is fast disappearing from the scene. Needless to say, we can't sell it out of the family, even if we were to find a buyer, so we can't move away. We are like the rulers of a tiny rural kingdom. Is it outdated? Yes. But old is not always necessarily bad.

I'm happy to take care of something that has survived for close to four hundred years. It's an honor.

Village and Town Society

Village life is much less cohesive than it was when I first came here. This is part of a continuum that has been going on probably forever. When my mother-in-law was a young girl, women would gather at the canal to wash clothes, baths were communal, and there were many more occasions to get together (such as to watch the first TV in the village, which appeared in 1963). Things are very quiet now compared to that. For example, there was the monthly ritual of "paying the tax" at the village hall in the evening. Everyone came, lining up to pay the local taxes with cash, chatting with neighbors, children running around — it was a group event. Now it's either paid automatically from one's bank account or collected by block captains once or twice a year.

There used to be several groups in the village with semi-mandatory participation, according to one's age, gender, and situation. Hence a woman would start off in the Women's Association and the PTA, then graduate to something called the Elders, before washing up on the final beach of the Old Folks' Society. Also, though decreasing in number, public village tasks continue to be undertaken today. According to a strict system of rotation, village residents clean the trash pickup areas, the shrine, the playground, the village hall, and the grassy verges of the roads; they stand at corners to remind drivers and cyclists about traffic safety, and put on annual athletic meets and culture festivals. Some escort children to school, join the volunteer fire brigade, or take office in the PTA or the municipal government. In addition, most people belong to a local Buddhist temple, which demands more time from them, cleaning the grounds and managing funerals. Even now, the expression "free time" has a slightly disreputable ring; "looking busy" is much more virtuous. So, as elsewhere in Japanese life, busywork wins out over logical allocation of jobs. Who really needs people to give up an hour of their busy morning to wave signs reading "Traffic Safety" in their neighbors' faces as they drive to work? But it was so decided at some point (most of these group labor imperatives date from the early post-war years) so it must continue. As in the past, it is extremely difficult to change or abandon this kind of activity, because one must keep up the tradition in order to honor those who have done it before. This reluctance to change is one of the most pernicious aspects of a society based on groups.

School and Childhood

Until about twenty-five years ago, Japanese schools met six days a week, including Saturdays; when this was phased out, many people complained. "Who is going to babysit children on Saturdays when there is so much else to do? Also, won't kids get soft because they have so much free time?" In reality, of course, extracurricular activities, such as soccer, swimming, and tutoring, have more than filled this gap, and children now have less "free time" than ever. This has changed since I was a young mother. My sons grew up mostly running around outside with a crowd of friends, but now the neighborhood, even on holidays, is eerily silent. This is due partly to the low number of kids residing in the village, partly to the rise of gadgets that keep kids inside and activities that keep them away from the house, and partly to the necessity for coaching classes to prepare for entrance exams that children must still endure before high school and university.

Today there are many fewer children. There were nine children from the village in my elder son's class in primary school; by my younger son's time this had decreased to three; and now, depending on the year, there may be none. In the past, the entire school was about two hundred kids. Currently it is around seventy. I am still glad my kids grew up with a little more elbow room, and more friends, than village children have now. In the "old days" of my first years in the village, children who came home from school were greeted either by their mothers, or, if she went out to work, grandparents. Now, with two-job families and nuclear families on the increase, there are after-school gathering places for kids to study or play under supervision until the parents return home. In my own case, I worked teaching English some evenings, and my mother-in-law shouldered the babysitting burden with many complaints. Hiring a babysitter from outside the family, and paying them, was unheard of. It still isn't common.

The People

What kind of people are they, these neighbors of mine? Many are elderly, and increasingly living alone. They struggle with their rice fields and vegetable patches until their considerable endurance and strength give out. Below them is my generation, people in their fifties and sixties, who work in various capacities, as public servants or construction workers or company men, until retirement. Many of them are two-job families. The wife may work on the cash register of a supermarket or in the office of a small company. Debts, many related to children or aging parents, and the race to amass a suitable amount before retirement, keep people's noses to the grindstone.

Those in the next rung of society, in their thirties or forties, have largely moved out of the village and live somewhere else, many less than an hour away. Why do they leave to become homeowners in quasi-suburban housing estates rather than make their homes with the old people? For one thing, they consider our community to be too remote, either for working or for bringing up children.

Grown kids leave to get jobs in urban areas and seldom return, except for obligatory summer and winter visits to the old people. How are you going to keep them down on the farm after they've seen Paree? And Paree is right at their fingertips now, with mobile phones and the internet. The women who marry these young men from rural areas have also seen Paree in the movies, magazines, and internet. They aren't about to choose inconvenience, lack of urban amenities like yoga classes and department stores, and the burden of caring for elderly in-laws, over all that even slightly more urbanized centers have to offer. They feel they can assert their own choices and desires much more than women of even one genera-tion ago. And it's true: there is more choice, thanks to advances in technology, communication, and psychology. This widening of individual lives is definitely a good thing in my opinion (though the old guys at the meeting would disagree, calling it "selfishness").

Meanwhile, there is another, opposite trend, visible for about the past ten years. This is the move from urban centers to the rural areas, sometimes by couples who retire to the country, buy a big house, and start a café or restaurant; and sometimes by younger people (whom I call "alternative Japanese") who would rather live in a wider, cleaner environment, let their kids run free, and till the soil or work in a small place, than become tie-strangled salarymen

The owner of the last shop in our village on her last day of business

at the beck and call of some faceless company. People from elsewhere who come here to live (*iryuusha*) find empty houses — of
which there are many — on the internet, and move in, bringing
their vegetarian or natural food-based lifestyle with them, and
band together in outdoor markets (which have now sprung up
everywhere), selling homemade bread, artisanal beer, reflexology
massages, and handcrafts, strumming guitars in the sunshine, and
dressing their kids up in handmade clothes. (Why do I get a whiff
of the sixties from these people? They may have arrived late to the
party, but at least they came — I applaud them for that.)

This trend is deeply confusing to hidebound rural society, but
I think it's good. The countryside needs new blood, and because
of them, the old regimented way of social congress in rural Japan
is starting to crack around the edges. They have brought a breath
of fresh air to rural communities. They demand (and start) things
like public spaces, cafés, and classes to enrich their lives. Because
of them, things in my town are much more colorful and hopeful
than they were when I first came. Now there are at least six decent
cafés, where there used to be just one; and there are more than
ten restaurants of varying ethnicities, where there used to be just
a noodle shop. Other changes I've seen since I've been here are
the construction of a concert building with two halls and numerous rental rooms, a sizeable library, and a nice, wide park with
a spreading lawn where kids can run around outside. Classes of
various kinds, playgroups, music groups, art groups: a lot is going
on here for such a small place (the township population is pretty
stable at around twenty-three thousand).

Business and Demographics

Don't worry, I'm not going to start spouting statistics. Still, it might be good to have some idea of what local people do for a living now compared to the past. First, even though this is a rural community whose products are overwhelmingly agricultural (beef, rice, and pickled turnips head the list of things the area is famous for), almost no one is a full-time farmer. From postwar times, men went off to work in companies at varying distances from the village, squeezing the rice planting and harvest into several weekends and holidays in spring and autumn. No one could make a living and feed his family solely on his rice crop — either then or now. At present, only a handful of rice farmers take care of everyone's fields (our own fields have been tilled in the past thirty years by a neighbor now in his eighties). There just isn't enough money in farming. The government, in the form of the "Agricultural Co-op," enforces crop rotation, usually from rice to soybeans to wheat to fallow; in the past, there have been both surpluses and shortages, since no one can really predict the success of any crop from year to year, especially now with global climate change.

As for peripheral crops, vegetables and so on, they have traditionally been the work of the wives; but vegetable patches are gradually being abandoned as young wives have neither the time nor the inclination to slave away in the fields for vegetables that are readily available in the supermarket. My mother-in-law was an assiduous vegetable grower, and I have tried to continue this, because I like knowing where my veggies come from (also, fresh veggies taste better). But women my age or younger would rather get a job that brings in cash money, and use some of that money to buy veggies in the supermarket, many of which come from miles away or even overseas. Very few people in the village now even make their own pickles or pound their own *mochi* (sticky rice cakes). To be fair, the "alternative Japanese" are more open and enthusiastic about these things than "ordinary" citizens are.

What does the future hold for the agriculture of Japanese rural communities? What I'd like to see is the two opposite camps of rural society, now divided by age, tradition, and outlook, banding together to create an entirely new paradigm. Farmers in Japan now average seventy years of age. At this rate, in the future there will be little manpower to feed the country, especially in rice; the Japanese have amply demonstrated how attached they are to their particular type of short-grain sticky rice, so they would be resistant to imports in this category anyway. More people are urgently needed to farm the land, and the "alternative Japanese" and other young people are perfect for the job. The older people have the know-how and the younger people have the energy. Break free of the stranglehold of the agricultural co-op system and forge new networks that respect the land as in previous times, respect community, respect human beings. Learn from the wonderful old agricultural systems that were in place long before mechanization, with efficiency, environmental savvy, and sustainability. You can tell I feel strongly about this issue.

Other businesses in the area are mainly in industrial parks set up in the rural parts of Japan by companies far away. These provide a certain number of jobs, so are valuable for keeping families in the area. There are also small firms of varying sizes producing traditional foods or craft objects, and other firms that take care of local demand for services: mechanics, roofers, carpenters, plasterers, road construction, and the like. In our area, there is little tourism, probably because we are off the beaten track transport-wise. These things have remained largely the same during the time I have lived here, although small businesses regularly fail and are replaced by large modern stores.

People here are relatively healthy, long-lived, with a little extra money to change their cars or modernize their houses when needed. The main demographic trend that I think is most dangerous to the community is the population drain to the big cities, resulting in ever fewer amenities for those who remain. About thirteen years ago the national government imposed a centralization system to bring together small local governments in units called "cities" (this word borders on the ironical in most areas, where the actual landscape is anything but urban). Before that, each small community had its police station and post office, and each village had a wide variety of shops. When I first came to our village, there were (going from west to east) a tobacconist and small post office, a futon maker and clothes shop, a place that made box lunches for events, a household goods and sweet shop, a fish and produce shop, a tofu shop, and a large housewares shop. Now all these shops are gone. Older people with no means of transport (many old people, especially women, never got a drivers' license) cannot do their shopping by walking around the village any more. The only businesses left are those of the carpenter and plasterer. Loss of these village shops means loss of a certain culture, a group feeling. Now to go shopping one must go by car or, less commonly, bicycle. The nearest shop is about three kilometers away — not walking distance. Older people rely on the kindness of neighbors or relatives or order by telephone from the supermarket.

When the nationwide centralization occurred, our town, along with a scattering of others, opted not to participate. In the aftermath, we lost our police station, and some other amenities; what we retained was the centuries-old name and identity of the town, which would otherwise have been swallowed up in the "city" that included many townships nearby. The centralization, at least in the case of rural areas, is now admitted to have been generally a failure. Rural communities have been splintered; life has become less convenient instead of more; the trend toward rootlessness and anonymity has quickened because of it. What is needed in Japan is less centralization, not more. The gradual withering of country life is largely due to this kind of thinking on the part of the government.

Changes in Rural Psyche and Gender Roles

In conclusion, I would like to say something about changes in psychology I have observed in individuals around me, with particular reference to the issue of gender.

The differences I have seen in forty years of living here basically come down to two words: *choice* and *change*. There is much less lockstep conformity and much less stoic endurance around than before. Two examples of this are refusal to attend school (*toko kyohi*) and reclusiveness (*hikikomori*), which, although less prevalent than in cities, are definitely part of life. Both trends, though unsettling and certainly painful for those involved, I consider somewhat encouraging, because at least these people feel they have the choice to opt out of what they consider untenable situations. That wasn't the case a few decades ago.

There is a considerable gender gap in the countryside, as well as in Japan overall, which was given a miserable grade in a recent worldwide ranking of countries by gender equality. Since I came,

I have seen very little change; there are now, as then, almost no divorces, and in my area, it is unheard of for a woman to become a block captain or a village head, since she does not possess the all-important male appendage. This is too bad, as women are the ones who really understand how the village is, and should be, run.

Women are feeling and showing their strength more. Of course women have always wielded a behind-the-scenes power that does not appear in demographics. But compared to forty years ago, I feel that women my age are using their newfound empty-nest free time to do things that interest them. (I believe that were someone to discover how to harness the power of middle-aged women, this world would soon be a lot different!)

When I first came, I was both amused and appalled at the way groups would divide along rigid gender lines at meetings, festivals, athletic meets, etc. It was almost as if there was an unwritten rule that men and women should not even speak to each other. There is more social intermingling now than before — although a lot of shyness and "bad boy" sexist remarks are still in evidence. Recently, on a bus trip I was one of only two women. One of the men called me "Rebecca-chan" using an ending reserved for children and cute young girls. I said, "Please don't call me that — I'm sixty-four years old." Perhaps he thought he was flattering me. But treating women like cute little pets, no matter what their age or mental capabilities, remains a popular male sport.

Younger women, as far as I have been able to observe, no longer go in for demure silence in the home. If they want help, they go ahead and ask their husbands for it — and the husbands do their best. Young fathers are much more likely these days to care for and carry their babies; whether because their wives insist on it, or whether they themselves are more comfortable in this role than before, it's good to see. Younger men in the countryside these days are much less likely to stand on their sexual pride. Older men, of course, have much more difficulty changing their habits in this area. And I think, mostly, they are the ones who want to "put things back the way they were" — for obvious reasons.

As I have said, a lot of what is going on in the rural Japanese psyche these days is related to the management of increased choices in life. Perhaps these young people don't feel they have much choice; but if they were to journey back in time four decades, they would definitely see the difference. Why, in those days, it seemed like everyone was wearing a uniform: the salaryman, the housewife, the student, the craftsman, the outdoor worker. There is much greater variety in appearance choice today.

Changes, and choices — the widening of the arenas of life — this sums up the contrast between now and forty years ago in rural society. Of course, a lot of people don't really want either one; they just want to live their lives in comfortable familiarity. But for those who have felt trammeled by tradition, it's time to learn how to fly.

About the Author

Rebecca Otowa was born in California, USA, in 1955 and grew up in Australia. After graduating from the University of Queensland, she travelled to Japan on a scholarship and has been there ever since. In 1981 she graduated from Otani University in Kyoto with a master's degree in Japanese Buddhism and that same year married the nineteenth-generation heir to a large traditional farmhouse in central Japan. Since then she has taken care of the house as well as writing, drawing, teaching English, and gardening. She and her husband now share the house with the next generation, her son and his family. Her books are *At Home in Japan* (2010), *My Awesome Japan Adventure* (2013), and *The Mad Kyoto Shoe Swapper and Other*

Short Stories (2019). All three contain illustrations by the author and are published by Tuttle. She is a member of Writers in Kyoto and has written for various publications, including the *Kyoto Journal*. She has a website and blog at **rebeccaotowa.com**.

12

For the Love of Yuki: A Winter Affair in Japan

By Sam Baldwin

Sam Baldwin was undergoing a premature mid-life crisis. The twenty-five-year-old laboratory technician could see decades of boredom rolling out ahead of him with painful predictability: he needed a change of career, a change of scene. He found it teaching English in Ōno, a pretty mountain-ringed town in Fukui Prefecture. As Sam describes in his upbeat memoir *For Fukui's Sake*, the Englishman's two years there were the best two years of his life, a time when "every day was an adventure into the unknown," and the local people's "generosity and openheartedness" made him feel more at home than he had ever felt. His account of working on the JET Programme is unusual in that he does not describe the ups and downs of culture shock. He seems to have been too busy for it. Whenever he had free time he headed out and made the most of the natural surroundings, and no more so than in the snowy depths of winter.

* * *

WITHIN the world of winter sports, Japan is a renowned powder paradise. Bordered by the Sea of Japan to the west and the Japanese Alps to the east, Nihon's "snowbelt" lies in the path of Siberian winds that sweep down from mainland Asia every winter. These winds pick up moisture as they pass over the Sea of Japan but are impeded in their eastern advance by the spine-like ridge of the Central Alps, which run the length of Honshu, Japan's largest island. Upon hitting this barrier, the moisture-laden fronts drop their cargo, at first as heavy rain and then, as temperatures plummet, as the most incredible and spectacular volumes of snow imaginable.

Though not the only reason for my desire to visit, the tales of fantastical snowfalls certainly played their part in my decision to venture to Japan. Four years prior, I had spent a winter working in Whistler, a Canadian ski resort. That happy period had opened my eyes to the joys of mountain life and ever since then I had been searching for a way to get back to snow-rich terrain. Japan offered plenty of that, and when it came to selecting exactly where I would spend the next two years, snow was the only thing I had on my mind. My research had consisted of calculating which prefectures had the most ski resorts and the highest snowfalls. Equipped with this information, I had applied to live and work as a teaching assistant on the northern island of Hokkaido (first choice) and in Nagano Prefecture (second choice), both of which boasted Winter Olympics fame and were renowned as the best that Japan had to offer when it came to snow.

Destiny, however, had other plans. In 2004, I had been posted to Ōno, in Fukui Prefecture, an area not known for its snow sports excellence. Indeed, the prefecture was seemingly not known for much at all, apart from accidents at one of its fourteen nuclear power stations. But the Japanese snow gods had big plans for me. After worrying about missing out on Japan's renowned powder, I would experience a winter with snowfalls so heavy that trains would be derailed, houses would be crushed, and over a hundred people would perish in its wake.

* * *

Before even drawing the curtains, I could tell it had come. The glow that spilled from the window on that December morning betrayed its presence; the snow had arrived. A joyous euphoria welled up inside. I slipped on my slippers and stepped onto my balcony. Yesterday, the land had been dull and dark. Now the rice paddies and mountains glittered with a gilding of white gold. Although I was a twenty-five-year-old man, snow still filled me with the breathless delight of a child. Even the most uninspiring landscapes are transformed to scenes of sheer splendour by applying a glaze of snow. Nature's layer of foundation makeup, snow covers all acne and scars, creating the perfect complexion.

Despite the snow, school was still on and I had to get to work. I decided to skip breakfast. I was too excited to eat, and it would take me extra time to uncover my car and escape from the carpark anyway. I grabbed my new aluminium shovel that had been waiting patiently for this day, stepped into my boots, and out into the snow. The snow was already shin deep and squeaked satisfyingly as I trudged over to the vending machine to exchange a few yen for my regular can of hot coffee.

I began to shovel. The snow was light and soft, and it took me fifteen minutes to clear a path to the road. With the escape route now open, I switched my car to 4×4 mode and exited the parking lot. I drove cautiously along the snow-covered roads but began to regret missing breakfast, so I pulled into a convenience store. The refrigerated shelves were stocked with sushi boxes and the Japanese version of a sandwich (which I feel has been lost in translation somewhat). I needed something hot and so headed for the counter. There, a stainless-steel water bath sat, steaming. It looked like something I would have used during my former life as a laboratory assistant in England. But it didn't contain conical flasks or centrifuge tubes. It contained *oden*, a popular winter food that contains triangles of gelatinous *konnyaku*, parcels of processed fish, and *daikon*, a vegetable that, when boiled, smells and tastes like a fart. I had already ascertained that oden (and in particular *oden daikon*) was my least favourite Japanese food, so I asked for a *karé pan* instead, a deliciously doughy dumpling filled with curry sauce.

I was at my desk in the staff room a few hours later when the electrical snowstorm began. It was only midday, but the sun had vanished, leaving a darkened, moody, gunmetal-grey sky. Thunder started to growl in the distance. Lightning flashed from afar. The rumbles grew louder and louder as the storm approached, eventually becoming thunderous explosions as the tempest enveloped us. The cracks were so loud that I would have been frightened if I hadn't been so excited.

Japan's snowbelt is one of the few places in the world that experiences "thunder snow." It's a spectacular, humbling and rare phenomenon, occurring only when an immense pool of very cold air forms above warmer, moister air at ground level, and it is seen only during the most powerful of winter storms.

Then came the snow. So much snow. Great big, fat flakes the size of Pringles potato chips, swirling and whirling as the blizzard took hold. It continued all day. By the time I left work, clearing my car took another fifteen minutes. I drove back home, carefully negotiating the snowy roads. Ploughs were working hard, and the sprinklers that sprayed water onto the roads (a surprisingly effective method of snow clearance, seeing as winter temperatures in the town didn't fall too far below freezing) were also assisting. I went to bed watching the flakes fall.

The following morning it was still snowing heavily. Half a meter now lay on the ground. My boots were no longer high enough to keep the snow out. I spent thirty minutes clearing a path from our carpark to the road. The tarmac was now completely covered, but at least the snow there had been compacted, creating a smooth white road. All day the snow continued; all the while the drifts grew. The flakes were like feathers, big and soft, and coming in such numbers that it was as if an enormous pillow had exploded in the sky.

After two days of continuous snowfall, cars that had not been cleared were just smoothed-over shapes in the snowscape. By the fourth day of the storm, giant walls of snow had appeared on the roadsides where ploughs had carved canyons. These dwarfed the pedestrians, who were now forced to walk on the road because the sidewalks had long since disappeared.

By day six, all but the most vital roads had become impassable. The clearance teams were unable to keep up with the snowy onslaught; there was simply no space left to put the ploughed snow. By day eight of the storm, the whole of Fukui had ground to a halt under the weight of the white. Neither car, train, nor plane could leave or enter the prefecture. We were completely shut off, cocooned by the snow.

* * *

Japan's snowbelt was generally well equipped to deal with heavy snow, and preparations had started early. By mid-November most houses had installed *yuki gakkoi,* or "snow shields," constructed from sheets of metal or plastic and secured to the side houses to deflect snow from walls and windows and keep a path to the outside world open. Trees were also not left to fend for themselves; most shrubs and bushes in parks and gardens had been protected from the weight of snow by wooden tepees known as *yuki tsuri.*

My school had switched to its winter timetable, the whole day set back by twenty minutes, allowing extra time to dig out cars and drive on snowy roads. Most of my colleagues constantly grumbled about our snowbound situation.

"I don't like snow, Sam-san. I must get up early to clear my car," said Mr. Yamada, the math teacher.

"Yes, we must also clear the roof of our house," added Ikigawa-san, the school nurse.

Growing up with such heavy winters had left them completely loveless for snow. For them it just meant miserable cold, constant inconvenience, and endless shovelling as they struggled to keep their car parks and roofs clear. For me, though, with my childlike love of snow, it was a winter of dreams. I found it hard to believe that the sky could contain this much snow, yet I had no complaints. I'd lived in Whistler, Canada; I'd seen the mountains of New Zealand; and I'd visited the French Alps and Andorran Pyrenees; but never, ever, had I'd realized that snow in such great volumes could exist. I was in white paradise.

In fact, I loved the snow so much that I actually looked forward to coming home from work and spending two or three hours, shovelling, scraping, chipping, and digging away the snow to keep our car park open. Not that it made much of a dent; three of us would spend an evening toiling to clear our cars and exit route, only to wake up the following morning and find a fresh two feet on the ground that locked us in like a cold white prison. After a couple of weeks, several residents of my apartment block gave up. Believing the fight was futile, they simply left their cars to become buried, planning to dig them out again weeks later when the weather warmed. I, however, continued to dig; it was almost a matter of survival. The entrance to my apartment block was under threat from being sealed off completely from the outside world. Every day, upon opening my front door, I would be confronted by the ever advancing "glacier" that would creep inward. Only daily shovelling kept my lifeline open.

That night at Yumeya, my favourite bar in Ōno, Yasu the owner told me it was like a "winter of old." The older patrons nodded knowingly as they sipped steaming sake from little cups. When they were children, the snow fell so deeply that the ground floors of their houses would be completely buried, they told me. The only way they could get in or out was via their balconies.

It was Yasu who would later enable some of my fondest Japanese experiences. Under his guidance, with snowboards strapped to our backs and snowshoes on our feet, we became acquainted with the backcountry snow spots of the Okuetsu and Hakusan ranges. Our friendship, based on a mutual love of mountains, snow, and music, quickly blossomed during the long winter nights over cups of *nihon-shu* (rice wine) and his famous home-smoked cheese. Somewhat of a local legend, Yasu had gained "man of the mountains" status after summiting some of the Himalayas' gnarliest peaks. His bar was a cosy hangout for local lovers of snow. The walls were adorned in climbing paraphernalia: the ice pick, snowshoes, and pictures of sabre-toothed peaks all proof of his past expeditions. Owning a bar gave Yasu the freedom to climb and ski mountains, sometimes for days at a time, whenever the desire presented itself. Sometimes we would turn up at Yumeya ready for a night of revelry, only to find the lights off and the door locked; Yasu was out hiking through snow on some remote Japanese peak again.

* * *

I was eager to explore the frozen world I was living in and so began a mission to visit all of Fukui's ski areas after school and on weekends. The snow was hurrying down from the night sky one evening as I drove toward the tiny ski area of Kadohara. I felt like an arctic explorer as I excitedly wove my way up the white roads, braving the storm, when few others dared leave their homes. The route was thoroughly covered. Black tarmac had become white snowpack. My headlights couldn't penetrate far into the mass of whirling flakes, but my four-wheel drive Suzuki Wagon R kept me on track as I passed through the giant red gate that spanned the road above the Kuzuryū River gorge. A little farther on, I drove by a huddle of homes snuggled under a thick duvet of snow, before pulling into the Kadohara ski area's empty car park.

I stepped out of my car into the deep drift. The slopes were bathed in the sodium glow of floodlights. I expected total silence, but instead muffled J-pop — Japanese pop music — floated from the ski area's PA system. Puzzled by the lack of people, I donned my gear anyway and trudged to a ramshackle hut to buy a ski ticket. I asked the young lift attendant where everyone was, but he just shrugged. Either my attempt at a literal translation of the English phrase made no sense, or he was also at a loss as to why not a single other person had ventured out to ski the exceptionally snowy conditions.

Yasu Matsuta – owner of Yumeya bar in Ōno, Fukui (and mountain climbing legend) wearing "kanjiki" –traditional Japanese snowshoes made from bamboo

I clambered aboard the rickety two-man lift, which rumbled me to the top through the ever-falling flakes. As I stepped off and sat down to strap on my snowboard, I saw no tracks other than my own. The snow was completely untouched; the entire mountain was mine. I had never been so privileged. I set off through the deep, deep snow, greedily devouring this local delicacy. My board hissed as it glided over the surface, parting the crystals and spurting smoky waves of snow into the air as I made big, slow turns in the pillow-soft powder. The air was so full of flakes I couldn't help breathing snow. The pines groaned as I passed, as if to complain about the ever-increasing burden they were being forced to bear. Three lifties watched from the cosy glow of their wooden huts. They loyally dashed into the storm to dust the snow from the lift seat and bow to me each time I lapped them, but they were in for a quiet shift. I was their only customer that evening.

In the world of winter sports there is a saying: "No friends on a powder day." Light, fluffy powder snow is considered the nirvana of all snow conditions, so the saying means that when powder is on offer, you don't hang around waiting for lagging friends; instead, you make the most of this rare commodity. But that night at Kadohara, the phrase took on a new meaning. There I was with snow falling so fast and thick that my tracks were being covered almost as quickly as I could make them, yet no one else was willing to join me on that snow-stormy January night.

* * *

It might seem strange that a person native to England, a country that receives little in the way of snow and is not blessed with mountains of any great height, should have such a strong affinity for this particular form of precipitation. Perhaps it is snow's very rarity in my own country that made me fall for it so deeply. I was now living in a place that got more snow in ten days that England gets in ten years, and I wanted to make the most of it. Back in summer I had discovered the existence of a cross-country (or *kuro-kan*) ski club at my school, and I had been eagerly anticipating the start of the winter since then. Now the time had come for me to add a new string to my snow bow.

At 3:30 p.m. lessons finished, and I hurried to the ski club's head-quarters, a small wooden shed that sat just beyond the now-frozen koi pond. Rows of ankle-high boots, toothpick-thin skis, and long, lightweight poles lined the walls of the wooden hut. The students seemed happy to have me join their club, yet they did have a press-ing concern. It was well known that all foreigners have massive, foreign-sized feet; would they be able to find ski boots big enough to accommodate mine? To their surprise, a suitable fit was found, and we were soon trudging over the snow, kitted up and en route to the school ski trails.

After a few warm-up stretches, I clipped on my skis and set off. I thought the transition from one plank to two would be easy, but it seemed my six years of snowboarding experience counted for nothing. My first attempts at moving forward simply resulted in me flailing around. I fell over repeatedly, and when I was moving in the right direction, I resembled a new-born giraffe. This was of great amusement to my students. Most of them were already pro-ficient cross-country skiers and zipped off, gliding over the trails that had been carved out over the baseball pitch and surrounding rice paddies, now buried under almost a meter of snow.

Though my Japanese was improving all the time, it was insuffi-cient for me to understand the finer details of *kuro-kan* technique as relayed by Takeuchi *sensei*, the club supervisor, so I had to teach myself. Over the coming weeks I picked up enough to wobble my way around the circuit. Despite my frequent falls, the *kuro-kan* club soon became the highlight of my day. I couldn't wait to clip on the skis and practice my stride. Even when it was snowing so hard that practice was cancelled, I would venture out alone anyway — goggles on, hood up — and try my hardest to improve my *kuro-kan* ability. It was a full-body workout, in a gymnasium far more scenic than a sweaty room of fancy treadmills and exercise bikes. That winter I spent as much time as possible on the ski circuit, practicing my Japanese and my skiing, chatting and joking with the students. My technique never became entirely polished (by the end of the winter I was still getting lapped by thirteen-year-olds) but I didn't care. I was content just to be out on the white paddy plateau under the eyes of the soft, wooded mountains.

* * *

Winter continued and the snow kept coming. Nights were cold. Given the onslaught of cold weather and heavy snow that would fall every winter, the apparent bad design of the local buildings was an ongoing mystery to me. Although Japan is hailed as one of the most technologically advanced nations in the world, the vast majority of houses, schools, and other buildings in Fukui seemed ill-equipped to cope with the extreme climate.

My apartment had single-glazed windows that were large and drafty. My front door was made of metal, a material not known for its insulating properties. My woven straw tatami mats certainly looked fancy, but they didn't keep feet warm like a plush carpet would. My apartment had no central heating system; my only sources of warmth were two paraffin heaters. These did belch out fumy, smelly heat; but when your internal walls are made of paper, any heat you do manage to muster doesn't hang around for long.

I imagined the conversation between two Japanese architects who had designed my apartment block might have gone something like this:

Architect 1: "This area is one of harsh climatic extremes. In summer it is hot and humid, yet in winter it is sub-zero with heavy snow."

Architect 2: "Then how shall we design these homes to protect from the elements and create comfortable living spaces?"

Architect 1: "This is indeed a difficult problem, but I have an idea. Let us build them with no insulation, no central heating, and no double glazing."

Architect 2: "Yes, this is surely the best way to ensure the comfort of the inhabitants."

Due to the toxic fumes, paraffin heaters cannot be left on all night, so sleeping was particularly chilly. I slept not just fully clothed but with an extra hooded top on, inside a sleeping bag, under a duvet, and pinned by a weighty assortment of additional blankets. This may have prevented hypothermia, but still I was cold. The thermometer that sat inside my kitchen reached a low of four degrees centigrade numerous times that winter. But I had it warm compared to others. My friend who lived in an older and draftier home frequently witnessed freezing point inside his abode.

Given the lack of adequate central heating systems, many people in Japan take a more local approach to keeping warm. For example, small, disposable warmers called *kairo* can be adhered to your back or legs, and provide a few hours of warmth. In Japanese households and some traditional restaurants, heated tables called *kotatsu* are a favourite weapon of warmth; and those who have a Western-style toilet may enjoy a heated seat.

I often asked my Japanese friends why central heating, double glazing, and insulation did not come as standard, considering

Japan's extreme climate. The explanations I received were inconclusive. I was told that stagnant air is the greatest enemy of the Japanese home; thus, houses are designed to be as drafty as possible to deter mould. While drafts may help keep fungi at bay during the humid summer months, unfortunately this means that winters are exceptionally cold in the Japanese home.

* * *

The big winter storm that kicked off a record-breaking winter was the worst (or, in my opinion, best) single storm to hit the country in twenty-five years. Japan's self-defense force was drafted to help dig out buried houses and remove snow from slopes in avalanche-prone zones. The job of shoveling snow, however, generally fell to local residents. It was common to see even elderly people shoveling snow at first light and continuing late into the evening, and students were made to clear school grounds during the daily ritual of *soji*, the mandatory cleaning period.

Snow is a heavy substance: a cubic meter of freshly fallen snow weighs about 100 kilograms (approximately 220 pounds). After compaction, its weight triples. Several lives were lost that winter when buildings collapsed under the weight of snow, and an entire factory was crushed in Fukui Prefecture. The cost of snow removal from roofs was not cheap, and prices as high as 130,000 yen (US$1,093) were reportedly charged. Residents who could not afford to hire professionals were forced to shovel snow themselves, a hazardous practice during which several elderly people slipped and fell to their deaths. A number of people were crushed by snow falling from roofs into the streets below, and avalanches also claimed some lives, blocked roads, and severed power lines.

Ironically, though, the massive snowfalls that Fukui received had a dual effect on accessibility. On one hand, the snow made hundreds of miles of sidewalks and roads impassable, but on the other, it opened up thousands of acres of previously inaccessible land. How? Well, Fukui, and indeed many parts of rural Japan, is covered in rice paddies. If a piece of land in Japan is not a building or a mountain, it's probably a rice paddy. Rice paddies give the impression of countryside and nature, especially during the harvest season, when they become a bright green sea of rice that ripples and dances as the breeze ruffles its surface. Yet there is a certain deception to this scene; rice paddies are very much of the "look but don't touch" type of nature. They are not somewhere you can throw down a blanket and have a picnic, kick a football around, or go for a walk. They are strictly off limits and provide no use for recreation.

My little town of Ōno, which means "the big field," is known for its paddies. Indeed, my apartment was surrounded by great swathes of greenery. But I could not enter this world. I often longed to immerse myself in nature, but I was largely confined to the tarmac roads and sidewalks. Back home in England, grass was everywhere, but in Japan it was a rarity; there were almost no lawns, pastures, or parks in Ōno; sports pitches were made of gravel or sand. Because of this, I sometimes felt hemmed in by my surroundings and missed being able to roam the green and pleasant fields like I had done in my homeland.

The snowy winters of Fukui altered this balance; although the snow blocked roads, cut off railways, and prevented pavement access, it also opened up the huge expanse of rice paddies, creating one massive footpath to anyone with a pair of snowshoes.

Snow has the unique ability to transform a fairly uninspiring landscape into one of the most beautiful scenes imaginable.

Suddenly, I was able to wander across the vast space of the rice paddies, which for so long had been taunting me. I snowshoed around beautiful wooden shrines that perfectly complimented the natural scenery, past miniature statues of Buddha dressed in red winter hats and scarves, and through bright-green bamboo groves, a particularly surreal scene, bamboo being a plant associated with tropical weather. It was on days like these I felt happiness could be inhaled, simply by breathing the cool, crisp air.

That winter I indulged in an intense affair with *yuki*, a truly cold-hearted lover, around which my life completely revolved. If I wasn't snowboarding in it, I was driving my Suzuki in it. If I wasn't walking the school dog in it, I was cross-country skiing in it. If I wasn't snowshoeing around ancient wooden temples in it, then I was sitting at my desk, mesmerized by it falling from the ominous clouds above. If I wasn't shovelling it, I was thinking about it; and if I was doing none of the above, I was probably dreaming about it.

When I first arrived in Fukui on a sweaty August day, it was hard to see how a snow lover could ever find satisfaction there. But with that extreme winter, one of the heaviest in recent history, I can only say *domō arigatō gozaimasu* — thank you very much — to the Japanese snow gods for showing me the deepest, most incredible snowfalls that I'm ever likely to have the pleasure of living through.

About the Author

Sam Baldwin is the author of *For Fukui's Sake: Two Years in Rural Japan*. The seeds planted during his time in Japan led him to seek out a home in another mountainous, snowy location. Eleven years after leaving Fukui, he settled in Slovenia. You can read about his adventures restoring a 300-year-old house there at BregHouse.com.

13

Call Me a Dog

By Iain Maloney

From Fukui we travel east to neighboring Gifu Prefecture. The name might not be familiar, but you've likely seen pictures of villages in northern Gifu with beautiful thatched steep-roofed farmhouses, a design indicative of the heavy snowfall.

Iain Maloney left Scotland for Japan in 2005 to teach English as a means to subsidizing his writing career, and fell in love with a Japanese woman and married her. After years of urban living and a long time looking for the ideal house, in 2016 Iain and Minori moved into a village in central Gifu.

* * *

M Y village is equipped with a PA system for public service announcements. A combination of volume, treble, and the surrounding hills reflecting the sound in seemingly chaotic directions means that they are rarely understandable, at least to me. I can occasionally make out verbs in the mush but usually have to rely on my wife for a translation. I will consider myself fluent in Japanese the day I understand one of these announcements without help. The most common broadcast concerns elderly people who have wandered off.

Counterintuitively, these disappearances seem to increase in the winter. I'd have thought that regardless of the grade of senility, the depth of the Alzheimer's, or the degree of confusion, the bitter winter temperatures would have tweaked some subconscious survival instinct and kept them indoors. Apparently not. Or perhaps the number of wanderers is constant, but in winter the waiting time before calling in a missing person is much reduced. Whatever the reason, the end of 2019 and the start of 2020 saw a plethora of PA blasts.

One day in particular stands out. The low temperatures, the lack of decent insulation in Japanese houses, and the environmental impact of electric or kerosene heaters means on the weekends we tend to stay in the warmth of our bed far later than is decent in non-students. Minori, after years of refusal, has belatedly got into *Game of Thrones*, so every waking moment is another episode. I'm reading Patti Smith's *Just Kids*, and a standoff is underway over who will make the coffee. Around nine the tinny BING-BONG of the PA reverberates around the village. I make out the verb "missing."

"Who is it?"

"An eighty-four-year-old woman is missing."

I go over to the window and peer out.

"She isn't in the garden."

"We've done our bit. Since you're up, get the coffee."

"Dammit."

I'm no sooner back upstairs with the tray when BING-BONG.

"They've found her."

"That didn't take long."

"She was probably just in the garden and no one wanted to go out in the cold and check."

We settle back in to our respective distractions. Reading about young romantic poets and artists in 1970s New York doesn't really work with a soundtrack of dragons, violence, and sex, so I soon give up and watch along with her.

"Where's Arya at the moment?"

"Shhh."

"I just want to know where you're up to."

"No spoilers."

"But I can pinpoint exactly where you are in the story by where Arya is in her travels."

"Shhh."

"Who's died recently?"

"You if you don't shut up."

BING-BONG.

"Another one?"

"Yes, a seventy-six-year-old man."

"Yamada-san is seventy-six."

"If he's wandered off, it's because he wants to. He isn't senile."

"He was asking me about some English phrases the other day. Apparently he unearthed some of his university textbooks."

"Maybe he's off travelling. What phrases?"

"Mainly 'I have a mind to....'"

"Did he want lessons?"

"No, I —"

BING-BONG.

"Again?"

"Yep, they found him."

"What's going on this morning?"

"Probably as soon as they hear the announcement they go 'Wait, that's me. I'm not missing, I'm right here.'"

"They need to be more careful. You know the story of the boy who cried wolf?"

BING-BONG.

Again? I figure we don't have to listen this time.

"There was a story doing the rounds a while ago. In this town in America, a woman went missing, so the whole town turned out to look for her. They were out for hours, all through the town, the hills, and forests, tramping through the brush, looking for her. It was only when they gave up and regrouped that they realised the woman they were looking for was part of the search party."

"Would you shut up?"

"Seriously?"

This time is different. The announcement goes on. And on. They usually repeat twice, but this one just keeps on keeping on.

"What the —"

"Shhh."

"Is someone missing?"

"Shhh."

"Is it about a wolf?"

"Shhh. No, a dog, she says."

"What?"

She starts laughing. The message finally ends and loops back to the start.

"It was the police. One of their dogs has run away."

"Are you joking?" I say.

"Nope. It's run off, and they're telling everyone not to approach it. Aren't those things really well trained? Why would it be dangerous?"

"They're trained to obey only their handlers. They wouldn't be much use if a criminal could just yell 'sit!' and the dog obeyed."

"It can't be that well trained if it ran off," she says.

"Maybe the training is brutal and the dog saw a chance to leg it."

"Maybe it wants to travel. It's a working dog, so it might need a holiday."

"Not much of a holiday in Gifu in mid-winter."

"It'll go north into the wild. Live like a dire wolf," she says.

"You've been watching too much *Games of Thrones*."

"I want a dire wolf."

"They'd be good if we had burglars. Maybe it's looking for sex. *Nampa shiteiru*. Off on the hunt."

"You've been watching too much *Game of Thrones*."

* * *

The area around the village is perfect for hiding, especially if you're a clever dog. Minori's right: it would head north. To the north it's all hills and forests. There's cover to the horizon where the Southern Alps start. I wish it all the best, on the run from the cops. Its training can now combine with its instinct. I picture it as an Alsatian, bounding through the snow, ducking branches. Run! Be free! I hope you find what you're looking for.

In Furukawa Hideo's novel *Belka, Why Don't You Bark?* the descendants of Kita, a Japanese military dog, spread around the world, mixing their blood with the descendants of Belka and Strelka, Soviet space dogs. Some become military dogs, some do more clandestine work, some are sled dogs, others win competitions. Two of them, Ice and then Sumer, roam the wilderness of North

America in search of safety, in search of freedom, in search of a life away from the world of men. Ice dies on the way, hit trying to cross a highway, leaving seven puppies behind. Sumer, a show dog whose puppies have been sold is in the truck that hits Ice, on her way to be destroyed. She escapes, takes Ice's puppies under her guardianship and leads them south, to Mexico.

There is a history of books that focus on animals, usually pets: Soseki Natsume's *I Am a Cat*, Virginia Woolf's *Flush*, George Orwell's *Animal Farm*, Richard Adams's *Watership Down*, Robert C. O'Brien's *Mrs. Frisby and the Rats of NIMH*, to name a few of the more famous. They tend to fall into two camps: books for children or satires on the human world using the non-human perspective to defamiliarise whatever it is the author has a beef with. *Belka, Why Don't You Bark?* is neither. It is only tangentially connected with humanity, and then only the criminal fringes. It is, in many ways, a new form of literature that opens the animal world up to fiction in a way that sidesteps basic anthropomorphism. Science fiction without the need for inventing aliens. The dogs aren't humanised animals; they are dogs with their own voices, own perspectives. It's a special book, entertaining and groundbreaking in a subtle way. It's also given me a framework in which to fantasise about the police dog's emancipation.

As I lie in bed waiting for the inevitable pattern to reform itself, for the BING-BONG saying the police dog has been found, I imagine her — I've decided she's female — stretching her muscles, running like she's never been allowed to run before. Summer — I've named her Summer, after Furukawa's Sumer, and because while winter is here, summer is coming — has the forest in her nostrils, the mountains in her eyeline, the wind to her back, and the snow under her paws. She's free in a way only the incarcerated can experience, and in that moment I envy her that thrill, that vital experience. Run,

Summer, run. I grew up in the woods. There's a hum, a vibration of life and energy between the trees. We came from there, from up in the branches. Our DNA remembers.

* * *

Summer's escape touched me because it cast light on the disappearance of my own pet. Ten years ago, we bought two turtles, each no bigger than a ten-yen coin. One died years ago; but the other, Lincoln, lived on. Specifically, he lived on in a huge plastic tub with a series of rock islands and bridges. I've been meaning to dig a pond in the garden since we moved in; but being thoroughly untechnical, I can't quite get my head around the series of pumps I need to stop it from turning into a primordial soup that produces endless mosquitoes. So Lincoln remained in his plastic home. Last summer, during the rainy season, I bought a few huge ceramic pots for the garden. Once they'd filled with rainwater I added a few plants and some goldfish. In the tall, deep ones, the fish seemed happy; but the shallower one for some reason wasn't ideal, and the fish soon died. I thought Lincoln might like a change, so I experimented with different sizes of rock and soon built an Atlantis that gave him places to hide, places to bask in the sun, places to eat and defecate. Everything except a means of escape.

See, Lincoln had long showed signs of edging towards emancipation. Eating and swimming were clearly not enough for him, and as someone who suffered through numerous family holidays poolside with three natural born sunbathers I could see his point. I sympathised, but not enough to cast him out into the wilderness. I suggested buying him a mate, like a cowboy celebrating his son's first birthday as a man, but Minori put me off such pimping and procuring, pointing out the problems of breeding turtles. So

Lincoln's urges remained unfulfilled. Like so many other reptiles, he was an involuntary celibate, an incel, but luckily had no access to the internet to share his failure.

Instead, like Summer, and like my elderly neighbours, he did a runner.

I'd made sure that none of the rocks he basked on were anywhere near the edge, and the sides of the ceramic bowl aren't just vertical, they curve back inside so only the most attention-seeking of Californian climbers would attempt to scale them. Unfortunately, I hadn't taken climate change into account.

* * *

This part of Japan is relatively mild. Typhoons rarely make it this far inland; but in the last couple of years, as climate change plays havoc with the usually predictable weather, encroachment of the more extreme forms of precipitation has increased. We battened the hatches, cleared the garden of anything that could take flight, and slept through the worst of it. Come morning all was sunny and serene. The aftermath of a typhoon — assuming no damage — is a moment I enjoy. The air crackles with spent energy, like things are falling back into place, like the whole world is breathing a sigh of relief, stretching out, and throwing the windows open. I took a stroll around the garden, tidying up anything that had shifted, sweeping leaves from the road, breathing in the crisp air.

It was Minori who noticed first.

"Lincoln has gone."

"You sure he's not under his rock?"

"Check."

Sure enough, his hideaway was empty. I pulled all the rocks out just to make sure.

"Yep, he's gone."

It hadn't occurred to me that the rain would raise the water level to the brim, spilling over, enabling Lincoln to tip himself over the edge. We hunted around the area, overturning anything he could hide under, but there was no sign. He's no bigger than a saucer, with tiny little legs, so he couldn't have gone far. There are no rivers or streams near the house, nothing like a natural habitat for him; but as wide a search area as we tried, he had gone to ground. Perhaps literally.

"My dad says they dig into the sand in winter."

"It isn't winter."

"Yes, but I mean they can dig. Maybe he's done that."

"He can't stay there long. They have no gullet, so he can't eat unless he's in water. He's going to starve."

As we searched, a few of the neighbours, Yamada included, came out to see what was going on. A small search party assembled but uncovered little beyond mushrooms and stray litter. I made a joke about using the PA system to announce Lincoln's disappearance, but my neighbours don't usually get when I'm joking and told me that the system couldn't be abused like that. Yamada laughed. He gets my jokes.

* * *

Yamada is seventy-six and very proud of the fact. He is happy to have achieved this age and retained his health and marbles. In every conversation he quickly turns the topic to his age, crowbars it in whatever the subject. It's strange then, given how much he acknowledges his age, that he seems to consider himself in the full flush of youth. His neighbour Koizumi-san is seventy-seven, but Yamada refers to him as "that old duffer next door." Clearly that year matters a lot to Yamada, and he defines himself in part by his relative youth. To be fair there is a big difference between them. Koizumi shuffles along, rarely has much to say for himself, and never strays far from home. Yamada on the other hand takes long walks every day, keeps up his piano playing, and, it seems, has picked up his English textbooks after decades of neglect.

English education in Japan is a complicated topic and one I won't get into here, other than to say this. At school the conversational side of English is ignored in favour of translation, memorising vocabulary and grammar forms, and listening to recorded exchanges. It's understandable from a teaching perspective in a country where class sizes are regularly in the forties, but it has two drawbacks: one evident, one less so. Obviously this means that students who get the best marks in English at school may be unable to hold even the most basic conversation. It also means that as students progress from elementary school through junior high school and high school, the vocabulary and grammar forms they are forced to learn become increasingly obscure. There simply isn't enough language to fill hours every week for nine or ten years. Hence Yamada having a textbook with a lesson that focuses on the structure "I have a mind to...." Yamada can't speak English. I had no idea he'd even studied it; although it's compulsory now, it wasn't always. When we talk it's entirely in Japanese, not even the code-switching hybrid most of my conversations are these days. If Yamada is keen to converse in English, "I have a mind to" is probably not the most useful place to start.

"When would you use this?"

"I wouldn't really. But it's used when you are thinking of doing something that you probably shouldn't, or something that may be surprising to the person you are talking to. For example, 'I have a mind to tell my boss exactly what I think of him.' Or 'I have a mind to quit my job and go travelling.'"

He thinks for a minute.

"So I could say, 'I have a mind to tell Koizumi to cut his bushes'?"

I laugh, "Yes, something like that."

* * *

The day of Summer's escape I finally haul myself out of bed. As always, it's much warmer outside than in. I go down to the end of the garden where I've been pruning trees. This is where I'd build my pond, Lincoln's pond. Far enough from the trees that the roots wouldn't interfere with the lining or be damaged by my digging but close enough for the cherry blossom to hang poetically over the water. It would back against the wall, follow its straight line, before curving out unevenly like a misshapen B. I like the misshapen. Geometry has no place in nature. I might put mesh across the middle, so I could have fish and turtles, without the former being lunch to the latter. I have a cairn of rocks kept to line the perimeter and to form islands in the stream. I have it all worked out, apart from the mechanics. The other thing that's stopping me is the neighbours.

"Cold today, isn't it?"

Yamada is returning.

"You must have warmed up on your walk?"

"Yes. It does me a world of good. Keeps me young. What are you up to? Tidying the garden?"

"I have a mind to build a pond," I say in English. He laughs, recognising the form but then shakes his head.

"Koizumi has a pond."

"Does he? I haven't seen it."

"Round the back. It stinks. He never cleans it. And in the summer the mosquitoes are everywhere. Every year I tell him, and every year nothing."

"Yeah, I was worried about the mosquitoes. I thought with a pump and a filter, with the right plants it would be okay."

"Maybe," he says, not looking convinced. By association with Koizumi, the very concept of a pond has been tainted. "Did you hear about the police dog?"

"Yes. Were you okay out walking? They said it might be dangerous."

"I didn't see anything. It's probably long gone."

"Where would you go if you were a dog? I thought it would head for the hills."

"Straight to Kawai-san's."

"Kawai-san?"

"The butcher in N—— Village."

"Ah. Yes, that would make sense."

"He has very good meat. You should try him next time you have a barbecue."

"I will, thanks."

* * *

I hadn't realised that dire wolves were real things. They lived in North and South America during the late Pleistocene and early Holocene epochs (150,000–9,500 years ago, thanks Wikipedia), the canine companion of the sabre-toothed tiger. Unlike their fictional cousins in *Game of Thrones*, they weren't giants, perhaps a touch bigger than modern wolves. Japan, like Scotland, used to have wolves but hunted them to extinction. There were two types of wolf in Japan, the Honshū and the Hokkaido. The latter was also known as the Ezo wolf, Ezo meaning foreign or outsider — the old name for Hokkaido, home to the Ainu people before full colonisation in the nineteenth century. When Hokkaido was brought into Japan proper, the wolf was exterminated with a bounty system and mass poisoning.

The Ainu too are all but extinct, their culture and language hanging on in Hokkaido mainly as a tourist attraction. I visited an Ainu village in 2018. At the time I had a huge beard that had gone untended for close to a year, a big bushy mess. One old man in the village told me I looked like an Ainu elder. I was inordinately pleased. I bought a two-metre square wall hanging from him that keeps demons from the door. For the Ainu, the wolf was a holy creature, divine, to be worshipped. To kill one with poison or firearms was taboo. They were considered to be beneficial animals across all of Japan — they kept wild boar numbers down, helping farmers. They were thought to protect travellers. There are shrines to them around the country. Now they are all gone.

In Scotland, wolves are part of the rewilding discussion. The UK is the only place in Europe that doesn't have wolves. They are good for the environment, helping bring ecosystems into balance, keeping an equilibrium among animals. They are also good for our spirits. The wild should be wild. Untamed, out from under the heel of man. Wild doesn't mean chaotic, not when we're talking about ecosystems. Wild is balanced. Order is unnatural. When we try to order nature, things die, go extinct. Hokkaido was brought into line. The wolf had to go. That's the price of order. Extinction. But we are part of nature too; our spirits were born in the wild, evolved in the wild. There is wolf in us.

Alex Martin wrote in the *Japan Times* in 2019 about a potential wolf sighting in Saitama, north of Tokyo. Rumours that packs survive have been around since the last known wolf was killed in 1905. There's romance in the article, an underlying dream that somewhere among all the controlled sterility of modern life something as raw as the wolf is holding on. An underlying wish that the animal that represents the feral nature of our origins — see the founding of Rome by the wolf-suckled Romulus — still exists in places it's thought to have been eradicated from gives us secret hope that our true nature, the wandering, nomadic, adventuring humanity, survives in the antiseptic twenty-first century. That we too, like Summer, can one day, metaphorically at least, run free through the woods, feeling the wind at our back and the snow under our feet.

We have a mind to flee. We have a mind to run. But we don't, because we have jobs and mortgages and responsibilities, bills and payment plans, and kids that can't fend for themselves. We aren't wolves; we aren't even dogs or turtles, but that instinct is still inside us. While I read about the poverty-stricken freedom of Patti Smith and the artists of the Chelsea Hotel exploring their freedom of the mind, and Minori watches Arya Stark crisscross Westeros exploring what it's like to be a woman freed from societal conventions around her gender, free to follow her desires and ambitions, we dream in our modern human way about a freedom Summer and Lincoln are experiencing. Perhaps this is the drive that kicks in when senility breaks the narrative: movement, travel, adventure. The elderly around here are off, exploring their natures, until the PA system lassos them home.

Or is it mortality? Many animals take themselves off when death approaches. Was this instinct also once in us, back when we were in the trees? Is it there, a behavioural appendix, after all this time, only surfacing when age withers consciousness and its defences? A slow countdown that powers our legs.

Maybe all of this is age, even though Yamada still considers me a kid, a young 'un, a whippersnapper. I'll be forty in a few months and I'm keeping a weathered eye out for any clouds that resemble a midlife crisis. Is envying a dog and a turtle their freedom a sign? I ended up in rural Japan by following that adventurous nomadic spirit, leaving Scotland behind to see what the world had to offer, tipping myself out of a familiar, safe environment and diving head-first into the storm. I catch myself looking at job adverts. Minori and I discuss a vacancy in Abu Dhabi. I recall one in Kazakhstan a few years ago and wonder what would have happened had I applied. I've settled down, house, mortgage, the works; but that wolf in me isn't asleep. He yearns to run for the hills. I can see the same thing in Yamada, a restlessness, a sparkle. He envies his daughter her experiences in China, envies me mine in Japan. His return to studying English may be a symptom of that — dreaming of travel through the pages of a textbook. But he's also happy where he is. A few days before New Year I find him sweeping up leaves outside his house, trimming the bushes, applying a very human order to things.

"My daughter is on her way," he says, "with the grandkids. This place is a mess, I want everything to be perfect when she gets here."

"How long will they stay?"

"Two nights. They have to visit his parents too." His disappointment is palpable. Every journey involves leaving someone behind. This is a pain we didn't evolve to deal with. We would have been nomadic together, extended families traversing the steppes in each other's company, and later being born and dying in the same village. The idea of heartstrings, of the tugging. Every journey means a stretching of bonds, a breaking of ties. In Philip Pullman's *His Dark Materials*, taking a child away from their daemon causes both physical and emotion wrenching. Distance equals pain.

Does Summer look back as she runs? Does Lincoln think about that big shape that fed him and washed his home, giving him fresh water when he'd shit the whole place green? Is this what defines us as modern humans, the tension between the wolf's urge to run and the bird's urge to nest?

"Are you going home for New Year?" Yamada asks me.

"No, I don't these days. Travelling at this time of year is too much trouble, and so expensive."

"Your mother must miss you."

Arya Stark is free to roam only because she thinks everyone is dead. The heartstrings permanently severed.

* * *

Inside, Minori has the heater on. I have a bottle Japanese whisky made in the traditional Scottish way. Arya is going back to Winterfell, her brothers and sister already there. Lincoln never came home. Neither did Summer. At least, there was no follow-up announcement, no BING-BONG closing the circle. If they tracked her down, they kept it to themselves. I hope she made it to the mountains. I hope Lincoln made it to a river. I keep expecting to overturn an empty shell while I'm digging the vegetables or the compost heap. So far, nothing. I hope whatever thought or instinct that drove Lincoln to take advantage of the storm, to pull a Tim Robbins in *The Shawshank Redemption*, to risk his life for the dream of freedom, that it was fulfilled.

I have a mind to travel. I have a mind to see more of this world. But it's weaker now than it used to be. I no longer have a mind to dive over the edge and head out into the storm without a thought for what I'm leaving behind, without an idea of where I'm going. From the window I watch the birds collect on the edge of Lincoln's former home. They take a drink, tip their heads back, and let the water run down their throats. They shake their heads, look around, take another drink. These birds are from Mongolia and northern China. *Jōbitaki*, Daurian redstarts. Every year they leave. Every year they come back. The fly over the Sea of Japan, over the Koreas, over China, into Mongolia, where they build nests, lay eggs, and raise their young. Then, when the temperature drops and the north winds come, they climb into the skies, their internal sat-nav set for my garden, for Lincoln's ceramic bowl where they can refresh themselves and sit out the worst of the winter.

As I age, I'm less like a wolf and more like a jōbitaki. Horizons shrink. Yamada could visit his daughter in China but doesn't. Instead he follows his circuit past the temple every morning, complains about Koizumi, travels through his English textbook, and talks to me about the world beyond the village. It's enough. At New Year and during the Obon holiday in August, she comes back and he prepares. It is enough. Maybe one day, many years from now, the PA announcement will be for Yamada and we'll find him up behind the temple instinctively following his old path, muttering "I have a mind to travel." Maybe. None of us know what is out there in the storm, what's in the mountains on the horizon. But for those about to wander off, I salute you.

About the Author

Iain Maloney is from Scotland but now lives in Japan. He is the author of the memoir *The Only Gaijin in the Village*, as well as three novels and a collection of poetry. He can be found at @iainmaloney and iainmaloney.com.

14

Sticky Ghosts and Other Missteps

By Thersa Matsuura

A common shorthand explanation of how religion in Japan combines both Shintoism and Buddhism is the truism that the great majority of Japanese have a Shinto wedding and a Buddhist funeral. Another important element is what we might call superstition, whether that be considerations of luck and misfortune connected to astrology, numerology, and geomancy, or the warding off of evil spirits. Thersa found this out the hard way when she married into the Matsuura family in Shizuoka Prefecture.

* * *

"YOU'RE sticky and you need to get help," my mother-in-law suddenly announced one winter night over dinner. There were four of us seated on the floor around the low *kotatsu* table, blanket pushed up on our laps, the heater underneath keeping our legs warm. It was me, my mother-in-law, my father-in-law, and my husband. But judging from the look she was giving when she made her statement, I knew exactly who she was talking about. Me.

Still, my Japanese was far from fluent back then. Had I heard her correctly?

"Sticky?" I asked.

"Yes," she continued. "There is something about you that is like glue. It attracts spirits and ghosts, and they don't want to leave."

I had only been married a year, but I felt that now-familiar sinking sensation in my gut when she made one of her announcements — something she did often when I was around.

"Here we go again," I thought.

A year earlier I had married a Japanese man and moved from Shizuoka City to Yaizu, a quiet town by the sea. Yaizu has since merged with the nearby city of Oigawa, and the population has more than doubled; but back then it really was the tiniest, most old-fashioned place I could imagine and I loved it.

Every summer there were local festivals with *obon* dancing, goldfish catching, and fireworks. In the fall with cooler weather came the autumn celebration, when the children dressed in fancy attire and played *taiko* drums or flutes as they paraded through the streets chanting and pulling a brightly lit, jangling *omikoshi* (portable shrine). I loved the *oni* (ogres) who came knocking on our door at night every February third, and how we had to throw beans at them while chanting "*oni wa soto*" (go away ogres) to shoo them away. If someone harvested extra vegetables, they were sure to share them with the neighbors; and if one of the elderly people in our neighborhood group passed away, everyone took a day or two off work to participate in the wake and funeral. That was one part of living in small town Japan.

But there was another part, and it was my mother-in-law who taught me the ins and outs of this deeper, more superstitious, and sometimes frightening Japan. I realize now her lessons started early.

Before my wedding ceremony I was excited to learn that a distant relative of my soon-to-be husband had an old Japanese-style house that he would rent to us while we found our feet. That excitement, however, faded only days later, after the wedding and on the plane ride back to Japan, when my husband explained to me that we couldn't move into that house right away. No, there was nothing wrong with the place. It was perfectly ready and waiting for us. The problem was he had just been informed by his mother that the direction we were traveling from Omaha, Nebraska, where we were married, to this lovely empty and totally ready-for-us-to-move-into home wasn't fortunate.

The *direction* wasn't fortunate?

Not only was it not fortunate, he said, it was unlucky.

This began a long explanation about how, according to some Japanese beliefs, when a person moves from one place to another, depending on the day, month, and year, there are fortuitous directions to go as well as less fortuitous ones. People, he explained, must check the charts before moving house, changing jobs, or even going on holiday.

Well, okay, I said. But what were we going to do? A hotel? And for how long? And if we go to a hotel, why not pick a hotel with a favorable moving direction toward the new house, stay one day, and then move into the house right away?

It wasn't so easy, he admitted. But it was okay because his mother had already come up with a plan. She told him that we could live with them for several months and then, from there, the direction would turn auspicious again and we could move into our new house safely, the fates smiling favorably on us.

It was a long several months.

"Sticky?" I mulled it over. Here it was over a year since we'd married and six months since we moved out from under my in-laws' roof. I had made a lot of mistakes along the way but was enjoying my time in that distant relative's old home with all the tatami matted floors and paper windows and doors. In the grand scheme of things, I thought this sounded kind of cool. Wouldn't it be good to have ghosts and spirits like you? But she continued.

"Recently, since you've come into our family, there has been a run of bad luck," she said. "My father passing way in spring. And remember that bad cold I caught that lasted for ages? And I probably didn't tell you, but my bicycle got a flat tire last month."

I couldn't say anything. If she had made up her mind that I was somehow bringing bad luck into the house, then anything even slightly unfortunate would be blamed on me. This is an argument I couldn't win.

"But don't worry," she said. "I have a plan. I know someone. She is a seer, quite powerful, and has a good reputation with things like this. I've already made an appointment for tomorrow night."

That decided it then.

The next evening, I stood in a stranger's narrow foyer with my mother-in-law, father-in-law, and husband, quietly removing my shoes. There was nothing particularly special about the house so far. It could have been any house in any neighborhood. I remember it being very dark and shadowy. The smell of incense was over-powering, even there in the entranceway. Underneath the sweet sandalwood fragrance was a hint of something else — boiled daikon-radish, I guessed.

My mother-in-law called out that we had arrived. The answer from deep inside the house was to please come in and follow the hallway to the main room. I was stepping up into a pair of slippers when my mother-in-law grabbed my arm and whispered to me that the seer was blind. It makes her powers stronger, she said.

So the four of us shuffled down the hall and filed into a tatami-matted room where we knelt in front of the old woman, who was sitting on a stack of several cushions and leaning against an unusually large altar. It wasn't strange that instead of one, she had several brass bowls filled with ash and stuck with handfuls of smoking incense sticks. It wasn't strange that even though she was blind, she had flickering candles set here and there, some spilling their wax all over the dark wood of the altar. It wasn't even surprising that there were unopened gifts of laundry detergent, canned tuna, and colorful hand towels stacked everywhere. What was surprising, though, were all the photos. Photos everywhere, in frames, out of frames, propped up or taped up. There were no shots of Mount Fuji or a cherry tree in the spring either. They were all taken of people: men, women, and children, not groups but individuals. I didn't ask, but I assumed these were people she was praying for or helping in her special way.

We all bowed, and my mother-in-law greeted the seer and thanked her for taking our appointment on such short notice. Next my father-in-law introduced himself, then my husband, and finally me. After I finished, though, the seer tilted her head to the side, waiting, as if listening.

"And who's the fifth?" she asked.

Fifth? We all looked at each other, confused. The old seer then said that she felt the presence of a fifth person in the room. She said she could feel five people from the time we first entered the house, actually, and all the way down the hall. A chill shot down my back, and my mother-in-law gave me an I-told-you-so look and an elbow to the ribs.

It was decided that I needed to receive a purification ritual. A week later on the prescribed day, after much cleaning on my part, the seer arrived at my house via taxi with a small case. Without much fanfare, the purification ritual began. I sat in front of her while she chanted, rang a bell, and sprinkled me with water for what felt like a very long time. I think maybe my mother-in-law was expecting something more dramatic, because when the rite was over she asked me how I felt. Did I feel sick, lighter, like something had left me? No, I pretty much felt as fine as I did going in, except my legs were really, really asleep. We all thanked the seer, my mother-in-law pressed an envelope into her hands, and that was that.

But not really. No matter how hard I tried, I continued to make cultural missteps.

There was the day I came across four little saucers at an outdoor market that I was sure my mother-in-law would love. I bought them and presented them to her, only to be reprimanded that four is a very unlucky number. "Four," *shi* in Japanese, is a homonym for the word for "death." Giving someone something in fours meant you wished they would die. She refused to accept my gift. I felt terrible.

Then there was the time our refrigerator broke and I was so proud because all by myself I managed to buy a new one at a decent price and even have it delivered. Only, unfortunately — very unfortunately — the delivery arrived on a day my mother-in-law was visiting me. She quickly pulled out her calendar and consulted it. Extremely flustered, she asked the deliverymen if could they take it back to the store and bring it back in two days. Of course they couldn't. But what did I do this time?

That was when I learned about *rokuyō*, the belief that every day of the year falls under one of six sequential categories. They go like this: *senshō* (good luck in the mornings, bad luck in the afternoon), *tomobiki* (good luck all day, but not at noon, no funerals on this day), *senbu* (bad luck in the morning, good luck in the afternoon), *butsumetsu* (unlucky all day, best not go out at all), *taian* (lucky all day), and *shakkō* (luck all day except around noon).

I didn't even realize it, but my mother-in-law and indeed many people from her generation and older checked with their rokuyō calendar before they did anything at all. Even a seemingly innocuous matter such as having an appliance delivered to their house needed to be checked so as to not invite bad luck in.

Needless to say, for a very long time I felt I could do nothing right; no matter how much I learned, I would invariably get something wrong and have to endure the lecture and embarrassment that came with it. Even something as harmless as naming my son with no other thought than I liked the name infringed on my mother-in-law's strict rules. I was floored to learn that when choosing a name for your child you have to consider the number of strokes in the characters and whether they are indeed an auspicious number or not. My husband and I spent days going through our list of names we liked, counting the strokes it would take to write the name, thumbing through a book, and taking notes. Then I learned that maybe the first name was fortuitous, but if you added the last name, you'd get another number and that had to be lucky too. Oh, and I wanted my son to have a middle name, so then came all the different combinations of names, and number of strokes to write each. It was maddening.

After a couple years, I began to get depressed. How could I live like this? Never doing anything right? Perhaps I didn't believe that the fact that I cut my fingernails at night would cause something horrible to happen. But if I was found out, and then a week later my father-in-law put his back out while weeding the garden, or our pipes burst because of a sudden cold snap, then my mother-in-law would point to my indiscretion as the cause. I couldn't win.

Then something changed.

After years and years of living like that, the day came when we had to move from that distant relative's old house and build our own. At that point I was holing up, not seeing anyone, just quietly raising my son, going to the park with homemade obentos, and watching *Ge Ge Ge no Kitaro* on TV when we got home. We were excited about the new house, and I threw myself into planning it: the layout of the place, the wallpaper, the wood color, the lights. My blues lifted.

Then the day came. After months of discussions, debates, and meetings, everything was finalized. The contractor brought over the blueprints, and we called up the in-laws and told them we had a surprise. I was so excited with all the work I'd done and couldn't wait to show them. After I spread the plans out on the table, my mother-in-law brought over her magnifying glass that she always used to read the newspaper and study coupons, and began to examine them. She didn't get far before she dropped the magnifying glass, pushed the plans away with a gasp, and declared that I had a door on my *kimon*, which was the worst possible thing I could do.

I was dumbfounded. What on earth was a kimon?

A kimon, or "devil's gate," I quickly learned, was the northeast direction of a house. It was thought to be the direction that ogres or devils entered your home or property. It was best to have a wall there, or closet — never something that could be opened like a window or door. Also, nothing to do with water: no bath, sink, or septic tank. And definitely nothing to do with fire, such as a stove, because that would aggravate the devils and make them more angry.

I also learned they sell compasses in Japan that are marked with lucky and unlucky directions. Why hadn't I bought one? I was angry but also felt absolutely defeated. This wasn't a set of saucers I could take back. I couldn't change anything. The workers were coming to start building the house in a few weeks.

It's okay, my mother-in-law said. She had a plan. We made another visit to the seer. She was older and didn't seem as mysterious as she had that first time; she just seemed like a nice old lady. When we arrived she didn't feel any extra ghosties hanging on. That was a relief. So after the usual greetings, I sat there listening to my mother-in-law go on and on about what I had done. My ignorance this time would surely bring a huge bout of bad luck on the entire family. I kept my head down, waiting for the sentence. But to my surprise, the seer was calm.

"Well, if you can't change the plans, I'll just give you an amulet to hang over the door," she said.

That was it?

"But," my mother-in-law began, "she doesn't need another purification ritual?"

"No, of course not," the woman replied. "She's fine."

And just like that a huge weight was removed from my shoulders. There are ways around some of these superstitions. Everything is not so black and white.

I bought the *kimon ofuda* and hung it up as directed. I was surprised that it was a thing at all. So I'm not the only person in all of Japan who has put something offensive on their devil's gate. There are other transgressors out there.

While the younger generations are moving away from such superstitions as rokuyō and kimon, the beliefs really were important back in the day. As a matter of fact, the idea of kimon was so predominant that not only houses but temples and even entire cities were built with this in mind. If you look at the Imperial Palace in Kyoto, you'll find a notch or indentation at exactly the northeastern corner. If you examine a map of Kyoto itself, you'll see on the kimon the Enryaku Temple complex on Mount Hiei has been put there to ward off evil. Another thing I learned was that those ogres hate holly. If you're out walking around a neighborhood anywhere in Japan and spot a holly bush, whip out your compass if you have one and check. It's a pretty good guess that it has been planted on the land's devil's gate.

From that day when I was told I could put an amulet over my door to protect my luck, something changed in me. Instead of feeling I was constantly making mistakes and bringing waves upon waves of misfortune to my family, I was able to see that it was my mother-in-law finding fault with me and whatever I did. It wasn't the fault of all these fascinating superstitions and old wives' tales at all. They are a wonderful peek into an older Japan and a different way of thinking. I began to study more on my own and try to guess why perhaps they were believed.

Yes, grandmothers told their children not to whistle at night or else snakes would come or bandits would swoop in and carry them away. But maybe it was a colorful tale that children listened to, related because walls were thin and neighbors close. Whistling and otherwise making noise at night disturbed people; and in a time when everyone depended on each other, from sharing food to helping with funerals, it was a good idea to keep the peace.

It might have been a baptism by fire, but I really appreciate all those glimpses into old Japan that my mother-in-law showed me. Maybe I'm sticky for ghosts, maybe not, but thirty years later and I am still captivated by these old superstitions and tales. I continue to study them, do podcasts on them, and write stories involving them. It's very easy to learn the top, shallow part of any culture:

it's just a Google or YouTube search away. But if you want get to the really interesting stuff, you've got to dig deep, because it lies down below the surface, often where the ogres hide.

About the Author

Thersa Matsuura is the author of two short story collections, *A Robe of Feathers and Other Stories* and *The Carp-Faced Boy*, the latter of which was nominated for a Bram Stoker Award. The American, drawing on her decades in Japan, deep interest in the culture, and life in Shizuoka, produces the Uncanny Japan podcast, which delves into legends, folktales, and superstitions.

15

One Time, One Meeting

By Mei Ling Chiam

From Yaizu we travel in the direction of Japan's highest peak, the 3,776-meter Mount Fuji, in the north of Shizuoka Prefecture, first following the Pacific coast and then heading inland into the lush hills that are the heartland of the nation's tea-growing industry.

* * *

IT all started with a packet of tea leaves. I was in my early thirties at the time and had been drinking tea for as long as I could remember, but mostly using teabags (in other words, largely imbibing tea dust and fannings, the "leftovers" in the manufacturing process). In 2013 a friend gave me a packet of loose-leaf *gyokuro* from Uji, a well-known tea-production area south of Kyoto, and things would never be quite the same. I'd drunk matcha, the powdered tea used in tea ceremonies, and tasted *sencha*, the most common Japanese tea, in loose-leaf form, on a trip the previous year. They were good but not life changing; after returning to my home in Sarawak, I went back to teabags.

The gyokuro my friend gave me was stunning, like no tea I'd ever tasted before. It had a rich aroma and a savoury taste that reminded me of kelp. Praising a tea for having notes of seaweed might seem funny, but thus began my tea journey. I started doing some reading and soon found out that gyokuro was not the same as sencha, and I also learned about the many types of Japanese teas, which are differentiated by the ways they are grown and processed. A whole new world opened up for me. I began making annual trips to Japan, combining sightseeing and the search for different teas. Among the highlights have been finding shaded green teas like gyokuro and *kabuse-cha* — I'm fond of their umami taste — and rarities such as a double-fermented tea called *goishi-cha*, which, complimenting a slight savory aroma, has a smooth, sour taste reminiscent of lemon.

Any tea, whether black or green, whether from Kenya, Sri Lanka, China, or Japan, comes from the leaves of a single plant: the evergreen shrub *Camellia sinensis*. The differences in teas are mainly from the processing; black tea leaves are fermented — more specifically, oxidized by being exposed to the air — whereas green tea is not, and oolong tea falls in between these. What chiefly distinguishes Japanese tea is that the leaves are steamed, typically right after picking, rather than being pan-fired.

In the case of gyokuro, some of its taste characteristics come from a pre-harvesting technique whereby it's cultivated under a sun-shielding covering made of straw or cheesecloth for several weeks before harvesting. Gyokuro accounts for only about 0.3

percent of tea production. Sencha is the most popular type of tea in Japan, with a 58 percent share.

Although tea is the embodiment of Japanese tradition, the national drink is ailing. Except for bottled tea, consumption is down. Old-style tea culture is out of sync with fast-paced twenty-first century lifestyles; young people don't want to brew a simple cup of tea, let alone bother with the tea ceremony, and they're more likely to be found in a Starbucks than in a tea house.

With consumption goes production. Tea farm acreage has been shrinking by about 1 percent a year. Old farmers are not being replaced, and when they go, so do the farms: the number of tea farms plummeted from 53,687 in 2000 to 19,603 in 2015. The move to bottled tea from loose-leaf tea has shifted the focus of farming from quality to quantity, and tea production on a small scale is often unprofitable.

The tea industry is trying to reverse or at least staunch the decline; the main approach seems to be accepting that traditional tea has had its day and instead diversifying into new tea-related products: everything from canned and bottled teas, some with added fruit flavourings, to bathing powder and lip balm, and most successfully, matcha, or powdered green tea flavour, in a variety of food products such as cookies, chocolate, candies, cake, and ice cream.

From my home in Kuching, Malaysia, I routinely scour the Internet for tea farms to visit. My trips have taken me to much of Japan, and in particular to the prefectures of Kyoto and Shizuoka. The latter lies along a coastal region between Tokyo and Nagoya, its mountains perfectly placed for the moderate temperatures and spring rainfall ideal for growing tea. More than 40 percent of Japan's tea comes from Shizuoka Prefecture, which is even more dominant in the tea-processing sector.

One tea farm in Shizuoka called Houkouen recently caught my eye. The tea fields of Houkouen sit at an elevation of 350 meters above sea level, with a cultivated acreage of 3.8 hectares, and a view to die for. On mornings when conditions are just right, there is the double treat of a stunning sunrise with a sea of clouds floating over the tea fields and the clear sight of Mount Fuji in the background. Instagram candy. I discovered that a small travel operator called the Tea Bridge offered a tea farm tour there, which I booked at the earliest opportunity. After attending the seventh triennial World O-Cha Festival held in Shizuoka, I took the tour and found not just award-winning tea but also some potential solutions to the decline in tea farming.

On a beautiful mid-November morning I was picked up from the Shimizu railway station by Ohashi Akito, the forty-year-old grandson of a tea farmer who co-founded the Tea Bridge in 2017. I told him it was the Instagram images of Houkouen that had first caught my attention. "That was how we started the Tea Bridge," he explained to me during the thirty-minute drive to the tea farm. He established the travel service after befriending an American woman. "I met Sandra, who found my tea photos on Instagram. She has a deep love for teas and has been to Japan a few times. She was looking for opportunities to learn about Japanese teas. I helped introduce her to my dad's friend, who is a farmer. He accepted Sandra, and we helped him at his farm and factory," he recalled.

Akito said that from this rewarding experience, Sandra discovered tea was more than just a drink. "She thought we should do something like this for other people, by connecting tea lovers to the farms and the farmers."

As we drove toward the mountains, Akito explained how he had started the Houkouen tea farm tour in January 2019 with Katahira Jiro, a third-generation tea farmer. "Jiro has an English-language website, but he cannot speak English. He has been getting a lot of requests to visit his farm after it was featured on some media platforms. So we spoke and he wanted me to help with the tours."

I mentioned the farm's slogan "tea with my whole heart," which is splashed conspicuously on the Houkouen website. Akito chuckled. "Jiro is really a great guy. He lives with tea and thinks about tea 24/7. It is always tea, tea, and tea. Together with his dad he is striving to make high-quality teas. Two years ago, Jiro bought a big tea factory in this area that was shutting down due to poor business. He decided to acquire it to protect the tea culture in this region, and now he and some of his friends are trying to promote their local teas," he said.

We were passing under the mega concrete bridges of the Shin-Tō-mei Expressway; even in these rural parts there is no escape from modernity. Suddenly, there was a bewildering sight on the road up ahead on the other side of the Okitsu River: a huge structure shaped like a *tokkuri*, or sake flask.

"A sake brewery?" I asked.

Akito laughed, "A water purification plant." The forty-five-meter tokkuri was the distribution tower.

Not long after, we reached Nunozawa Village and continued up the mountain where Jiro has his tea fields. Akito explained that teas in the mountains are usually harvested later, compared to teas in low-lying areas. "Because of that, some farmers in this part of Shizuoka often feel that their teas are inferior or not valued right, in comparison to those from other areas, even though mountain teas are of high quality.

"Jiro and his friends are trying to change the community's mindset. They do new things, like holding tea events to get people to know about teas here," he said, as he maneuvered the car around narrow winding bends. It was just us between the rough cliffside and the sheer drop to the valley below.

Farther on, Akito pulled over, parking on the side of the narrow mountain road with that Japanese brilliance for miniaturization. We had arrived. Out I stepped, taking a deep breath of rejuvenating autumn air, crisp and cool, and marvelled at the landscape glistening under an almost cloudless sky. From the steep slope, glorious layers of green, neatly trimmed tea fields, and then patches of lush vegetation stretched out to the east, where Mount Fuji shone majestically with a fresh coat of snow on its summit. No matter how many times I visit Japan, every encounter with this notoriously shy mountain is memorable.

We climbed a small path from which we could better see Mount Fuji. Looking around, adjacent to this tea field I noticed an overgrown one. It was untrimmed and unkempt, with weeds poking through the hedges. Clearly, the plot belonged to someone who had quit the industry. The tea plant, as the scientific name *Camellia sinensis* indicates, is a camellia, a genus known for bright showy flowers. Its white flowers with their striking yellow stamens are pretty to look at but are a sure sign of degeneration. A good working tea field has very few flowers because young buds are constantly harvested throughout the year, thus preventing the plants from flowering.

The tea bushes in the abandoned field were in full bloom. I observed that it was beautiful in its own decayed way. Akito shook his head and lamented the state of tea farming. The biggest problems in the Japanese tea industry, he said, were greying farmers and abandoned tea farms. This century the number of commercial tea farms in Shizuoka has more than halved. With a declining, aging population, many labour-intensive agricultural industries are suffering. The average age of the Japanese farmer is about sixty-seven. A less well-known problem with tea farms is the average age of tea trees.

"When tea bushes are old and weak, they get more flowers. Look, compare that with Jiro's tea bushes. You do not see many flowers on his. If you want good tea, you do not want to see flowers," said Akito. "Normally, tea bushes are replaced every thirty years or so; but Jiro is doing it more often, section by section. By doing this, the tea bushes will be rejuvenated and can produce better tea. Young bushes mean increased yield and quality," he said. And the average age of tea plants in Japan? According to 2011 figures, 55 percent of trees were twenty-one years or older, and a third older than thirty years.

Slightly above where we stood, there was a wooden platform I had seen in promotional photos of Houkouen; it is what the majority of visitors come here for. Known as a *chanoma* (tea space), this kind of platform is now being built at tea fields that offer elevated views. The idea, actively promoted by the local tourism bureau in their tea tourism campaign, is fast catching on in many hillside areas of Shizuoka and in some other tea-producing prefectures.

The chanoma, which is surrounded by rows of tea bushes and mountains, also makes for a good classroom. Akito gives visitors samples to drink and educates them on the complexity of green teas. Jiro plants twenty-five different tea cultivars in addition to the popular Yabukita cultivar, which accounts for most of Japan's tea production. (A cultivar is a plant variety that has been cultivated for specific qualities.) It's difficult to imagine how he keeps track of so many cultivars, each one with its own physical traits and requirements; it speaks of a whole hearted dedication.

Akito said he has been attempting to convince the local people to see that their tea is special by bringing tea lovers out here. "It is normal that we often don't see the beauty of our own place, but people from other places will remind us and make us realize that our own place is special, that our own tea is special. I hope more people come so that the locals will understand that and be motivated by it. The old business model of tea is not working. It really needs to change," he remarked.

After taking more photos of the scenery, we decided it was time to head to the tea-tasting session at Jiro's family house, which is about ten minutes away in the quiet village below. The Houkouen tearoom and the adjacent factory are just a few steps from the house. In comparison to the factory that Jiro recently acquired, the older Houkouen tea-processing factory is a very small one, homely and rustic. Akito took me into the factory for a quick tour, pointing out the various machines, some of them very old, and detailing Jiro's hands-on approach.

"Most farmers sell *aracha*, or unrefined tea, to wholesalers, who will be doing the refining and blending work. At this factory, Jiro refines and sells his own tea under the Houkouen brand name. It is considered a single-origin tea because it is not blended with others," he explained. Akito added that wholesalers have the tendency to believe that consumers want the exact same taste as what they drank in the previous years. I nodded my understanding.

Blending tea from different producers is a way to standardize the taste as well as to adjust costs. I strongly believe that this mindset is misguided. Tea should not taste the same every year. Wine differs from year to year, and yet people still buy a particular brand that is known to be of high quality. Surely, tea can establish such brand power and encourage a shift in consumer perception.

We headed over to the tearoom, where Akito started preparing the tea wares for the tasting session while I seated myself on a log-stump stool in front of a wood-slab tea table. A *kakejiku* (hanging scroll) hung unobtrusively on the wall beside the entrance to the tearoom. It read "*cha ni kokoro wo nosete*" and seemed familiar. Then it came to me: it translates into "putting (one's) heart into tea" or *tea with my whole heart*, the slogan on Houkouen's website.

While waiting for Jiro, we began our tasting session with tea produced from a cultivar called Yamakai, which is a cross between Yabukita, the most widespread tea cultivar in Japan, and an unknown cultivar. The tea was presented in a tiny glass tea cup.

I sampled a mouthful. "There is a rather interesting flavour or aftertaste, but I can't pinpoint it," I said.

Akito took a sip from his cup and asked a question that threw me, or rather my senses, off guard. "Did you get the mayonnaise taste? It is unique to the Yamakai cultivar."

"What? No, I didn't. Was I supposed to?" I took another sip and tried to identify the flavour notes. There was a very slight hint of sourness, but certainly there was no mayonnaise. I felt annoyed that I could not detect it, that my tongue was incapable of tasting tea like an expert.

We moved on to try three other teas of different cultivars. The one that stood out for me was a tea made from the popular Yabukita cultivar. This was a kabuse-cha (shaded tea), and it was hand-rolled, a rare process in today's tea production, where machines do most of the tedious work. As expected, the taste was exceptional, brought forth when served in a shallow cup, resulting in a very concentrated and umami-filled brew that left me craving more.

The sliding door to the tearoom opened, and Houkouen's young owner stepped in. He was of medium height and athletically lean, with sharp facial features softened by an easy smile. I stood up, greeting Jiro formally despite knowing that he is a little younger in age. Greetings and pleasantries done, Jiro sat down with us and started chatting like we were longtime friends. He was obviously more than happy to share his thoughts about tea and life on the farm. The conversation was in a mixture of Japanese and English, with Akito often translating to help out with my intermediate Japanese proficiency.

Jiro said when he started the tour of his farm two years ago, following constant requests for visits from customers, he didn't charge any fee. This was not because he did not want to, but because he expected the demand would be short-lived. Eventually he realized that a tea farm could be a tourist destination if things were done right, particularly in a sustainable way. However, he was wary of turning the village into a tourism spot, as some farmers would find crowds descending upon their humble backyard *mendokusai* (bothersome).

"The impact of so-called tea tourism for the local community here is still very small. There is nothing for sightseeing in the village, and our farmers are so busy with making their teas. The thing is, some visitors come just for the scenery of the tea fields. We have the chanoma for people to rent so that they can enjoy the scenery and tea tasting, as well as to take photos for social media. But not all of them know tea. Many come but don't buy any tea. They have no impression of our teas. It is only a place with a beautiful view to them," he noted, with a tinge of wry mirth.

"It has become a norm for people to drink tea from a plastic bottle," he continued. "I want to create tea that makes people feel like they want to drink again and again. I want to get them interested in the tea, so that they will truly enjoy it."

Jiro gestured at the teas laid out on the low table in front of us and held up a cup. "You know, this cup of tea is only here for this moment. Using the same leaves, same water, same tea ware, and same environment in making the tea, yet there will be a difference in the next cup. It is not the same cup of tea. You cannot meet this cup of tea again. It is very precious. That is why I always think of how to produce the best tea so that people will remember each cup for a long time," he said.

A Japanese idiom came to mind: *ichi-go-ichi-e*, literally "one time, one meeting," which carries the meaning of "an encounter that could happen only once in a lifetime" or "only for this moment." This is a concept most popularly associated with *chado*, the Japanese tea ceremony; it reminds us to cherish any gathering because it can never be exactly replicated.

Jiro was right. The cup of tea I was drinking now would not be the same as the next. Even with the same type of production method, the taste of a tea varies depending on its cultivar, the terroir, from one harvest to the harvest, and so on. Conversely, the same type of cultivar can be processed into green tea or black tea. And then there's the brewing and serving. To me, this variety makes every tea worth tasting, because you never know what you'll discover about it. The distinctiveness is something to be cherished. An emphasis on consistency, standardization, and mass consumption is against the essential nature of tea and detracts from the natural variation that makes tea fun and interesting. Trying to iron out this variation diminishes tea. Each tea should be accepted for what it is.

Savouring the subtlety of the tea in my cup, I felt grateful for the opportunity to be there at that very moment. It did strike me, however, that there are practical limits to the *ichi-go-ichi-e* philosophy; it doesn't exactly lend itself to being scaled up. Rather than relying on one-off encounters, there had to be other ways for people to better know the teas from this part of Shizuoka.

As if reading my mind, Jiro said that he uses social media to create interest and awareness about the teas from his area, and he always makes sure to state that his teas are Ryogochi teas. Ryogochi is no longer found on maps, even though it is one of the more established tea-production areas in the prefecture. As part of the merger of territories in the early 2000s, the name of Ryogochi Village was lost.

"Our tea already has established its own identity, which is the pride of the local community. That is what we want people to remember always. Not just visitors or tea drinkers, but our own community. We want to remind everyone of the fact that even though the name Ryogochi is no longer on the maps, the tea from here is still as exceptional as ever," he said.

Too soon it was time to leave, as Akito reminded me of the hour. It was past lunchtime. We had eaten nothing but drunk a lot of tea and talked a lot about tea. Before leaving, I bought a pack of the exquisite hand-rolled kabuse-cha.

The sky darkened suddenly, thunder rumbling in the distance. We took our leave, with me thanking Jiro profusely for taking time off from his busy schedule to meet me and offer his first-hand insight into the industry. It began drizzling the moment we got into the car, the dark clouds getting ominous. Akito and I waved goodbye to Jiro, who was still standing in front of his house to see us off.

"Wow, you are really lucky. It didn't rain the whole morning," Akito said as he carefully drove out of the narrow street. The car's windshield wipers screeched a little in the rain. The raindrops got bigger, the leading edge of a thunderstorm that would last into the evening.

As we put Houkouen behind us, I thought of what Akito and Jiro had shared with me. I would try to tell people about Houkouen and the other tea farms of the mist-shrouded village of Ryogochi, the name that had disappeared from the maps but is fighting to retain its identification with high-quality teas.

I'm relatively positive about the future of Japanese tea farming. My own personal story highlights various ways forward. Since discovering Japanese loose-leaf tea in 2013 I've been an enthusiastic drinker and buyer. As the domestic tea market in Japan declines, international sales are growing. With only about 5 percent of Japanese tea being exported — the largest markets are the United States and Taiwan, then Germany and Singapore — there is great potential, especially for organic teas, which account for barely 3 percent of total production.

Tourism and the Internet allow producers to reach a wider market. The Tea Bridge was co-founded by another foreign woman who became hooked on Japan's tea culture and made connections through Instagram. My own fascination has brought me to Japan multiple times, and I've been spreading the word with a tea blog, *The Floating Tea Stem*. In 2018 I took my interest to another level when I signed up for a correspondence course administered by Japan's Nihoncha Instructor Association, a non-profit organization working to promote the country's tea culture. The course was tough; the study materials and the tests were in Japanese, and the curriculum covered everything about tea, including history, cultivation, production, brewing and drinking, health benefits, and current trends. I surprised myself when I passed the course last year and was certified a Nihoncha Adviser. I consider this certification not the end but only the beginning of my immersion in tea.

I wanted to wrap this chapter up with a sentimental harking back to "Tea with my whole heart" — the Houkouen tea farm slogan, which captures so well my own philosophy, a cup of kabuse-cha by my side as I wrote, but just two months after the visit, my thoughts are currently more along the lines of "Tea with not all my nose." I wrote this chapter under strange conditions, struggling with a minor but unusual health condition called anosmia, which is defined as the loss of the ability to detect one or more smells. In layman's terms, it's smell blindness. The first warning sign was not smelling the garlic in a dish my mother was stir-frying, and the clincher was not being able to smell durian. Even though tea drinking has more to do with taste, smell plays a vital part in providing the full experience. Tea aromas are fainter than before for me, and it has become harder to identify certain notes. Hopefully this is just a passing annoyance.

About the Author

Mei Ling Chiam is a writer based in the Malaysian Borneo city of Kuching, where she works as a journalist. She is a Nihoncha (Japanese Tea) Adviser, as certified by the Nihoncha Instructor Association. A frequent traveler to Japan, she aims to spread the appeal of Nihoncha through telling stories of teas and their growers.

16

Ibaraki, Inaka, and the In-laws

By Tom Gibb

I~N~ the annual *miryokudo* (attractiveness) rankings, a survey of
public opinion and awareness regarding Japan's forty-seven
prefectures, Ibaraki consistently comes last: even neighbouring
Fukushima, the site of a catastrophic nuclear accident, places
higher. Partly at the instigation of radio presenter Tomoya Aoki —
a self-styled "Ibarakist" whose show is called "Ibaraking" and who
moonlights as the Ibarapper — the prefecture and its tourist board
have attempted to make a virtue of this fact. After all, there is no
such thing as bad publicity, and in 2015, Ibaraki-born celebrities
Naomi Watanabe and Yuji Ayabe appeared in a promotional video,
the catchphrase for which was "No. 1 in Japan for Potential."

As the video pointed out, the prefecture has plenty of tourist
attractions: the sea of brilliant blue nemophila flowers at Hitachi
Seaside Park, the billowing white sails of traditional *hobikibune*
fishing boats on Lake Kasumigaura, and the carnival floats and

dancing lions of the Ishioka Festival, to name but three. Through a quirk of geography, you have to drive through both Saitama and Chiba Prefectures to get here on the Joban Expressway, but Ibaraki's southwestern border is less than forty kilometres from Nihonbashi — the point from which distances around Japan are measured — meaning that it is regularly employed as a film and television location.

Proximity alone, however, will never make Ibaraki fashionable or cosmopolitan. And like pretty much anywhere outside the twenty-three wards that constitute central Tokyo, it is perennially regarded as being in the countryside, or, to use the Japanese word, *inaka*.

The two kanji used to write "inaka" (田舎) mean, respectively, "rice field" and "cottage" (or "inn"). Aside from its definition, inaka carries the implied — and pejorative — meaning of "the sticks," or what we British refer to as "the arse-end of nowhere." Inaka is so widely used and loaded with its own distinct connotations that like *onsen* (hot springs) or *onigiri* (rice ball), it is a word with which expats sprinkle their conversation untranslated, and English speakers will often say, "I'm stuck in the inaka," while sipping on a Frappuccino at Starbucks, or write, "That's so inaka!" in a Facebook comment.

I live with my wife, Mieko, and our daughter and son in Naka City, which despite the resemblance has no direct connection with the word inaka, and is also not to be confused with Hitachi-naka, Hitachi, Hitachi-ōmiya, or Hitachi-ōta, fellow municipalities in the north of the prefecture whose names even the natives find confusing.

In reality, Naka is two small towns that in 2004 merged to form an administrative entity that calls itself a city, and its area of around a hundred square kilometres has just fifty-three thousand inhabitants. When they are older, our daughter and son may well find the slow pace of country life uninspiring, and another potential disadvantage to growing up here is that as mixed-race children, they look noticeably different from their peers.

In Japan the standard response to seeing a young child is "*Kawaii ne!*" ("Isn't he cute!"), although this is such a reflex action and *kawaii* so omnipresent that one should not take its use at face value, as even the most bawling or vomit-encrusted infant will be its recipient, more often than not before the person uttering the supposed compliment has properly set eyes on them. "*Orikō-san desu-ne!*" ("Isn't she a good girl!") is another, while babies in particular will be told "*Me ga bacchiri!*" ("His eyes are beautiful!"). Often, however, we will overhear passersby say something like, "*Yappari, chigau yo-ne,*" which means, "Of course, they're different, aren't they?" — the "they" being mixed-race people — and while this, too, is meant as a positive reference to their appearance, it is something that our children would not have to deal with if they lived in Britain.

As a Westerner in the inaka, I have long since become accustomed to standing out: on one occasion a local was so surprised to see me emerge from a convenience store that he crashed his car into a lamppost. But once you get used to this, living here as a foreigner has much to recommend it, in that people are curious in a good way and keen to treat you to the kind of hospitality usually reserved for a guest: that is a short-term visitor or a tourist, as opposed to a father with a full-time job and a permanent residency visa.

In line with the national demographic, however, our children are also in a minority because of their age. More than a third of Naka's population is over sixty-five years old — that is even higher than an already high national average — and at the risk of stereotyping, like British old age pensioners with their carpet slippers and tartan blankets, the elderly in Japan tend to be stylistically homogeneous.

There is a very funny scene in the 2004 film *Shimotsuma Story* (aka *Kamikaze Girls*), which makes a joke of the fact that everyone in the eponymous Ibaraki city of the title (like Naka, Shimotsuma is in reality a collection of villages masquerading as a city) buys their clothes at the local Jusco. Partly to divest itself of such ridicule, at the time of the film's release Jusco was already in the process of rebranding itself as Aeon, and is reminiscent of Tesco in the United Kingdom or Walmart in the United States.

A day out at an Aeon mall is the cultural highlight of many people's lives, and while youngsters buy their clothes at its boutiques, which have names like OPAQUE.CLIP, Alphabet's alphabet, and — my particular favourite — Starvations, parents and grandparents purchase theirs from the Aeon clothing department, or at one of a dwindling number of neighbourhood clothes shops.

The district of Naka in which we live is called Urizura, and its main thoroughfare is a typical example of the *shattaa-dōri* (shutter street). Such streets thrived until the coming of Aeon and its ilk, and most of the shops that lined them have now closed; indeed, you really can hear the rattle of a succession of store-front shutters from the rush of air created when vehicles pass through. Two of the businesses still clinging on in Urizura sell clothes and, alongside the frumpy, floral-patterned trouser suits beloved of old ladies, stock a garment essential for any woman over the age of about forty: the apron.

What is referred to in Japanese as an apron is more like a smock that extends around the wearer's back. Its purpose is to protect your frumpy, floral-patterned trouser suit when you are cooking, cleaning, or gardening, and although kawaii Hello Kitty aprons are an unofficial uniform for nursery school teachers, women in the countryside will wear theirs — usually with a check design in more low-key colours — all day, every day. When a friend of ours was visiting from abroad a few years ago we drove to a nearby onsen, and as we set out I jokingly predicted that we would see at least ten women wearing aprons along the way. We saw eleven.

So apart from hanging out at the nearest Aeon mall, what exactly do the few youngsters who live in rural Japan do? Well, customising your car is one option. The boy racers in my Devonshire hometown would have a Confederate flag on the roof and a Colonel Bogey horn to sound while driving around the local council estate. Here in Ibaraki there are plenty of drivers who negotiate undulations in the road with extreme care because the bodywork of their car is about a millimetre off the ground, or who adorn the bodywork itself with depictions of manga characters — more often than not, young, doe-eyed, female ones. These days you will see "camber" wheels, which can be adjusted to slant away from the chassis. But when I first came here, aficionados of hydraulics would gather to show off how high in the air their wheels could jump, preferably to an accompaniment of blaring hip hop or R&B.

Speaking of noise pollution, a sound as redolent of the Japanese countryside as croaking frogs or chirping cicadas is that of the *bōsōzoku* (motorcycle gangs), who ride around revving their engines as loudly as possible, often on sunny weekends but sometimes — and to the consternation of anyone living near a main road — in the middle of the night.

Aside from the lack of a muffler, a distinguishing feature of a bōsōzoku bike is its extended seat back, often upholstered in white leather and protruding from the rear at head height. Many bōsōzoku groups have a military feel, with members designated as "head of the imperial guard" or "commando unit leader," and their jackets embroidered with the old Japanese army flag of a rising sun emanating red rays. Back in the eighties there were an estimated forty thousand bōsōzoku nationwide. Fights between rival gangs and other instances of anti-social or criminal behaviour led to a crackdown; for example, the raised metal reflectors along the centre line of many Japanese roads were introduced partly to prevent bōsōzoku from weaving from side to side and into the path of oncoming traffic. Nowadays, bōsōzoku are unlikely to be reprimanded for any infringement more heinous than failing to wear a helmet.

Another youth subculture closely associated with Ibaraki are the so-called *yankii*. Yankii wear skin-tight jeans, winklepicker shoes, and pompadour hairstyles, and are most visible at summer festivals, where they perform twist-style line dancing to fifties and sixties rock 'n' roll. The yankii in Mieko's hometown of Hitachi-ōta have been using the same worn-out speakers for years and take a perverse pleasure in the fact that the music they dance to is thereby horribly distorted. Also known as *rōraa-zoku* (the rock 'n' roll tribe), yankii such as these were a common sight in the Tokyo district of Harajuku — Japan's epicentre for young fashion — back in the eighties and nineties, and yet another phenomenon that makes Ibaraki seem so behind the times.

There is a festival in Urizura that the yankii do not attend, and it is the one time of year when the aforementioned shutter street is restored to its former hustle and bustle. Because the festival is organised by a Buddhist temple, you will see parishioners queueing to say a prayer and place a coin in the collection box, or chanting along to a mantra before the temple dais. We recently attended a smaller-scale festival at a children's home, where we danced the *bon-odori* (part of the annual memorial service for one's ancestors) and ate homemade *onigiri* at fifty yen apiece. Our children were chaperoned by the residents, and came away at the end of the evening with the gift of a boxful of pet stag beetles.

Particularly in the summer months the countryside is teeming with wildlife. Along with frogs and cicadas, there are dragonflies, bees, butterflies, lizards, snakes, spiders, and, of course, mosquitoes. Few, though, are venomous, and statistically speaking, the most dangerous is the *suzumebachi* (hornet), whose sting can cause a lethal allergic reaction. The number of people who lose their lives this way averages in double figures annually, and a friend of ours nearly became one of them. Stung by a hornet that flew in through his car window, as he was receiving treatment in a local hospital his heart actually stopped for a few seconds; he now carries an EpiPen and spends a lot less time outdoors.

Apart from wild boar, raccoon dogs, and the occasional monkey, larger mammals are rare, partly because Ibaraki lacks the rugged mountain scenery of other parts of the country. This plain-ness, as it were, is another reason the prefecture is considered unappealing, although the high proportion of arable land means that it is near the top of the table in terms of agricultural production.

A Japanese phrase, *kengyō-nōka*, meaning to have a proper job during the week and to farm on weekends, applies to many in Ibaraki. Even acquaintances of mine who work at Nissei — a manufacturing centre for the Hitachi Corporation and the largest employer in this part of the prefecture — are likely to own a rice field and to dedicate much of their holiday time to rice planting and harvesting. This proliferation of small-scale farmers is one of the reasons Japanese roadsides are home to so many coin-operated rice hulling machines and *chokubaijo* ("direct sell place").

As the translation suggests, chokubaijo sell local produce directly to consumers. Wooden shelves and handwritten signs give them the feel of warehouse-style grocery stores or indoor farmers' markets,

and they carry such unique foodstuffs as *yuzu* (Japanese lemon —
this has a wonderfully subtle, bittersweet taste with a fragrance
somewhere between that of a lemon and an orange, and is used
not just to flavour food and drinks but to add fragrance to a hot
bath), *nanoana* (rapeseed — more often used for its oil in the West,
when lightly boiled and seasoned with soy sauce and bonito flakes,
this makes for a tangy, bitter-tasting salad vegetable), and *inago*
(grasshoppers — yes, you read that correctly, grasshoppers — sau-
téed in soy sauce, sugar, sake, and mirin until crunchy and sweet).

Japanese cuisine has a reputation for being healthy, but this is
something of a myth, and many staple dishes contain artery-con-
stricting quantities of salt, fat, and sugar. Take, for example, *daigaku-imo* ("university potatoes"). Daigaku-imo were originally beloved
of cash-strapped students — hence the name — and are roughly
chopped sweet potatoes, deep-fried and coated in treacle and
sesame seeds. While their main ingredient is tasty, versatile, and
contains three times as much fibre as an ordinary potato, it also
has a significantly higher calorie content, and in my experience
can weigh down your stomach like a sack of quick-dry cement.

Indeed, the aforementioned soy sauce, sugar, sake, and mirin
— also a variety of sake but sweeter: think sherry as opposed to
wine — are the holy, er, quadrality of Japanese cooking, and used
in the preparation of an enormous range of dishes, so that eating
a main meal here can feel like you have skipped straight to dessert.

When we visit Mieko's family home, my mother-in-law — or
Okaa-san, as we call her — will serve fish or eel simmered in sweet
sauces, deep-fried rice cakes, Japanese curry given depth and a
mahogany-like lustre with a few squares of plain chocolate, and
similarly hearty fare. Not only that, but winter brings with it a
regular supply of *hoshi-imo* (dried sweet potatoes), from a family
business based on the farm where Okaa-san grew up. Combined

with sea breezes along the Ibaraki coast, the unusually low humidity of autumn and winter in Japan is conducive to the drying process, which more than doubles the concentration of sugar: a friend who has competed in the 170-kilometre Ultra-Trail race around Mount Fuji tells me that hoshi-imo are ideal for on-the-run refuelling.

You have probably seen photographs of traditional houses with tatami mat floors and sliding screen doors, moodily lit and enhanced with little more than a flower arrangement or calligraphy scroll, their floor-to-ceiling windows looking out on an ornamental rock garden and intricately sculpted pine trees. But another myth worth dispelling is that the Japanese live minimalist lifestyles, for if you enter a typical residence, you might be forgiven for thinking there has been a burglary or, perhaps more likely, an earthquake.

While superstitions relating to the layout of a house and its contents do exist — for example, *kitamakura* ("north pillow") dictates that it is unlucky to sleep on a futon with one's head pointing northwards — feng shui is only a recent import from China, and the fact that Japan gave us organisational guru Marie Kondo arises, I suspect, not so much from a desire but an inability on the part of many Japanese to tidy their homes. At my in-laws', for example, doorways are blocked, corridors almost impassable, and because cupboards, chests of drawers, and so on are already full to overflowing, the floor is piled high with odds and ends, making it impossible to open the cupboards and chests of drawers in the first place.

The kitchen, in which Okaa-san spends such a lot of her time, is perhaps the messiest room of all, and over the years the area within it for preparing food has been reduced to one no bigger than a tea tray, as the worktop, windowsills, draining board, and dining table are piled ever higher with crockery, gadgets, and ingredients, not to mention plates of half-eaten food wrapped in cling film.

My own childhood home was similar, in that my mother rarely cleaned and was a compulsive hoarder: a result, it would seem, of having grown up after World War II, an era of food shortages and rationing, during which people had neither the money nor the online shopping to replace the old with the new. In the same way that our fridge would be full of leftovers — a couple of string beans here or half a boiled potato there — so Okaa-san's is the same, with all kinds of indeterminate items relegated to its far reaches, many either mouldy, dehydrated, or several years past their sell-by-date.

In addition to performing most of the household chores, Okaa-san grows her own fruit and vegetables, so that along with *hoshi-imo* we are given lettuce, onions, and parsley in spring; cucumbers, cherry tomatoes, and football-sized watermelons in summer; pumpkins and potatoes in autumn; and Chinese cabbages and daikon (large Japanese radishes) in winter. These are grown in what she calls the *hatake* (field), a plot of land purchased by my father-in-law — aka *Otō-san* — in the mid-nineties, partly so that Okaa-san could hone her gardening skills, but mainly in the hope that my brother-in-law — *Onii-san* — would one day build a house there.

The Japanese have specific words to describe siblings, denoting who is the oldest, the second oldest, and so on, and when you ask about a person's family, this information will be inherent in their description of it. Because a *chōnan* (eldest son) is expected both to care for his parents in their old age and to inherit the family business, his is the position that carries the most pressure and expectations. While at vocational school and in his first full-time jobs, Onii-san rented an apartment, but when he was in his late twenties — and, being the chōnan, he had no doubt anticipated this — Otō-san asked him to work at the family barbershop.

It was around this time that Otō-san purchased the hatake, although the problem was, whenever Onii-san introduced prospective wives to his parents, Otō-san would disapprove. One was too young, one was too old, and another was — as Otō-san so diplomatically put it — "ugly," meaning that Onii-san eventually gave up, and at the time of writing is in his late forties and still single. In contrast with this, when Mieko broke the news that not only was she thinking of getting married to a foreigner, but of moving to the U.K., whatever reservations Otō-san may have had, because she is both female and the younger sibling he made no attempt to prevent her from doing so.

At a traditional barbershop like Otō-san's, customers will typically pay three or four thousand yen for a service that encompasses not just a haircut but a wet shave with a cutthroat razor, shampooing, massage, and specialised hairstyling — for example, the so-called iron perm, which results in a quiff solid enough to withstand a force-ten gale. But once the so-called bubble economy had burst, *sen-en katto* (thousand-yen haircut) establishments — with their high customer turnover and no-frills approach — were on the rise, and the family ended up with an overpriced vegetable patch and payments on a second mortgage that were due to continue into the 2020s.

I have always assumed that Otō-san was slightly disappointed upon discovering that when Mieko and I first met, my hairline was already receding like the tide on a north Devon beach. Still, I always look forward to my monthly haircut, as it gives Otō-san and me the chance to talk in the uncluttered, air-conditioned environment of the shop. (The messiness in the household occurs out of customers' sight.)

As he shaved my head with a set of electric clippers, I once asked Otō-san when he was going to retire, to which the reply was, "Never!" But partly from the strain of maintaining the same posture day after day, he has for a long time suffered with a bad back, and recently there have been times when Onii-san has to put the finishing touches to one of Otō-san's haircuts because he has been unable to complete it to his usual high standards.

Okaa-san says that when she was more regularly called upon to attend to customers, Otō-san's overly blunt way of giving orders was such that she sometimes contemplated stabbing him with the scissors. But she and Onii-san have begun to suspect that there could be more to his moodiness than an old-fashioned, patriarchal attitude, and more to his making mistakes than the forgetfulness of old age.

Particularly outside the big cities, information is disseminated to communities via telegraph pole-mounted speakers and what are known as *bōsai-rajio* (disaster-prevention radios), for instance to summon volunteer firefighters to an emergency, or to warn residents if a crime has been committed and the perpetrator is at large. By far the most common announcements, however, are those regarding elderly people who have gone missing, either from their own or nursing homes, and one day soon it may just be Otō-san's description being relayed to all corners of Hitachi-ōta, asking them to contact the police if he is found.

Partly with this in mind, Otō-san's younger sister paid off some of the mortgage on the *hatake* from a sum of money she had inherited, and Mieko and I paid off the remainder using our savings from Britain. This has opened a new and equally complicated chapter in the family's story, with Otō-san none too keen on Onii-san's ideas to revamp both the barbershop's interior and the way it is run. But at least they can now live without the millstone of several more years of loan repayments to deduct from their ever-dwindling wages, and Otō-san can pop upstairs for his afternoon nap without having to worry if and when another customer will trigger the chime on the smoked-glass shop door.

*Tom and his son getting their hair cut by Okaa-san and Otō-san
at the family barbershop*

By coincidence, Ibaraki was the first place I visited on my first
day in the country, way back in October 2002. At the time a friend
from London was in Tsukuba on a workplace exchange programme,
and having been dropped off at his apartment, I went for an aimless,

265

jet-lagged stroll around the nearby university campus. Autumn is the ideal time to be in Japan, as the heat and humidity of summer have died down, and almost every day is cloudless and pleasantly warm. That first afternoon — and indeed most of the ten-day holiday I spent here — was no exception, and the leaves of the ginkgo and Japanese maple trees were cast in a particularly golden glow by the afternoon sunlight.

Through a rather convoluted chain of events I have ended up not very far from where I started, and fashionable or not, this much maligned prefecture — with its unhealthy diet and its untidy homes, its boy racers and its bōsōzoku, its retro line dancing and its frumpy aprons — is where I shall stay ... at least until our children have left home or I feel the urge to return to my roots in the southwest of England. Dare I say it, from the very beginning, I believe that I may even have found Ibaraki attractive.

About the Author

Tom Gibb has worked in Japan as an English teacher for more than a decade, so far with no discernible effect on the language ability of the population as a whole. Partly for this reason, he is plotting his escape from the education system to become a freelance translator. He has travelled to more than half of Japan's forty-seven prefectures by bicycle, and is presently writing an account of his first and longest tour, with the provisional title of *Gaijin on a Push Bike*. His blog can be found at muzuhashi.com and his family can be found at the local Costco.

17

Following in Bashō's Footsteps along the Narrow Road to the Deep North

By Lesley Downer

Traveling north from Ibaraki we pass into Fukushima, the first of the six prefectures that make up the rustic, formerly remote region of Tohoku. This northernmost part of Honshu is noted for rural ways and spectacular scenery. Its sacred peaks, mountain temples, and coastal views were immortalized by Japan's most beloved poet, Matsuo Bashō (1644–1694), in *The Narrow Road to the Deep North*, his evocative account of wanderings in Tohoku toward the end of his life.

* * *

ONE day in late summer I was walking toward the hills in Japan's northeast region, Tohoku. The road wound between paddy fields packed with brilliant green rice shoots and the sun was shining. I was following in the footsteps of the poet Matsuo Bashō, who had come this way some three hundred years earlier, in 1689. But what had been a narrow earthen track in his day was now a motor road. I could tread where Bashō had trodden, visit the temples he visited, see the monuments inscribed with haiku he had written, but the world he had known seemed to have changed beyond recognition.

Then I caught sight of a little road winding off enticingly into the hills and disappearing into the pine trees. A road like that demands to be followed. There was no choice.

I turned off along it. Soon I was in desolate country, tramping through a gorge between high hills tangled in forest. The road grew wilder and narrower, overgrown with gorse and long grass and wildflowers, and quickly dwindled to a footpath. I rounded a corner alongside a shed full of cows, an odd thing to see in Japan. I crossed a bridge, skirted a waterfall, turned another corner, and suddenly was out of the pass, standing on a sunlit hillside.

Between the shifting leaves I caught glimpses of a valley far below. It was hugged by forested hills and carpeted with glistening paddy fields, with thatched roofed farmhouses tucked into the folds of the hills. A child's voice floated up through the silence.

It felt warm and welcoming, like a homecoming. One of Bashō's haiku drifted through my mind:

uma ni nete
zammu tsuki tōshi
cha no kemuri

Dozing on horseback:
Lingering dreams, distant moon,
Smoke of breakfast tea.

Nearly thirty-five years have passed since that day.

I first encountered Bashō in the Penguin *Anthology of Japanese Literature* when I was just becoming interested in Japan. I was captivated by him and by his marvellous haiku, seventeen-syllable poems that capture a mood or a feeling or an experience in a Zen-like flash and imbue it with clarity, wit, and wry humour. There are always two parts — a statement and a punchline — with a word that communicates the season. Bashō perfected the form. His haiku can be profound and moving or playful and humorous — or all of these at once.

Now that I was hooked on Japan there was no going back. I had to find a way to live there. Early in my stay I was invited to the small town of Iga Ueno by a family who thought their young sons would benefit from rubbing shoulders with a foreigner, a rare beast in those days. Iga Ueno was where Bashō had been born. I was thrilled when they took me to see his little house with its clay walls, wooden door, and latticed window. In the garden someone had planted a banana tree, a *bashō*, his favourite tree, from which he took his pen name, Bashō.

Iga Ueno is also famous for its spectacular rough-hewn pottery and as the home of the ninja, the famous spies of Edo times. There are those who say that Bashō too was a ninja, which is why he was able to travel so fast and so far, and that the secret purpose of his travels was to report back on the most far-flung parts of the country.

There are many reasons to travel. Some people are born with the itch to be up and off, to see what's across the horizon. As Bashō wrote:

tabibito to
waga no yobaren
hatsu shigure

"Traveller" —
Let that be my name.
First rains of winter.

I too suffer from that restlessness. After five years in Japan I
ended up back in England. But there was something nagging at
me, something left undone. I'd always wanted to follow Bashō's
footsteps, tread the ground he had trodden, see the places that
inspired his haiku. I'd never been to the north country and wondered what I would find.

Back then it was long before earthquake, tsunami, and nuclear
disaster had carved the name Fukushima into everyone's conscious-
ness and made us all aware of Japan's north country. In those days
no one went to Tohoku. There was nothing there, nothing to see,
no reason to go there, or so people said. It was poor, that was all.

The same had been said in Bashō's day, three centuries before.
As far as he was concerned, he was venturing into wild, dangerous
country. "Though the hardships of the journey will pile up snowy
hairs on my head, I will see with my own eyes remote places of
which I have only heard. I cannot even be certain that I will return
alive," he wrote as he set off on a journey he was to chronicle in
the last of his great travel diaries, *Oku no Hosomichi,* most famously
known in English as *The Narrow Road to the Deep North.*

At forty-five, Bashō was an old man and didn't expect to live
much longer. But he was also determined. Nothing was going to

stop him from traveling. He wanted to go everywhere and see and experience everything.

yase sune mo
areba zo hana no
Yoshino yama

Thin shanks! Still,
While I have them — blossoms
Of Mount Yoshino.

So he wrote at the start of another earlier intrepid journey.

Bashō was a hugely celebrated poet with a coterie of disciples and admirers around the country, and he had only recently returned from his previous travels. But he couldn't resist the call of the road. "The spring mist filled the sky," he wrote, "and in spite of myself the gods filled my heart with a yearning to cross the Shirakawa Barrier."

He set off from his modest home in Edo, now Tokyo, with his traveling companion and assistant, a budding poet called Kawai Sora. In those days wheeled vehicles were banned except for transporting goods. Travel was on foot or horseback and often perilous. It took the two of them nearly a month to reach the legendary Shirakawa Barrier, where travellers crossed from the civilized south to the untamed north. Today Shirakawa is on the bullet train line just over an hour north of Tokyo, heading for Fukushima.

For Bashō, his was not just a journey through time and space. Every stone, every place on the road was overlain with layer upon layer of history, poetry, and legend. As he travelled he passed places that had inspired poets of old, saw ruins that evoked the distant past, and presided over gatherings of local poets to compose linked verse. He wrote of the flowers and trees and landscapes he saw, and of the people he encountered along the way, weaving the prose account of his travels and experiences together with the haiku they inspired in a poetic tapestry.

When he crossed the barrier at Shirakawa he felt his journey had begun at last. He composed a haiku to mark the moment:

fūryū-no
hajime ya oku no
ta-ue uta

Culture's beginning:
Rice-planting song
Of the far north.

Three hundred years later, I too arrived at the barrier at Shirakawa. In Bashō's day it had been a bustling place staffed by intimidating guards who checked travellers' papers and, armed with hooks on long poles, grabbed them by the obi if they tried to sneak through. Nevertheless, as you stepped through you couldn't help feeling the bracing air of the north country, that exhilarating sense of barriers lifting, of the nets of constraints imposed by civilisation falling away. As Bashō crossed the famous barrier, he wrote that he felt as if he were seeing it through the eyes of all the poets who had passed through before him. He could almost hear the murmur of their voices as he remembered the poem that each had written.

By the time I arrived, there was nothing but a moss-covered stone pillar, half hidden in grass. But I couldn't help sensing that link with ancient times, that feeling of eras colliding, of the gap of time between us collapsing. It sent a shiver down my spine. Bashō had stood here and seen this and now I stood on the same soil and saw this same stone.

And so both our journeys began.

Bashō and Sora meet the mountain guide who led them across the high pass that led to the remote North Country. One of Yosa Buson's illustrations to The Narrow Road to the Deep North, *painted around 1778 (Kyoto National Museum)*

From the Shirakawa Barrier, Bashō travelled north, stopping to admire the rubbing stone of Shinobu and visit the temple that houses the great sword of Yoshitsune and the satchel of Benkei, in reality a huge wooden box. For he too was on a poetic pilgrimage. While I was following in his footsteps, he was following the footsteps of Japan's great twelfth-century hero, Yoshitsune, who had travelled that same road though in the opposite direction in 1189, exactly five hundred years before Bashō. First of all Yoshitsune, then Bashō, brought fame and resonance to these small obscure towns where the hero's relics are treasured and his exploits remembered and where everyone can recite the haiku Bashō wrote there.

North of Sendai, Bashō stopped to admire the legendary beauty of Matsushima, a glorious inlet where pine-clad islands dot the bay and which fortunately survived the Fukushima disaster. He was too lost for words even to compose a haiku. A few days later he and Sora got completely lost and ended up following a rough track "fit only for hunters or woodcutters." It was late at night by the time they arrived at the grim port town of Ishinomaki, where hundreds of cargo ships jostled in the harbor and smoke poured from the chimneys of all the furnaces. They "looked around for lodgings, but there was no one who would rent us a room. Finally we spent the night in a miserable little hut and as soon as it was light set off again on our confused wanderings along unknown roads."

But this whole colourful adventure, it turned out, was a piece of poetic license.

Sora kept his own diary, written not in poetic *kanji* characters but in the down-to-earth *katakana* alphabet. Every day he recorded the weather and what they ate. His prosaic account differed in many crucial respects from Bashō's. He wrote cheerfully in his guileless way that Ishinomaki was on their itinerary all along and they stayed at an excellent inn there. Travel writing involves creation and artistry, and Bashō was not averse to massaging the truth for the sake of a good story.

There was one place in particular that Bashō was eager to see: Hiraizumi, where Yoshitsune had holed up with a mere eight followers in the castle while an army of twenty thousand massed outside, charged with delivering his head. His retainer, the giant Benkei, a sort of Little John, single-handedly held them off long enough for Yoshitsune to commit honourable suicide (or, if the legend is to be believed, to escape to Mongolia, where he became Genghis

Khan). It's an event as resonant with history as the beheading of Charles I or Bonnie Prince Charlie's escape to Skye.

But when Bashō arrived five hundred years later, there was nothing but a hillside covered in grass. He sat down on his bamboo hat and wept. He recorded the moment in a haiku:

natsu gusa ya
tsuwamono domo ga
yumei no ato.

Summer grasses —
All that remains of
Mighty warriors' dreams.

It was this haiku with its thrilling drumbeat of syllables, akin to Anglo-Saxon poetry, and its sombre mood, its reminder that all things shall pass, that first spurred me to make this journey in his footsteps. Now I too sat on the hillside and gazed at the bend in the river where Benkei had stood, bristling like a porcupine with all the arrows that the enemy had shot into him, keeping his feet long enough for Yoshitsune to complete his suicide.

And from there like Bashō I turned inland into the hills until one day I found myself at the head of a pass, looking down into a beautiful unspoiled valley.

I gazed and gazed, unwilling to break the spell. When I finally set off down the hillside, I began to notice that close up the houses weren't so idyllic. They were all a bit more run down and shabby than when seen from a distance. Those that had thatched roofs by some inexorable logic had corrugated iron walls, and those with wooden walls had garish red- or blue-tiled roofs. But it was still a lovely unspoiled place, a tiny piece of Bashō's world.

On an impulse I dropped into the village store and asked the woman there if there was anywhere I could stay.

She didn't seem to notice my foreignness. "Somewhere to stay? See the headman," she said, or words to that effect; her accent was so strong it was almost impossible to understand her.

I found the headman up a ladder repairing the thatch on a rambling old house. He scrambled down, beaming at the arrival of a newcomer. He was small and cheery, with a crumpled face and bristly gray eyebrows permanently raised in an expression of good-natured bewilderment.

"I'm Kuroda," he introduced himself, revealing a huge hole in his front tooth. "We're all Kuroda here — those that aren't Hayashi, that is."

He insisted I go in, meet his wife, have tea. When the pleasantries were over, I made my request. Might it be possible to stay? Was there perhaps a *minshuku* (bed and breakfast) in the village or a family I could stay with?

As he'd been talking I'd been thinking. "If possible," I said, "I'd like to stay four days."

"Four days?" He gaped in disbelief. "You want to stay four days? But what for? There's nothing here. Of course, if you want to stay…."

Once we'd established that I definitely wanted to stay, unlikely though that was, he showed me round the village. The hillside stretched away, sculpted into shallow steps packed with rice plants that rippled gently in the breeze. Half hidden behind clumps of trees was a row of brown thatched houses. It was like a scene from an old ink painting, as near paradise as I was ever likely to see.

* * *

Kuroda-san, the good-natured old headman, arranged for me to stay with a widow who had plenty of space and needed a little extra cash. I had the empty upstairs room while the family slept downstairs in the normal way.

As I woke next morning, I smelled wood smoke — "smoke of breakfast tea" — and wondered if I was still dreaming. Sunlight dappled the tatami. I slid open the window. Outside were the misty hills and terraced paddy fields, much as they must have been in Bashō's time. Frogs croaked and water gushed.

Kojirō, my new home, was an imposing farmhouse with gables and a broad thatched roof. Wedged between the house and the hillside was a pond crowded with black trout. Water spouted into it through a bamboo pipe, then gushed out the far end and ran down the hillside through tiers of vegetable and flower beds into the network of channels that fed the rice fields in the valley.

"Look at the size of these," said my hostess, holding up three thick celery-like stalks. "Found them up in the woods on Mount Hayama. Big, eh? I'll cook them for you for dinner." She showed me the stalks she had collected, heaped on bamboo trays. "*Fuki*," she said. I looked it up: butterbur, coltsfoot.

She and I took to each other immediately. She was a strong, handsome woman with a broad face and sculpted cheekbones, a tiny nose, and huge welcoming smile. I knew immediately what to call her: *Okaasan*, Mother. She had a big hearty laugh, not the cramped, nervous giggle of a city woman. But her speech was barely comprehensible, a succession of barbarous sounds that scarcely resembled Japanese at all. I listened hard, trying to pair her syllables with standard Japanese so I could work out the sound changes.

While I ate breakfast she was busy on the telephone. There were two: one standard and one for local calls, which were free. The local phone played music night and morning and broadcast information about village events. "Wake up, wake up," it scolded in the morning. "Time to get up and sweep the road and clean the drainage channels!"

Okaasan wasn't clear quite where I came from. I overheard her telling people I was from the Philippines, Australia, Ethiopia, Italy. It didn't really matter. I was *yoso no hito*, an outsider, not much stranger than the people from the village across the next pass, on the other side of the mountains. Okaasan herself had never been further afield than a village a few miles away.

None of the villagers had ever met a foreigner before, and Okaasan was anxious to show me off. I was equally anxious to meet them. First she gave me a pair of her plastic outdoor sandals, several sizes too small. Then we shuffled off, shoving open doors, barging in, yelling *"O! O! O-sewa-sama-su!"*, which literally translates as "Thanks for taking care of us," though it feels more like, "Hey! Anyone in?"

The old man next door had a wasp's nest in his entranceway and bunches of dried herbs hanging over an ancient wood-burning stove. In the alcove was an extraordinary clutter: a stuffed badger on its hind legs, wearing a doll-sized cap and apron; a stuffed grouse; the seven gods of good fortune; two bonsai trees the old man had grown himself; colourful dolls in glass cases that one son had brought back from Okinawa; and a wooden bear that another son had brought from Hokkaido.

"Four sons and two daughters," he said wistfully. "All gone to Tokyo."

Last year the second son had come to visit, bringing the grandchildren with him. This year no one had come. The two old people sat alone in their big thatched house.

I listened to their tales of bear-hunting and eating bear meat, of silkworm-keeping, the rice harvest, the winter snows — "boars rooting up the rice shoots, plagues of rabbits in the bean fields." Here among these people I fancied I was in a world that Bashō would have recognized.

Back home we started preparing dinner. Okaasan's son sat at the low table in the living room watching television, a glass in his big carpenter's hand.

"Oi!" he shouted every now and then. "Saké!"

His wife would creep out from the kitchen with an enormous bottle and refill his glass. She never spoke and kept her eyes averted. She looked less than twenty. It was hard to believe she had been married ten years.

Kuroda-san told me their story. When his father died, the son brought home a bride. No one ever spoke of getting married. It was always "bringing home a bride" or "coming as a bride". But in ten years they had still not had children. That I knew was a tragedy, not in personal terms — that was irrelevant — but for the "house," the family. No children meant the end of the family line — no one to till the family fields, no one to tend the ancestors' graves and make offerings to them.

"No one knows whose side the fault is on," Kuroda-san said, hissing through his teeth and shaking his head.

* * *

In the end I stayed many more than four days at Yamanoshita, the village under the mountain. I came to love these people and for years afterward went back to visit whenever I was in Japan.

The first time I went back, I took careful note of the paddy fields in the neighbouring villages as I passed through. I knew the villagers would want to know how the harvest was progressing on the other side of the mountain. I thought it best not to mention

England. I didn't want to remind them of my foreignness, as if I had been home to Mars.

For a while after I arrived, Okaasan said nothing about where I'd been or the fact I'd been away. Then, once I'd settled in, instead of asking about the harvest as I was expecting, she said, "I've been watching the news all year, keeping an eye on what's going on in England. We all want to make sure you're okay. There's that Mrs. Thatcher, isn't there?" I was touched that she cared about me and half pleased, half sorry that I had opened her eyes to the outside world.

A couple of years after that she had stunning news to tell me. The sad daughter-in-law was sad no longer. She had had a little boy, Yoshi, the apple of everyone's eye. I was thrilled to meet him and dandle him on my knee. Okaasan was ecstatic. Now the daughter-in-law was in charge of the house and Okaasan was the matriarch.

Yet more years later the phone rang one day in the room in Tokyo that I was renting.

"Lizlee-san," came the familiar northern vowels. A house had come empty in the village, they said. Would I like to buy it?

Once again I took the train up to the north country. The path through the hills had become a road, and there was a bus now that stopped outside the village store. Everyone was there to meet me. Once I'd settled in we went to see the house. It seemed the old lady who owned it had lived there alone. Her whole family had moved to Tokyo and these days never came back. No one wanted it. If I didn't buy it, it would be torn down, which everyone agreed would be a terrible shame.

It was a small thatched house with corrugated iron walls and an outside toilet that even the villagers conceded was not the most salubrious. It was very cheap, about £2000 in 1990s' English currency. But I didn't have that sort of money. And even though the villagers assured me that they would take care of it when I wasn't there and would sweep the snow off the roof in winter, it would still have cost a fortune to make it habitable.

Most damning of all, it was below the road, just above the river. It would have been damp. So in the end, reluctantly, I decided not to put down roots in Yamanoshita, the village under the mountain.

* * *

Bashō's path led to the river Mogami, where I took a boat — not a rice boat, as Bashō had, but a tourist boat. The boats for transporting rice had gone out of use almost a hundred years before I set out on my journey. Summer was reaching its end, but the weather was still hot and humid.

We docked at the nondescript town of Karikawa, midway between the mountains that form the central spine of the northern provinces and the Japan Sea. From there the route led across an endless plain of rice fields toward the hills on the distant horizon, where a vast red-painted *torii* gate straddled the road, marking the crossing point onto holy ground.

And so I arrived at the Three Mountains of Dewa, the spiritual heart of the north. Visiting the shrines on these mountains was the culmination of Bashō and Sora's journey.

Mount Haguro is the gateway, the most accessible of the three. I crossed a curved stone bridge and passed a wooden pagoda encrusted with moss. From there 2,446 rough stone steps wound up through a forest of cedars, the trunks soaring upward like the columns of a cathedral. The oldest was a thousand years old, according to a plaque attached to its trunk. Looped around it was a rope hung with folded pieces of mulberry paper, marking it as sacred.

The tree was already old when Bashō passed through:

kono sugi no
mibaeseshi yo ya
kami no aki

In that age
This cedar was a seedling:
Autumn of the gods.

When I finally panted my way to the top, I found a vast complex of temples surrounding a large pond — the dragon pond. Dominating them all was a gigantic Shinto shrine with a thatched and gabled roof that towered above the cedars. White-clad priests flitted about, tiny against the dark recesses behind.

When Bashō was here, *yamabushi* — "mountain priests" — lived in caves in the mountainside and in the village at the foot of the mountain. Here they performed the mysterious rites and practices of Shugendō, a tantric Buddhist sect. Haguro was one of four yamabushi centres where acolytes were initiated into mysteries and secret rites. Pilgrims came in the thousands to worship the mountain and absorb its sacred spirit.

Bashō was deeply impressed: "Cloisters stretch row upon row where devotees carry out the Shugendō disciplines with immense zeal. The power of their austerities makes this a holy mountain and a sacred place, which fills men with admiration and awe. The wonders of this mountain are beyond measure: surely its prosperity will last forever!"

I didn't expect to find yamabushi in modern Japan. But as I strolled across the top, two crossed my path, leading a group of white-clad pilgrims. One was young, the other old and grizzled.

They strutted along on high wooden *geta* clogs, in baggy bloomers gathered at the knee. They were dressed in flowing black and white blouses, wore small black hats like miners' lamps tied to their foreheads, and carried a staff and an enormous conch shell under their arms. Both had mirrors hanging on their backs.

"Evening," said the younger one with a grin and nod. He was as brawny as a young sumo wrestler, with a beaming round face full of humour and a head shaved as smooth as an egg. He invited me to stay at the pilgrim lodge he ran in the village — the very village where the yamabushi had lived in Bashō's time.

Gassan is the second of the three mountains. The name means Moon Mountain. From inland it curves above the surrounding mountains like the full moon; but from the sea it is wild and forbidding, a formidable barrier protecting the third mountain, Yudono. Anyone that wants to worship at the inner shrine at Mount Yudono has no choice but to battle up Gassan's rugged slopes.

"On the eighth we climbed Gassan," Bashō wrote. "Hanging necklaces of white mulberry paper on our bodies and wrapping our heads in bleached cotton hoods, we followed a Strong One, a mountain guide, up onto the mountain." They climbed "through cloud and mist, over ice and snow, until we thought we must have crossed the barrier of the clouds and were treading the very path of the sun and moon." It took all day. That night they bedded down at the top.

I climbed Gassan with a group of pilgrims, all of us dressed in white robes with mulberry ropes around our necks and bells tied to our waists. We left before dawn and climbed in a long line, clothes flapping in the wind, bells tinkling.

Very little can have changed on this bleak mountain since Bashō's time. We walked on boards across sodden heathland, then climbed higher and higher. Patches of snow glistened in the hollows. It was silent, too high for cicadas. We clambered through a barren moon landscape of volcanic rocks scattered across the mountainside, some as big as houses, other smaller ones lovingly piled into heaps. At the foot of some, people had left coins and small images. Way below us wisps of cloud drifted.

Finally we arrived at a small grey building on the peak of a pyramid-shaped hillock six and a half thousand feet above the rice plains, surrounded by high black walls to protect it against the weight of the winter snows: Gassan shrine. We stood heads bowed, hands together, and chanted in unison. The sound of our voices hung for a moment in the still mountain air, and the tiny bells that hung from our belts tinkled faintly. A coil of smoke spiralled upward from the incense cauldron.

Standing on the summit of Gassan I congratulated myself that the journey was over. But the worst was still to come. There was still the descent to Yudono. We plunged down a staircase of massive boulders, scrambling from rock to rock, slipping and sliding across the shale. After two hours, the landscape was no longer alpine but tropical. As we scrambled across the rocks we pushed through bamboo and camellia thickets and thick ferns crowding across the path. The clouds had cleared and the sun shone fiercely out of a blue sky.

Around a corner the path came to an abrupt end. A cluster of pilgrims lined up to start down the first of what turned out to be a series of long rusty iron ladders, fixed precariously into the rocks. I hung above the void, feeling blindly for the next rung, gripping the sides of the ladder until my knuckles were white.

Pilgrims are forbidden to reveal what they see at the holy shrine at Mount Yudono. I approached the shrine with excitement. It was not my religion, it was not my god. But I was eager to see this mysterious and holy place. A priest swished a wand of mulberry papers above our heads to purify us. Then we took our shoes off and washed our feet and in silence passed one by one through the stone gateway and into the inner shrine.

Bashō wrote only a haiku, nothing else:

katararenu
Yudono ni nurasu
tamoto kana

Yudono
Of which I may not speak
Wets my sleeve with tears.

With that, he added, "I stop my brush."
And I too stop mine.

* * *

Bashō completed his masterpiece four years after making his momentous journey. He died the following year. On his deathbed he dictated his farewell haiku:

tabi ni yande
yume wa kareno o
kakemuguru

Ill on a journey,
My dreams wander on
Across withered fields.

About the Author

Lesley Downer is an English author, journalist, and historian who has lived on and off in Japan for about fifteen years. Her books on Japan include *On the Narrow Road to the Deep North*; *The Brothers*; *Geisha: The Secret History of a Vanishing World*; *Madame Sadayakko: The Geisha who Seduced the West*; and *The Shogun Quartet*, four novels set in nineteenth-century Japan.

18

The Wrong Way Round Hokkaido

By Tom Gibb

We finish our long traverse of Japan in the northernmost and largest prefecture. Hokkaido accounts for 22 percent of Japan's land area but just 5 percent of its population, which translates into wide-open spaces and lightly trodden wilderness. The human stamp on the land is more recent here too — you won't find ancient temples or shrines — as it was only in the late nineteenth century that this frontier area came under full Japanese control, a colonization that brought settlers and development, and forced assimilation for the indigenous Ainu people.

Hokkaido's winter charms attract tourists to Sapporo's annual Yuki Matsuri (snow festival) and sports enthusiasts to its ski resorts. It's during the comfortable summer months, however, when most visitors come, especially hikers and cyclists. In this chapter, Tom Gibb, whom we met earlier in his adopted home of Ibaraki, takes us on a summertime cycling circumnavigation of the island.

* * *

CYCLISTS in Japan are spoiled. We can ride on the pavement or on the wrong side of the road; and even when we are not riding, our bicycles are unlikely to be vandalised, stolen, or stripped of their parts. The roads themselves are well maintained, and when in need of sustenance we are never far from a vending machine or a convenience store.

Perhaps appropriately as it sits at the top of the archipelago, it is not too much of an exaggeration to call Hokkaido cycling heaven in an already cyclist-friendly nation. At least in summer, thousands converge on the island to explore it by pedal power.

My sojourn in cycling heaven came in 2008, and my trusty steed for the summer was a cross bike with the thoroughly uninspiring name of Transeo 4.0 GT 7005 City Cross Design. In order to make it seem a little more companionable I attached a mascot to the handlebars. In Japanese, the word for "frog" and the verb "to go home" are both pronounced *kaeru*, so this hundred-yen-shop plastic frog — which if you squeezed it made a squeaky honk — was my *buji-kaeru* ("safe frog" or "safe return"), a play on words and a lucky charm in one.

Having caught the Sunflower Ferry overnight from Ōarai in Ibaraki Prefecture, at Tomakomai ferry terminal I turned right and, for no other reason than it felt like a good idea at the time, set off in an anti-clockwise direction around Hokkaido.

In the countryside beyond Tomakomai's American-style grid of city blocks, wild deer flashed their fluffy white backsides as they scampered into the woods, and the roads were lined with windbreaks like big Venetian blinds, the slats in which can be adjusted to prevent snow drifts. Much of the island is snowbound for around five months of the year, so there were also pole-mounted arrows at the same height as streetlights to indicate the edge of the road, and on inclines grooves cut into the tarmac to prevent tyres from slipping.

Soon I began to pass pebble beds on which *konbu* (kelp) was being laid out to dry. Although less well known outside Japan than *nori* (paper-thin sheets of crispy, dark-green *nori* are used as the wrapping for rolled sushi) and *wakame* (a common ingredient in miso soup), konbu is probably the most palatable variety of seaweed for the uninitiated Westerner. Among other things it is used in *osechi* (a selection of semi-sweet appetisers eaten on New Year's Day), in *oden* (a peculiarly Japanese winter warmer consisting of fish cakes, vegetables, and eggs simmered in a light soup stock and garnished with mustard), and on its own as a simple side dish called *konbu-no-tsukudani.*

At the turn of the last century Kikunae Ikeda, a professor at Tokyo University, had for a long time wondered why his wife's homemade konbu soup tasted so delicious. One day in 1907 he sent her to buy as much konbu as she could find; upon her return, the two of them set about boiling and chopping up an incredible thirty-eight kilogrammes of the stuff. From this, Ikeda extracted just thirty grammes of *ajinomoto* (the "origin of flavour"), also known as monosodium glutamate. An acquaintance of Ikeda's built a hugely successful food business around *ajinomoto*, and by the name *umami* it has been added to the very short list of funda-mental flavours recognisable to the human palate (the other four being, as everyone knows, vanilla, strawberry, mint chocolate chip, and butter pecan).

Almost all of the konbu in Japan that is not farmed comes from Hokkaido, and along this stretch of coastline the harvest was in full swing. Its long, dark strands are picked either from small boats or by wading into the shallows at low tide, although if konbu is left on its pebble bed for more than a few hours it can become brittle, so it is then moved indoors for the flavour to mature, in some cases for up to a decade.

As I was leaving a public bath near Cape Erimo, which is the southeasternmost point in Hokkaido, a konbu farmer came over to say hello.

"Can you speak Japanese?" asked Mr. Village Middle (at the time I had only a rudimentary grasp of Japanese conversation and am almost certainly misquoting the people I met, so in order to maintain their anonymity they shall be referred to by literal translations of their names).

"Yes," I replied.

"And what are you up to now?"

"I'm going to the campsite."

"You mean you're going to put up your tent in the dark?"

"I suppose so."

"Not anymore, you're not," he said. "Come over to my place."

I have on several occasions been invited to stay at strangers' houses while on cycling tours, and this tends to happen after we have at least become acquainted in a restaurant or while sightseeing. Mr. Village Middle, however, did not appear to be bothered by such trifling matters as who I was, where I was from, and whether or not I would steal his wallet and do a runner.

"I can only fit two in the front, so you'll have to sit with your bike," he said, and enlisted the help of a friend to lift it onto the flatbed of his truck. We then headed north for a few kilometres, and I could hear their muffled chatter from the front seat as I gripped

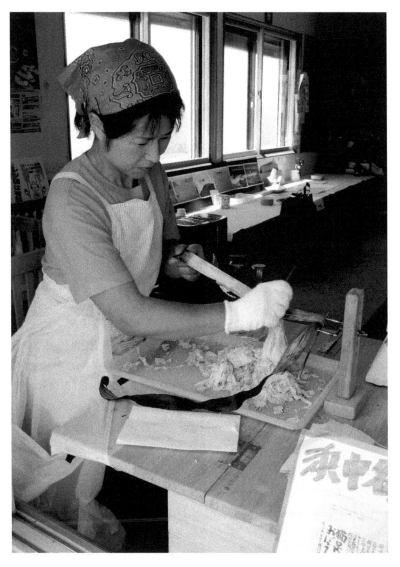

Konbu being grated at a roadside souvenir shop

the side of the truck and watched the red glow of its rear lights
on the road behind us.

Mr. Village Middle's house appeared to be very much that of a single man: the living room was used as a storage area for work clothes and old furniture; I saw at least one cockroach scuttle across the floor; and everything was tobacco stained and slightly sticky. Our evening meal, too, was suitably masculine, consisting as it did of rice, instant ramen, and fried meat (the latter was so tough that I could not tell exactly what kind of meat, and this did not seem to be the time to mention that I was a pescatarian).

On the television, a boxing match had just been won by the Japanese flyweight Daisuke Naitō.

"Naitō's from Hokkaido, you know," explained Mr. Village Middle with obvious pride. "He was brought up by his mum and he used to get bullied at school, but look at him now — that's his fourth world title."

Tall and well-built with craggy features and a mop of jet-black hair, if Mr. Village Middle was a boxer he would have been a heavyweight, although I could not help noticing that part of the little finger on his left hand was missing. Cutting one's little finger off is a common form of penance for members of the yakuza (more commonly referred to as *bōryokudan* or "violence group").

During the course of the evening, Mr. Village Middle mentioned that in his younger days he had travelled the world on a tuna fishing trawler. Because working on one is so hazardous — even if you do not get swept overboard, the possibility of serious injury is ever present — the wages are high: when the economy was booming in the eighties as much as ten million yen a year, although nowadays around half that is the norm. You are also stuck on board for months on end, with no means of escape should you decide the work does not suit you, or become so chronically seasick that you cannot fulfil your duties in the first place. Many such trawlers are owned by the yakuza, who take advantage of this by employing people who have fallen behind on their loan repayments. With few opportunities to spend money en route, such forced labourers ought to look forward to receiving a hefty wad of cash at the end of their contracts, but instead their earnings go straight to the loan shark, while they emerge from the experience in financial parity and a few credits closer to graduating from the school of hard knocks.

Not that I had the courage to ask him about it, but as far as I could tell Mr. Village Middle's shady past was just that, as nowadays he combined summers farming konbu with winter work as a truck driver — at least I think that's what he said, as Mr. Village Middle and his friend used only the crudest form of Japanese possible.

To give you an example, if you are talking to someone of a higher status, or who in the context of the conversation should be treated with a degree of respect, you might say something like, *"Nanika, meshi-agarimasen ka?"* ("Won't you do me the honour of eating something?")

Or if you wanted to be reasonably polite without going over the top, you could say, *"Nanika, tabemasen ka?"* ("Won't you have something to eat?")

If you were with friends or family you could be more familiar: *"Nanika, tabenai?"* ("Fancy some food?")

My host for this evening, though, asked, *"Meshi, ku'u?"* ("You gonna scoff some grub?")

In fact, I did not catch on at first when Mr. Village Middle's friend announced that he was leaving, which left me alone, in an isolated house, in the middle of the night, with only a possible ex-gangster for company. And at least one cockroach.

* * *

The next extremity on my circumnavigation of Hokkaido was to be Cape Nosappu to the northeast, heading for which would first take me along a thirty-three-kilometre stretch of Route 336 better known as the *Ōgon Dōro* (Gold Road).

The Gold Road was completed in 1934 and connects Erimo Town with Hiro'o Town. It took seven years to build and earned its nickname because of the astronomical construction costs, which rose even further when it was first tarmacked in 1960; this set the authorities back 900 million yen per kilometre, or ten times the going rate. Even now the Gold Road is still consuming cash: as I rode along it, the cliffs up above were being reinforced and workers abseiled between a network of scaffolding walkways, their safety ropes disappearing into the mist. Work had also commenced on the Erimo-Ōgon Tunnel, which at almost five kilometres was to be the longest road tunnel in Hokkaido.

While the majority of roads on the island are wide, comparatively traffic-free, and come with the added bonus of attractive views, particularly on the coast you will pass through countless such tunnels. These are hazardous for cycling because with a few notable exceptions they are narrow, poorly lit, and often devoid of a walkway. Even if they do come equipped with the latter, it will more often than not barely be wide enough to ride along, so high that should you veer off the edge your front wheel may buckle from the impact, and lined with SOS telephones that protrude from the wall just that little bit too far to pass them comfortably. Not only that, but the gutters you negotiate instead will be awash with a sludgy cocktail of drain water and engine oil. At the entrances and exits to tunnels on the Gold Road, you will therefore find boxes containing reflective wristbands, which can be borrowed by cyclists to make us more visible and less likely to be brained by a wing mirror.

Further up the coast and beyond the Gold Road I stayed at my first rider house. While not exclusive to the island, most of these are located in Hokkaido and primarily frequented by motorcyclists, although they enable anyone to sleep indoors without paying much for the privilege. Rider houses employ a variety of dining, sleeping, and bathing arrangements, and over the summer I stayed at one that metamorphosed into a karaoke bar after dark, another where guests were packed in like the proverbial sardines (perhaps dreaming about his wife, during the night the man in the next futon snuggled up to put his arm around me), and another whose bath was a so-called *goemon-buro* (essentially a big cooking pot with a fire underneath that in days gone by was also used as an instrument of torture).

Forlorn in the gloomy weather, the village of Chokubetsu consisted of little more than a few dilapidated buildings next to a disused railway station. I found the entrance to its rider house — named Mickey House, presumably to create an aura of Disney-like charm — hidden away across an overgrown back garden and through an unmarked side door, although the welcome within could not have been in greater contrast to the bleakness outside.

The proprietor of Mickey House was an old woman the guests referred to as "Mum." She showed me how to use the washing machine, introduced the other guests, and did not mind us tramping through her kitchen and lounge to use the bath. As I was unpacking, Mum said that when she was much younger, she would often complete a twenty-kilometre round trip with forty kilos of rice on the back of her bicycle, which made me feel a bit of a wuss for loading the Transeo 4.0 GT 7005 City Cross Design with just ten kilos of clothes and camping gear.

Because they open only in summer, many rider houses are run as side businesses, and the main attraction at Mickey House was Genghis Khan. No, not the genocidal Mongolian warlord, but a dish that for largely obscure reasons is named after him and was served in the adjoining restaurant.

Genghis Khan is lamb barbecued on a cast iron convex grill: while the meat cooks on top, its juices collect around the side to baste the accompanying vegetables. Lamb has never been a common source of protein in Japan, and sheep were initially farmed for their wool, which in the early twentieth century was used to make winter clothing for workers constructing the rail network (the Nemuro Line that no longer stops at Chokubetsu Station, for instance). But in the early 1930s, Japanese soldiers acquired a taste for lamb during the invasion of Manchuria, and Genghis Khan was reborn in his culinary incarnation upon their return to Japan.

Another of the guests, Mr. Middle Field, was in Hokkaido for his twelfth summer in a row. This year he was travelling not by motorbike but by car with his wife and baby daughter. Because Genghis Khan is cooked at your table and several people were smoking — not so much the cyclists as some leather-clad Harley enthusiasts who turned up later in the evening — it was not the ideal environment for a one-year-old, and I was awoken several times in the night by the sound of her crying.

Over breakfast the next morning Mr. Middle Field apologised, saying that in the end he had taken his daughter for a drive to quieten her down. "I think staying in an unusual place spooked her," he said, although it was just as likely to have been the lingering aroma of cigarette smoke and barbecued meat.

* * *

The roads around Cape Nosappu were mercifully tunnel-free, and after a week and a half on the coast it was something of a jolt to then be confronted with my first proper hill, in the shape of the 738-metre Shiretoko Pass. This particular section of Route 334 ought to be called the Platinum Road, as it took a full decade longer than the Gold Road to complete. It is the only national route in Hokkaido to close in winter due to the weather, and when reopened in April has to be cleared with snow ploughs, which leave white walls as much as ten metres high on either side. Even in mid-summer there was a noticeable difference in temperature between sea level and the upper slopes, but looking across the Sea of Okhotsk towards the Kuril Islands and inland towards Mount Rausu more than compensated for the steepness of the climb.

On the far side of the pass at the Shiretoko Nature Centre, bears — that essential topic for anyone coming to Hokkaido — were very much the dominant theme.

Around ten thousand *higuma* (brown bears) live in Hokkaido; and while the brown bear is smaller and less fearsome than, say, the grizzly, a full-size specimen can still weigh up to half a ton. It may surprise you to learn that its diet is 90 percent vegetarian, although as well as wild salmon, the other 10 percent does occasionally include domesticated human. Not only that, but a brown bear can run at up to 50 kph, which meant that even downhill and with a following wind, I would barely be able to out-pedal one on the Transeo (a freewheeling descent is the cyclist's reward for completing a climb, and on my way down from the Shiretoko Pass I clocked a new top speed for the trip of 53 kph).

As well as bear bells to warn unsuspecting bears of your presence, and bear spray — a kind of long-range, super-strength pepper spray — to ward them off in case they did not hear your bear bell, the souvenir shop at the nature centre sold bear candy, bear fridge magnets, bear warning signs, bear T-shirts, and even bear-in-a-can, which an assistant confirmed really was edible ... and accompanied with soy sauce and mushrooms.

That summer I met several people who had come face-to-face with a bear and survived to tell the tale. But the best way to observe one from a safe distance is by boarding one of the sightseeing boats that depart toward Shiretoko-misaki (Cape Shiretoko), which was the next goal on my trip.

The Shiretoko Peninsula is both a national park and a World Heritage site, and apart from the occasional jetty, log cabin, or dirt track is almost entirely untouched. Its ridge of 1500-metre-high peaks, and its forests, cliffs, and waterfalls, are truly awe inspiring. Some of the latter are even geothermal; that night I stayed at Iwaobetsu Youth Hostel, whose toilets were of the primitive, composting variety, but where the bath and shower taps ran with naturally hot water twenty-four hours a day.

On its return from the cape, our boat navigated to within a couple of hundred metres of the shore, where, sure enough, there was a family of bears scavenging for food. Even when photographed at the far end of a long lens they were no more than small brown blobs blending into a background of rocks and trees. Thankfully, that was as close as I came to a bear the entire time I was in Hokkaido.

* * *

From Shiretoko I detoured inland towards Lake Kussharo, views of which are renowned as some of the most beautiful on the island. The air temperature that night was forecast to fall below ten degrees Celsius, and after erecting my tent at a campsite near Kussharo's southern end I went for a hot meal at a ramen noodle restaurant.

"I was just about to close for the night," said Mrs. Bamboo Child, the smiling, white-haired old lady behind the counter, who began to tell me her life story almost as soon as I had taken my seat.

"Most of the families around here are originally from Honshu," she said, referring to the largest of Japan's four main islands. "My father was from Fukushima, and at the time there wasn't even a road — he came up the river in a boat he had made himself. It's too cold to grow rice, so that had to be carried by boat as well."

This difficulty in cultivating rice is one of many factors to have distinguished Hokkaido from the rest of Japan, factors that include a strong foreign influence and the relative prominence of Christianity. Colonisation from the south did not begin in earnest until the late nineteenth century, when the Meiji administration established a government office here and promoted industrial development. But tax reforms and the abolition of the old system of feudal domains encouraged a further influx of migrants, to the extent that at the end of World War II, Hokkaido briefly surpassed Tokyo to become the most populous prefecture in the country.

"My mother had twelve children and lived until she was ninety-two," continued Mrs. Bamboo Child. "And even now ten of us are still alive. I went to school only in winter because we had to work in the fields during the summer, and I left for good when I was in the sixth grade. Eventually I had three children myself, and all of them were born in April — in fact, two of them have the same birthday. Back then everyone did the same thing. If you were pregnant over the summer, you couldn't work, and we deliberately timed it so that our babies were born in spring."

Mrs. Bamboo Child's restaurant was full to the rafters with her collection of mementos, lucky charms, and lanterns, alongside celebrity autographs and handwritten menu items, curled at the

edges and stained brown from exposure to the steam from sim-
mering soup stock.

"It's been twenty-four years since I opened this place," she said.
"I can't walk around much these days because I've got a bad knee,
and my granddaughter helps me out for a couple of hours at lunchtime. We're busy at the moment, but there are no tourists at all
in winter, just locals. Even if people do have machines to do the
farming these days, Hokkaido's still a tough place to live."

Speaking of tough, along with tunnels and being pursued by a
bear that is running at precisely 50 kph, the other sworn enemy
of cyclists in Hokkaido is the wind. Cape Erimo, for instance, is
the windiest place in Japan outside the high mountains, with wind
speeds there exceeding 36 kph almost every day, and in Shiretoko
I had met a fellow Englishman who became so fatigued on his way
down the northeast coast that he packed up his bike and caught
a bus instead.

I would argue that riding into a high wind is harder than riding
up a steep hill, for although the effort involved is about the same,
the nature of it is different. In both cases you use a low gear and
sometimes stand on the pedals for extra leverage; but in contrast
with the meditative, often pleasurable quality of a climb, working
against the wind is supremely frustrating. Why, one thinks as
one struggles onwards, head down and teeth gritted, should it be
such a challenge to ride along a flat road on a fine day? On a climb
your muscles may be straining but your surroundings are calm.
Against a headwind, however, there is no escape: your ears ring
with white noise and your body is pummelled as if by an invisible
boxer. It feels, in fact, a little like those nightmares in which, try
as you might, you cannot run away from something.

That summer's descent from cycling heaven into cycling hell
came on Route 238 towards Cape Sōya, which as the northernmost

point in Japan was my next objective. Dark clouds rolled by after an overnight rainstorm, carrying in their wake a headwind that grew in intensity as the day progressed. Whenever I stopped to eat, to rest, or for what tennis players like to call a "comfort break," I had to cower behind the nearest wall or building to avoid the onslaught. At one point a line of hills provided some shelter, but on the downhill stretch of each the wind was so strong that if I stopped pedalling I remained — as if on an exercise bike — rooted to the spot.

In winter, ice floes reach across La Pérouse Strait to Cape Sōya, and it has become a tradition for a few hundred hardy (or, depending on how you look at it, foolhardy) souls to camp there on New Year's Eve, usually in a blizzard and sub-zero temperatures. The skies were clear enough when I arrived that the Russian island of Sakhalin, some forty kilometres distant, was visible across the strait. But instead of being elated at the achievement of having made it this far I was almost delirious with exhaustion, and even here — especially here, in fact — the wind was relentless.

I left as soon as I could, and the contrast between cycling north into a headwind and south with a tailwind could not have been greater: having covered the previous sixty kilometres in six hours, it took just an hour to cover the thirty to Wakkanai, and along the way I passed — surprise, surprise — one of the largest wind farms in Japan.

* * *

On the long journey down the west coast of Hokkaido I acquired a riding buddy of sorts. Mr. Warehouse was from Okayama Prefecture, and since quitting his job as a motorcycle mechanic three years before had embarked on various adventures, including walking the Shikoku-henro, a 1200-kilometre temple pilgrimage around the smallest of Japan's main islands.

"When I left Okayama in March, there was snow on the mountains," he said, "and I've cycled all the way up the Pacific coast to Hokkaido. Now and then I'll stay somewhere for a while and get a temporary job to make some money. The plan is to arrive home before Christmas."

Mr. Warehouse was younger, fitter, and faster than me — when the opportunity presented itself, he said, he would pop into a clinic and donate blood after a day in the saddle — and it soon became apparent that we would not be able to ride side by side. Instead we met several times over the course of a week or so, sometimes by chance and sometimes by design, and reached Cape Shirakami — Hokkaido's southernmost point — on the same day.

That evening as we sat together in a bus shelter (Hokkaido's bus shelters are luxurious enough to keep passengers warm in winter and to serve as free accommodation for cyclists in summer), Mr. Warehouse told me about his family.

"Back home in Okayama there are seven of us living in the same house," he said. "Me, my grandparents, my mum and dad, my younger sister, and her son."

"How old is your nephew?" I said.

"He's five. My sister got married when she was still a teenager. But her husband spent all of his money in hostess bars, and in the end she kicked him out. That's when they moved back in with us."

"You're not in a hurry to have kids yourself, I take it."

"Actually, I'd like to settle down soon. I've been going out with the same girl for a while now, and when I'm at home we see each other most days. Since I left Okayama, though, I only call her about once a month. If it was more than that we'd start to miss each other — plus the calls are expensive."

"Does she mind when you go travelling?"

"Of course she does! She didn't want me to go on this tour at all, but I just ignored her and came anyway. What about you, though? Didn't you just get married?"

"Yes," I said. "We're having a wedding reception in Ibaraki next month."

"How about a honeymoon?"

"That was a week in Spain earlier in the year."

"Five weeks in Hokkaido and only one week in Spain?" said Mr. Warehouse. "Your wife must be very understanding!"

Banter aside, my conversation with Mr. Warehouse raises an interesting point, namely that in Hokkaido, women cyclists — and for that matter, women motorcyclists — are vastly outnumbered by their male counterparts, many of whom have abandoned significant others to experience the freedom of riding all day and sleeping semi-rough at night. As is the case elsewhere in Japan, those travelling alone have very little need to fear for their safety, but besides a group of university students from Aichi Prefecture, I only met two female cyclists during my entire five-week tour.

* * *

Also on the west coast I had passed through Hokkaido's capital, Sapporo, and quite by chance came across a high-rise block that is home to perhaps the most important business on the island.

The word *seikō* means "success," and Seicomart is one of the oldest convenience store chains in Japan, although apart from a modest presence in Saitama and Ibaraki prefectures, it has yet to expand into a nationwide concern. From its inception, Seicomart specialised in upgrading independently run off-licences (that's liquor stores, for my American friends) and has maintained its connections with alcohol producers around the world, meaning that it stocks cheap, good quality wine. Alongside convenience store staples such as rice balls, sandwiches, and so on, many branches sell hot food prepared on the premises. More importantly, there are branches of Seicomart in even the most far-flung corners of Hokkaido, because rather than attempting to chase away its competitors by opening multiple branches close together — as is the policy of certain other chains — the company makes a point of establishing its stores in areas that lack retail outlets.

Seicomart thereby provides an essential service to cyclists, who are hungry, thirsty, and in almost constant need of a pit stop. The majority of those I met carried Seicomart loyalty cards, which they used when purchasing at least one meal a day, and sometimes all ten.

So a significant number of the conversations I had that summer took place in Seicomart car parks, and it was at the very last of these before boarding the ferry back to Honshu that I met Mr. Traverse Region.

On his fourteenth tour of Hokkaido, Mr. Traverse Region had a long grey beard and a red nose, which he assured me was that way due to sunburn and not cheap wine. His outfit of a waistcoat, T-shirt, and shorts was augmented with a pair of flip-flops.

"Wouldn't it be better to cycle with something more sturdy on your feet?" I asked.

"Nope," he replied. "I realised pretty quickly these are the most practical thing there is. It doesn't matter if they get wet, right?"

"That's true," I said, and wished I had thought of the same thing myself instead of avoiding rain altogether or wrapping my shoes in plastic bags like a homeless person.

"Where are you going today?" I said.

"Toward Muroran," said Mr. Traverse Region. "How about you?"

"Tomakomai. My ferry leaves at quarter to seven."

"Really? I'll let you into a secret. Another thing I've learned over the years is that clockwise is best."

"Why's that?"

"Well, you're always on the side of the road that's closest to the sea, so you get an unobstructed view."

He had a point: the Japanese drive on the left, so it makes sense to go clockwise if you follow the coast, not to mention being safer. After all, how many times had I needed to dart across two lanes of traffic to get a better look at a beach, an island, or a sunset?

Yes, all this time I had been going the wrong way round.

Then again, if I had travelled clockwise around Hokkaido instead of anti-clockwise, I may never have met Mr. Village Middle, the Middle Fields, Mrs. Bamboo Child, Mr. Warehouse, or for that matter Mr. Traverse Region. In this sense, it occurred to me that the tour was a rather neat metaphor for life itself. Like the outcome of a computer model for chaos theory, depending on arbitrary decisions such as which way to turn at a T-junction, where to stop and where to stay, where to eat and where to drink, how far to ride and how long to rest, one's destiny can change completely, not just that day or that night, but weeks hence and hundreds, even thousands of kilometres down the road.

And every summer Hokkaido is very much about meeting people, as the island is transformed into a kind of large-scale social club for cyclists. Many may claim to be here for the scenery or even the seaweed, but as much as anything else they come for the simple pleasure of talking to strangers.

About the Author

Englishman Tom Gibb lives with his Japanese wife and two children in Ibaraki Prefecture, where he works as a teacher and translator. He has travelled to more than half of Japan's forty-seven prefectures by bicycle, and is presently writing an account of his first and longest tour, with the provisional title of *Gaijin on a Push Bike*. His blog can be found at muzuhashi.com.